CRITICAL INSIGHTS

Macbeth

CRITICAL INSIGHTS

Macbeth

Editor
William W. Weber
Independent scholar, PhD from Yale University

SALEM PRESS
A Division of EBSCO Information Services, Inc.
Ipswich, Massachusetts

GREY HOUSE PUBLISHING

Publisher's Cataloging-In-Publication Data
(Prepared by The Donohue Group, Inc.)

Names: Weber, William W., editor.
Title: Macbeth / editor, William W. Weber, Independent scholar, PhD from Yale
        University.
Other Titles: Critical insights.
Description: [First edition]. | Ipswich, Massachusetts : Salem Press, a division
        of EBSCO Information Services, Inc. ; Amenia, NY : Grey
        House Publishing, [2017] | Includes bibliographical references
        and index.
Identifiers: ISBN 9781682175637 (hardcover)
Subjects: LCSH: Shakespeare, William, 1564-1616.Macbeth. | Shakespeare,
        William, 1564-1616--Criticism and interpretation. | Macbeth,
        King of Scotland, active 11th century--In literature. |
        Masculinity in literature. | Witchcraft in literature.
Classification: LCC PR2823 .W43 2017 | DDC 822.33--dc23

First Printing

Contents

Critical Contexts

Critical Readings

Resources

About This Volume

William W. Weber

The *Critical Insights* series strives to provide students and interested readers with original scholarship to help understand literature in fresh ways and from new perspectives. This volume, on Shakespeare's *Macbeth*, focuses on a single play that has had a profound influence on literature, film, and culture more broadly. Shakespeare's shortest tragedy has had a long and eventful afterlife, and like all of Shakespeare's works continues to accrue new and vital significance through both scholarly analysis and a series of continual reimaginings on stage and screen. This volume is intended both as an introduction to *Macbeth* for those encountering it for the first time and as an example of the many ways it can be interpreted for those embarking on their own original written interpretations of the play.

The first major section of this book provides a broad overview of the play and several of its contexts. In addition to a general introduction by volume editor William W. Weber, this section also includes a biographical sketch of Shakespeare's life and career in the theater, as well as a set of four original essays approaching the play from four different contextual perspectives. The first of these charts the origin, evolution, and current diversity of critical responses to the play, examining the multiple ways in which *Macbeth* has proven of immediate concern to readers over the centuries since its first performance. From William Davenant's moralized adaptation of the play for the Restoration stage later in the seventeenth century to today's interest in the play's gender dynamics and psychological complexity, the critical history of *Macbeth* can teach us as much about the play's readers—ourselves included—as about the play.

In the second essay in the first section, Bryon Williams turns our attention to the play's historical context, providing both a useful overview of the political debates surrounding James I's accession to the English throne and his fraught self-image as both a mortal man and, in his estimation, a divinely anointed monarch with virtually unlimited power. To give this complicated and crucial history added depth and nuance, Williams provides a detailed look at how James understood himself in relation to the ancient tradition of the royal touch and the King's Evil, a superstition holding that the rightful monarch was endowed not just with political authority but with the supernatural power to heal those suffering from scrofula. This admixture of royalty and magic is entirely foreign to our modern sensibilities but occupied a fascinatingly liminal significance in Shakespeare's day. As Williams shows, understanding this complicated cultural practice can help us gain greater understanding of *Macbeth*'s creative image of a world where raw political power and ephemeral supernatural forces coexist.

While reading the play with added attention to its historical context is an excellent method for understanding it more fully, modern scholarship has also added greatly to our understanding of literature by analyzing it via contemporary advances in intellectual practices across a number of fields. So-called theoretical readings approach texts from the precise point of view of a chosen critical methodology. The third essay in the first section of this volume provides an excellent example of how viewing a classic text through a particular critical lens can refocus our attention on aspects of the original work that might otherwise have been confusing or entirely overlooked. By reading *Macbeth* through Alfred Mele's influential psychological theory of self-deception, Mohammad Shaaban Ahmad Deyab demonstrates the depth and complexity of the tragic hero's compulsion to create a comprehensible, but ultimately illusory, version of his moral world in which his increasingly heinous actions are justified. Recognizing the techniques the character uses to deceive himself helps us see through the play's own layers of potentially deceptive representation, and casts both the natural and supernatural environments of the play in a new light.

The final essay of the first section exemplifies a type of scholarship that students of literature are often called upon to perform, but which is rarely the primary mode of professional scholars: the comparative analysis, sometimes better known as a compare-and-contrast essay. Volume editor William W. Weber provides an engaging discussion of the way that reading *Macbeth* alongside Shakespeare's earlier tragedy of *Hamlet* can help us understand both plays' thematic interest in the practical and moral challenges posed by the process of deliberation. Hamlet's famous thoughtfulness contrasts sharply with Macbeth's increasingly manic tendency to act purely on impulse, and yet both characters self-consciously engage with their own mindfulness. Even though *Hamlet* was written before *Macbeth*, this essay demonstrates how the latter play provides readers with clarifications of Shakespeare's own thinking on this issue that help resolve some of the most central problems readers have with understanding *Hamlet*'s notorious ambiguities.

The second section of the volume consists of nine new critical readings on a wide range of subjects touching on *Macbeth* and its broader cultural significance. The first, from David Currell, supplies an eloquent and erudite discussion of the play's sonic complexity. Looking at poetic and rhetorical devices like alliteration, rhyme, metaphor, and punning, Currell demonstrates just how much meaning Shakespeare's language contains within its sounds in addition to its straightforward semiosis.

Following from Currell's careful dissection of the play's original language, the second critical reading, from Fernando Gabriel Pagnoni Berns, turns to the play's performance history and how critics have made sense of adaptations of early modern plays into twentieth century films. In contrast to a traditionalist model of adaptation studies that privileged faithfulness to the original work over all other criteria, Pagnoni Berns argues that each adaptation should be considered an independent text in its own right, and that within this framework those adaptations that take greater liberties with their sources can actually provide the most rewarding and thought-provoking new experiences. Focusing on the film *Joe Macbeth*, which reimagines the story of the play within the gangster subculture of American film noir, Pagnoni Berns demonstrates how some of the biggest departures from Shakespeare's text can actually provide the most powerful commentary upon the same thematic concerns.

Blending the linguistic focus of Currell's reading with the attention to performance and adaptation in Pagnoni Berns's, Pamela Royston Macfie offers a focused and insightful account of the divergent ways in which *Macbeth*'s witches have been brought to life in various stage and film adaptations of the play. While each version Macfie describes is fascinating and important in its own right, the true discovery of the argument is how the etymological and descriptive ambiguity in Shakespeare's text correlates and even demands the diversity of imagination on display in historical and contemporary adaptations alike. No matter how unique the vision of a given director, no matter how ambitious a filmic adaptation, the ultimate creative credit is all Shakespeare's.

The last in a trio of essays focused largely on films of the play, the fourth critical reading, from Robert C. Evans, focuses on the character of Lady Macbeth and, specifically, how various films have depicted her response to the trauma of committing murder. Covering a wide range of films and cinematic periods, Evans combines his descriptive accounts of performances with a nuanced account of the play's representation of what Evans argues is its character's posttraumatic stress disorder.

Lady Macbeth is a character who herself pays great attention to gender dynamics, and no discussion of the play is complete without investigating them. Building on Evans's introduction to the character's psychic victimization, the next two essays take two different paths toward examining gender in *Macbeth*. Savannah Xaver focuses on Shakespeare's repeated invocation of the imagery of bodily fluids—blood, milk, gall, and so on—and investigates the ways in which these fluids reflect Lady Macbeth's desire for gender to be similarly fluid. Her desire to "unsex" herself in many ways reflects not a negation of gender so much as a privileging of masculinity. Jim Casey, on the other hand, argues that "masculinity" is a contested category that must be defined and maintained through repeated performative acts. Lady Macbeth's version of manhood requires the suppression of emotion and results in excessive personal violence, but this definition of gender is set in opposition to Macduff's view of masculinity, which allows for a full expression of feeling and uses violence only in the defense of the state.

Macbeth is a play obsessed with death, and Sophia Richardson demonstrates that this obsession was part of a broader early modern fascination with remembering, depicting, and moralizing mortality. By carefully combing the play's language for markers of this *memento mori* tradition, and analyzing these passages alongside contemporary paintings and engravings visually depicting similar messages, Richardson shows how fully invested Shakespeare was in examining and commenting upon death's disturbing proximity to early modern culture.

While Shakespeare's culture undoubtedly had a particularly self-conscious approach to engaging with mortality, death is one of the themes in Shakespeare's plays that is truly universal. The penultimate essay in this volume, from Rahul Chaturvedi, explores three different aspects of the play that exemplify the tension between the cultural particularity of Shakespeare and the universality found in his greatest works. By casting the discussion in terms of getting a modern-day class of Indian students to engage with a text far beyond their own cultural experiences, Chaturvedi elucidates the ways in which Shakespeare's text itself productively exemplifies the tension between in-group (*emic*) and out-group (*etic*) understanding.

Finally, Daniel Bender approaches these same issues of universality versus cultural distance by arguing for the immediacy of *Macbeth*'s significance within our own world today. Using the critical framework known as presentism, Bender explains how reading *Macbeth* helps him gain a fuller understanding of the cultural violence that permeates both the play's world of medieval Scotland and our own landscapes of Vietnam, Iraq, and Ferguson. History is circular; Shakespeare's time is our own.

The final section of the book includes several helpful resources, including a timeline of Shakespeare's life, a general bibliography combining the most fruitful avenues for further study, information about the editor and the contributors, and an index. All together, this volume should be a helpful resource for any and all who wish to explore all that is profound, disturbing, and fascinating about the worlds inhabited by Macbeth, by Shakespeare, and by ourselves.

On *Macbeth*

William W. Weber

Fair is Foul

From the very beginning, *Macbeth* announces itself as a play where meaning itself is subject to debate: "Fair is foul, and foul is fair" (I.1.12). This paradoxical assertion of the radical identity of two opposite terms is a perfect embodiment of the play's focus on uncertainty. Fittingly, this single line is spoken by multiple characters simultaneously, with the layering of voices echoing the layering of alliteration and chiastic repetition within the line. The similarity of the words—fair and foul, both four-letter monosyllabic f-words—ironically highlights their status as antonyms, and calls on us to question why such similar, easily interchangeable utterances can carry such wholly dissimilar meanings. We are thus reminded that language is arbitrary, that the words we choose to describe things and ideas originate within us, not the world we strive to describe. And if language is arbitrary, who is to say that the moral poles of good and evil, fair and foul, are not similarly open to subjective interpretation? Welcome to the world of *Macbeth*.

Shakespeare brought this world to life in late 1605 or, more likely, 1606, building on the groundwork of Raphael Holinshed's *Chronicles of England, Scotland, and Ireland.* This is the same source Shakespeare uses for his history plays about English monarchs, and as with those plays he lifts some details verbatim while condensing the overall historical timeline into the tight narrative arc of a tragedy. The story was an especially compelling one to dramatize, for both artistic and political reasons. Artistically, Holinshed's account of eleventh-century Scottish history includes all the elements of high drama: a brave warrior encounters mysterious witches, receives a prophecy that he will become king, follows his wife's advice to assassinate the current king, assumes the throne, rules justly for a number of years, spirals downward toward tyranny through a series of increasingly violent outrages, and is finally killed in combat with one of the noblemen he wronged. An inherently exciting narrative with a classic rise-and-fall tragic arc and a bit of the supernatural thrown in for good measure, Macbeth's story practically begs to be told. That Shakespeare chose to tell it when he did, early in the reign of James I—aka James VI of Scotland—speaks to an additional set of facts that made the story particularly pertinent to the times.

As a member of the King's Men theater company, Shakespeare was technically a servant of the new king, and had a vested interest in pleasing the taste of his patron. As a sharer in the company's profits from the Globe Theatre, he also had a vested interest in pleasing the tastes of the paying public. *Macbeth* appears to have been an attempt to do both, as it focuses on topics of pressing interest to the sovereign and his subjects alike. For the people, still getting accustomed to life under a Scottish-born ruler, all things Scottish were fascinating. For the king, there were two obvious points of individual interest: first, there was the fact that his family traced its lineage back to a character in the play, Banquo; second, James was well known to have a keen interest in witchcraft and the occult, as in 1597 he published *Daemonologie*, a philosophical account of dark magic and a justification for witch hunting—as well as a source for Shakespeare's depiction of the Weird Sisters and their rituals. If Shakespeare had simply wanted to flatter the king and entertain the masses, though, he certainly could have written a rousing drama with a clear promonarch message of moral certitude. Instead, he produced a dense, atmospheric, intensely psychological play where good and evil become so intertwined as to be at times indistinguishable. Ambiguity is the play's defining feature, with Shakespeare sending conflicting messages about loyalty, morality, kingship, gender, nature, and reality itself.

Overview

For all of its richness and complexity, *Macbeth* is a strikingly short play: the shortest of Shakespeare's tragedies, less than 62 percent the length of *Hamlet*. Many scholars believe that Shakespeare originally wrote a longer, fuller version of the play, and that the text we have today reflects a version that had been edited and revised for performance—perhaps a performance before James I at court. No version of *Macbeth* was published during Shakespeare's lifetime, so the text as we know it derives from that published in the First Folio. The First Folio was the collection of Shakespeare's plays published in 1623, seven years after Shakespeare's death, by Shakespeare's friends and colleagues from the King's Men, John Heminges and Henry Condell. Were it not for their work in memorializing their friend, *Macbeth* would likely have been lost.

No one knows for sure exactly how many years before it was eventually published the play was written, but, as stated above, 1606 is the most likely date of composition. Any time before 1603, when Elizabeth I died and was succeeded by James I, is difficult to imagine because the play seems so clearly suited to the accession of a Scottish king. 1607 is almost certainly the latest possible date, as in that year *The Knight of the Burning Pestle* by Francis Beaumont made an allusion to the banquet scene with Banquo's ghost. Most scholars agree that 1606 is the most likely date, as *Macbeth* includes a number of lines that are best explained as allusions to the Gunpowder Plot of November 5, 1605, and the subsequent trial of one of the alleged conspirators the following year. It is likely that the play was performed for James I himself in the fall of 1606, although there is no concrete evidence of a performance before 1611. Complicating matters further is the fact that the published text of the play includes cues for songs known elsewhere not from Shakespeare but from Thomas Middleton. Many scholars believe that the play we have today reflects Middleton's revision of Shakespeare's original play, with substantial material excised to shorten the running time as well as some new material added to meet the evolving tastes of theatergoers. Such revivals and revisions of old plays were commonplace in this era, and it is entirely possible that Shakespeare was never aware of the precise form his play took before it was immortalized in the First Folio. No matter how, precisely, *Macbeth* came to be what it is, undoubtedly its greatest mysteries are the ones within, the ones Shakespeare challenges us to confront.

What Is Real?

At its most literal, the witches' claim that "Fair is foul" refers to the weather, asking us to imagine a barren Scottish heath simultaneously wracked by storm and kissed by sunlight. For the original audience at the Globe Theatre, where the stage was exposed to the elements, this line would have served as a metatheatrical reminder that no matter the conditions in London, the weather on stage could be anything the players desired. This ability to manipulate the audience's belief, the very cornerstone of drama, is immediately compared to the black magic by which the Weird Sisters appear to be controlling the storm that accompanies and symbolizes the offstage battle at the beginning of the play. Rather than lull the audience into an unconscious suspension of disbelief, Shakespeare immediately foregrounds the almost magical artificiality of the performance, reminding us that we are being deceived. This questioning of the materiality of the play's world becomes a recurrent theme: Banquo asks the witches "Are ye fantastical" (I.3.53) and suggests that they may have been a hallucination caused by eating "the insane root / That takes the reason prisoner" (I.3.84-5); Macbeth questions his own senses repeatedly, both visual —"Is this a dagger which I see before me[?]" (II.1.34) and aural— "Methought I heard a voice" (II.2.38); Lady Macbeth famously hallucinates the "damned spot" (V.i.35) of guilt upon her hands. The inner workings of the mind seem to externalize themselves in the world sensed by the characters, and the insistence with which Shakespeare reminds us of the senses' unreliability makes us question whether what we see on the stage is to be understood as having literal existence within the play's world at all. Does Banquo's ghost actually come to dinner, or are we being shown the mad imaginings of Macbeth's guilt-racked conscience? Are there actual witches in the play's Scotland, or are they to be seen as symbolic representations of the characters' anxieties and desires? Of course, if a day can be both fair and foul then a witch can be both real and imaginary, a dagger can be both visible and symbolic, and a bloodstain can be both dirty and invisible.

Prophecy and Paradox

Whether the witches who deliver the inciting prophecy that Macbeth will "be king hereafter" (I.3.50) are themselves real or not, their prophecy takes on a life of its own. Evoking an ancient tragic tradition going back to Oedipus, a prophetic utterance prompts major interpretive challenges. The central question is whether the prophecies are glimpses into a future that is already set in stone, thereby eliminating the very concept of free will, or whether the subject of a prophecy possesses the agency to avoid what has been foretold. Secondarily, as Macbeth himself wonders, does a prophecy eliminate the necessity of conscious action in order for it to come true, or does it compel someone to act in order to bring it about? When told that he will be king, Macbeth immediately recognizes that the swiftest way for him to make the prophecy come true would be to commit regicide, and yet he balks at this horrible thought: "If chance will have me king, why, chance may crown me / without my stir" (I.3.143-4). Wishful thinking, perhaps. By minimizing the act of murder with the euphemism "my stir," Macbeth has already begun the process of rationalization, a necessary step on his way to ensuring the prophecy comes true. Ironically, by refusing to see whether "chance may crown [him]," Macbeth arguably takes power away from the prophecy—if every prediction prompted the hearer to takes steps to fulfill it, anyone could be a fortune-teller.

Macbeth's response to prophecy in the play is wildly inconsistent, however, as his active attempts to fulfill the prophecy about his own kingship do not stop him from taking active steps to prevent the prophecy about Banquo's descendants from coming true. Moreover, after having taken active roles in responding to the first two prophecies, Macbeth then acts upon his interpretation of the second set of prophecies in a way that suggests he has absolute faith in their veracity. Told that "none of woman born / Shall harm Macbeth," (IV.1.102-3) and that "Macbeth shall never vanquished be until / Great Birnam Wood to high Dunsinane Hill / Shall come against him," (IV.1.114-16) the king believes he is invincible and neglects to provide adequate defenses accordingly. In every case the prophecies come true, and each time their accuracy depends on Macbeth's actions, yet each time his actions reflect a different attitude toward prophecy. This combination of a dynamic character arc against the backdrop of consistent supernatural power makes for especially thought-provoking theater. Where does power really lie?

Unsex Me Here

Perhaps an even more fascinating depiction of power and agency in the play comes with its interest in gender. Shakespeare provides repeated images of gender fluidity: the witches are described as having feminine bodies as well as beards; Lady Macbeth repeatedly uses the language of emasculation to manipulate her husband into enacting their violent plot; conversely to these threats of emasculation, Lady Macbeth makes an explicit call for her own femininity to be erased—"unsex me"—and replaced with a pure distillation of masculine cruelty. Fair is foul, and the fairer sex is the fouler. This confusion over gender would have appeared all the more directly and metatheatrically on the original Shakespearean stage, as in this period all the actors were men, even those playing female parts. The witches may have had real, rather than costume, beards, and the actor playing Lady Macbeth could well have portrayed her in a more masculine light over the course of her unsexing soliloquy:

> Come, you spirits
> That tend of mortal thoughts, unsex me here,
> And fill me from the crown to the toe topfull
> Of direst cruelty. Make thick my blood;
> Stop up th' access and passage to remorse,
> That no compunctious visitings of nature
> Shake my fell purpose nor keep peace between
> Th' effect and it. Come to my woman's breasts
> And take my milk for gall[.] (I.5.39-47)

Her feminine nature, with its capacity to create and nurture life, becomes the target of her desire for metamorphosis; she wants hate to replace compassion, gall to replace milk, hate to replace heart. Whether the invoked spirits help her or the capacity for violence was within her all along, Lady Macbeth's bloodthirsty persuasion causes her husband to recognize her newfound masculinity: "Bring forth men-children only; / For thy undaunted mettle should compose / nothing but males" (I.7.72-4). Lest we see Lady Macbeth's masculine metamorphosis as complete, though, note that Macbeth describes it within the still-feminine context of childbearing—the very thing that Lady Macbeth herself seemed to scorn by rejecting her milk. Unsexing, ultimately, seems impossible in this play where states of being become superimposed rather than erased. The implications of this layering and alternation of gender within the play's characters are fascinating. As some of the men in Shakespeare's company could take on feminine qualities on demand, the highly masculine world of Scottish political history appears constantly under threat of invasion from an enemy within itself. By waging war against biology, against the need for society to include feminine as well as masculine energies, the play's primary characters attempt to set themselves above nature itself.

"Nature Seems Dead"

To be above nature, literally to be supernatural, is a dangerous ambition. It is one associated with the witches, of course, but also with both Macbeths' desire for political power. Over and over they assert a desire for the natural world to cease its natural functions, for the natural order to bend itself to their will:

> Come, thick night,
> And pall thee in the dunnest smoke of hell
> That my keen knife see not the wound it makes,
> Nor heaven peep through the blanket of the dark
> To cry, "hold, hold." (I.5.49-53)

So says Lady Macbeth, betraying the recognition that her desired enterprise requires the infernal "smoke of hell" to block the view of heaven. Similarly, Macbeth invokes a blinding of nature's omniscient vision: "Stars, hide your fires. / Let not light see my black and deep desires." In both these speeches nature takes on an ironically supernatural capacity for surveillance, symbolically representing the moral authority of an unnamed but palpable religious providence. To blind nature is to escape judgment, to transcend justice.

Justice is no more limited to the confines of the natural order than murder, however, as witnessed by Macbeth's reaction to the appearance of Banquo's ghost:

> The time has been,
> That, when the brains were out, the man would die,
> And there an end. But now they rise again,
> With twenty mortal murders on their crowns,
> And push us from our stools. This is more strange
> Than such a murder is. (III.4.79-84)

Indeed, to the world of medieval Scotland violence and death seem more natural than resurrection, and yet the human drive for vengeance overpowers all else: "It will have blood, they say: blood will have blood. / Stones have been known to move and trees to speak" (III.4.123-4). There is a certain hubris to this belief of Macbeth's, to assume that his own actions are so powerful as to cause a response from even inanimate objects. Kings, of course, are not known for their modesty.

The King's Two Bodies

Macbeth's kingship provides additional examples of the play's fixation on ambiguity, examples that were particularly pertinent to *Macbeth*'s historical moment. As soon as he assumes the throne, Macbeth changes the way he refers to himself in public, with his frequent use of the introspective *I* turning into the so-called *royal we*. Why did monarchs in this era refer to themselves in the plural? The answer comes from an ancient custom of seeing the monarch merely as a human individual, but also as a vessel for a second person entirely—an immortal royal personage who inhabits each successive ruler without interruption. It is his complicated metaphysical explanation that gives rise to seemingly awkward locutions like "Ourself will mingle with society" (III.4.4) where the singular (*self*, not *selves*) and plural (*our*, not *my*) coexist, and it is this concept that helped justify the theory of the Divine Right of

Kings, the belief that God chooses the ruler and to question his or her authority would be to question God's.

James I was, not without a bit of self-interest, a major proponent of this view. In a 1598 treatise, *The True Lawe of Free Monarchies*, James attempted to justify the divine legitimacy of his rule, arguing that there was no role for the people or their representatives in parliament in choosing a monarch or, in the event of a bad one, deposing him or her. Macbeth's situation calls this entire political world-view into turmoil, as we witness the protagonist seizing power through deceit and murder and in turn have authority taken away through violent revolt. Macbeth wants to believe that his reign is divinely sanctioned, but his conscience creates massive cognitive dissonance. The very fact that he obtained the kingship proves that the kingship is not the pseudomagical state of divine power that made it worth seeking in the first place.

The play also explores another crucial political question of both Macbeth's period and Shakespeare's: is monarchical power inherited or passed on by election? Traditionally medieval Scotland employed the latter method of choosing a new king, largely out of practicality: kings almost never lived long enough to have adult children capable of assuming authority, and therefore the nobles saw fit to elect the most powerful from their number—often a brother or nephew of the deceased king—to take up the crown. Duncan I, the king the historical Macbeth deposed, threw this system into chaos by announcing that his son Malcolm would succeed him and creating him Prince of Cumberland. This English-style political move, based on the tradition of the Prince of Wales, marked a major sea change in the political world of the time, and was likely part of the historical Macbeth's motivation for killing the king. Very little of this motivation, arguably rooted in preserving a traditional way of life from foreign corruption, manifests itself in how Shakespeare depicts the act—and yet by including the lines by which Duncan announces his intention to make Malcolm his heir, the idea is present all the same. The debate between election and inheritance was a crucial one in the years leading up to Elizabeth's death, and remained vexed as James took power and claimed that Parliament had nothing to do with it. As much as *Macbeth* could be read as an endorsement of hereditary monarchy through its celebration of Banquo's descendants and its moral privileging of Malcolm's invasion and reclaiming of his father's crown at the end of the play, significant questions remain.

Malcolm's accession is not quite as pure a happy ending as it may at first appear. Malcolm himself, even while claiming a birthright to the throne, goes out of his way to establish a limitation upon his legitimacy when he rather bizarrely tests Macduff's loyalty in IV.3. In so doing, Malcolm discovers that greed and lechery are entirely acceptable in a king—or at least preferable to the tyranny of Macbeth—while deceptiveness is a bridge too far. Why, exactly, a king's legitimacy should hinge on one moral failing but not another is not fully explored, but the very fact that both Malcolm and Macduff seem to agree that birthright alone is not enough to justify his rule is noteworthy. Kingship might be something one is born into, but it also appears to be something one can sin one's way out of—divine right or no.

National Identities

Malcolm's successful uprising against Macbeth, while led by the Scottish thane Macduff, is more than a domestic rebellion; it is also a foreign invasion. Malcolm would have had no chance of reclaiming his father's throne if he had not been given the command of an English army, and in the final speech of the play he makes it clear that the troops are more than mere mercenaries, they are representatives of a permanent cultural invasion as well:

> My thanes and kinsmen,
> Henceforth be earls, the first that ever Scotland
> In such an honor named. (V.8.62-4)

While this change in semantics may seem benign enough, it represents an important coda for the play, serving as a final reminder both of the theme of linguistic layering—fair is foul and thanes are earls—and the very type of cultural imposition that many in England feared upon the accession of a Scottish king. Malcolm is an inverted version of James, journeying from one British kingdom to another and bringing its dialects and values with him.

In *Macbeth*, of course, there is little doubt that this pseudo-English invasion is a good thing: Macbeth's Scotland has become a tyranny, a lawless land full of violence, darkness, and terror. England under its king, Edward the Confessor, is just the opposite – a realm of justice, peace, and wisdom. This historical self-portrait of Shakespeare's native land is not without its own complexity, however, as Shakespeare's audience would have been well aware that Edward the Confessor's reign ended in a very famous year: 1066, the year of the Norman invasion when William the Conqueror established an era of French domination over England that, in some dynastic respects, persisted to Shakespeare's day and, indeed, our own. Shakespeare's England was no longer a pure land of unadulterated British heritage, and perhaps by reminding his audience of this at the end of *Macbeth* the playwright was suggesting that the reign of James was less of a threatening anomaly than many had feared.

Religion, Terrorism, Equivocation

The single most powerful source of anxiety upon the accession of James was the question of what it would mean for England's religion. The Protestant Reformation, begun by Martin Luther and taken up in England by Elizabeth's father, Henry VIII, had thrown Europe into a period of chaos. In the sixty years before *Macbeth* was written England had gone from Catholic to Protestant under Henry VIII, then back to Catholic under Mary, then back to Protestant under Elizabeth. Each shift of official state religion was accompanied by widespread violence and unrest as many resisted being forced to alter their beliefs and practices, and those in power persecuted any caught disobeying their directives. James's mother, Mary Queen of Scots, had been executed by Elizabeth for attempting to lead a Catholic rebellion against Elizabeth's Protestant rule, and many feared that the new king James, while nominally a Protestant, would upon taking power institute yet another religious shift. In fact he did not, and his refusal to institute his mother's religion led a group of Catholic extremists to attempt to kill him and other leaders of England's Protestant government by blowing up Parliament. This Gunpowder Plot and its highly publicized aftermath, including the trial of conspirators and a bloody crackdown on suspected Catholics, hovers threateningly in the background through much of *Macbeth*.

One of the alleged participants in the Gunpowder Plot was the Jesuit priest Henry Garnet. Garnet, who was executed in 1606, had previously published a *Treatise on Equivocation*, instructing Catholics on how to deceive Protestant would-be persecutors without technically committing the sin of lying. Equivocation, etymologically "to call something by the same name," was the practice of using deliberately ambiguous language in order to lead someone to a false interpretation. The porter in II.3 speaks at length of an "equivocator…who committed treason enough for God's sake" (II.3.8-10). This line directly calls the divine right theory of kingship into question, as a conflict between political and religious loyalty should not be possible in a world where monarchs are divinely ordained. Can any would-be traitor, whether a Macbeth or a Garnet, genuinely believe that murder is part of God's plan? If their treason succeeds, as Macbeth's indeed does, does that in turn suggest that they were right in believing in divine sanction for regicide? Macbeth's success, taken alongside the evocation of equivocation, suggests that either God willed Duncan's death—in which case the king lacked any kind of divine favor—or that there is no God at all—in which case no king can claim power from anything other than mortal sources. Whether God fails to protect kings or lacks any power whatsoever, *Macbeth* is an exceedingly disquieting play for those who believe in a world guided by Providence.

Conclusion

If *Macbeth* refuses to provide the reassurance of a world where traditional hierarchies and power structures stabilize civilization, all the better for Shakespeare and his art. Drama is at its most dramatic when hierarchies implode, when structures erode, when convention explodes. Literature strives to be the opposite of equivocation: while the latter strives to deceive while telling apparent truths, the former seeks to illuminate the truth by presenting self-evident fictions. Fair *is* foul, and foul *is* fair. As Macbeth says,

> Life's but a walking shadow, a poor player
> That struts and frets his hour upon the stage
> And then is heard no more. It is a tale
> Told by an idiot, full of sound and fury,
> Signifying nothing. (V.5.24-8)

Life is theater, theater is life, and that which signifies nothing means everything.

Works Cited and Consulted

Halley, Janet E. "Equivocation and the Legal Conflict over Religious Identity in Early Modern England." *Yale Journal of Law and the Humanities,* vol. 3, no. 1, 1991, pp. 33-52.

Kantorowisc, Ernst. *The King's Two Bodies*. Princeton UP, 1957.

La Belle, Jenijoy. "'A Strange Infirmity': Lady Macbeth's Amenorrhea." *Shakespeare Quarterly*, vol. 31, no. 3, 1980, pp. 381-86.

Shakespeare, William. *Macbeth*. Edited by Stephen Orgel. Penguin, 2016.

Stuart, James. *Daemonologie*. Waldegrave, 1597.

_____. *The True Lawe of Free Monarchies*. Waldegrave, 1598.

Biography of William Shakespeare_____

William W. Weber

Historians, biographers, critics, and others have been writing about Shakespeare's life for hundreds of years, ever since the actor and playwright from the small market town of Stratford-upon-Avon rose to his elevated position of acclaim. The desire to know everything about a figure who means so much is profound, and profoundly frustrated by the fact that the documentary evidence that survives falls short of giving us the richly detailed history we crave. Speculation and unverified traditional stories fill these gaps in the record, with entire books being written on what might have happened to turn Shakespeare into the man and the writer he was. What kind of relationship did he have with his wife and family? What was he doing during the years between attending grammar school in Stratford and beginning his theater career in London? How much of his personal life appears in his sonnets and plays? What provided the inspiration for his most famous lines? What were his religious beliefs? These questions cannot be truly answered, and yet that has not stopped thousands of fascinated commentators from doing their best to answer them. If you want to know more about what kinds of answers have been proposed, start with Peter Ackroyd's thorough *Shakespeare: The Biography*, and work your way through his bibliography as deeply as you like. For the purposes of this present biographical sketch, I will strive to stick to the facts as much as possible.

Sticking to the facts when telling Willing Shakespeare's story becomes immediately unsatisfying, as we do not even know for a fact what day he was born. We do know, however, that he was christened in Stratford's Holy Trinity Church on April 26, 1564. We also know that infants at this time were usually, though by no means always, baptized three days after birth, and therefore tradition celebrates Shakespeare's birthday on April 23—a date that fits the evidence better than any other, and that has the additional significance of being the same as Shakespeare's death 52 years later on April 23, 1616. So what happened in between these two fateful April 23rds? Quite a bit, both in the literary world and across the great globe itself.

Shakespeare's relatively short lifetime began early in the long reign of Queen Elizabeth I and ended midway through that of James I. This was an era of religious upheaval, political strife, global exploration, intellectual advancement, and literary revolution. It was an era of glory and plague, of coronations and beheadings, of peace and war. In a word, it was an era of drama, and Shakespeare played an indelible role in it.

It was at the King's New School in Stratford that the young Shakespeare began learning the linguistic skills that would serve him so well as a playwright. In Elizabethan England, a grammar school education like the one afforded the sons of prosperous citizens—like John Shakespeare, a glove-maker and municipal official—consisted of rigorous training in, fittingly enough, grammar—Latin grammar, to be precise. Students learned the language through translating passages from ancient authors into English, and then translating their translations back into Latin. Through this disciplined course of study students received training not just in reading and writing, but also in argumentation and oratory. Many would go on to be merchants, lawyers, and priests; Shakespeare took his familiarity with poets like Ovid and playwrights like Terence and Plautus and strove to surpass them.

Shakespeare did not just leave his hometown of Stratford when he went to London, however—he also left his wife and children. In November of 1582 Shakespeare, only 18, married the 26-year-old Anne Hathaway. Six months later she bore him their first child, Susanna, and two years after that the couple had twins, Judith and Hamnet. We know very little about the private life of the family, and speculation abounds as to why Shakespeare's wife and children remained in Stratford when William made his way to the metropolis. Was he trying to escape an unhappy marriage? Or, as he returned to Stratford regularly and maintained property and business dealings there throughout his life, was it a separation necessitated by simultaneous commitment to both his hometown and his career?

Shakespeare's career in the theater could only have happened in London, and his timing could not have been better. The entertainment industry as we know it today arguably had its modern start in Elizabethan England. Drama in the earlier medieval period was predominantly religious in nature, and with mystery, miracle, and morality plays staged in villages across the Catholic countryside during feast day celebrations. The actors in these plays were often amateurs or quasi-professionals, and seen as little more than vagabonds when not performing. It was not until the late sixteenth century that permanent public playhouses began to be built in London, with permanent professional acting companies performing newly written secular plays in them.

We know from a 1592 attack by the early playwright Robert Greene that Shakespeare had by that time already made a name for himself as an actor and, as Greene parodies a line from *Henry VI, Part 3*, a playwright. While Greene and some of the other so-called University Wits (gentlemen educated at Oxford or Cambridge who were active in the nascent world of professional literary writing) may have initially looked down on a relatively uneducated young man from a provincial town competing with them creatively, Shakespeare's success as a writer came quickly. He appears to have had little trouble in finding theater companies to write for or more experienced dramatists to collaborate with, as his early works were staged by multiple companies and were often the result of multiple authorship. *Titus Andronicus*, Shakespeare's first tragedy, was written with George Peele; the three *Henry VI* plays, Shakespeare's first histories, were collaborations with several playwrights, most probably including Christopher Marlowe and Thomas Nashe.

The year 1593 marked a major turning point both in Shakespeare's career and in the Elizabethan literary world, as it saw both the closing of the theaters due to plague and the violent death of Christopher Marlowe—at the time inarguably the most famous and successful of all playwrights, surpassing Shakespeare's output up to the time in quantity and, arguably, even quality. Without a professional theater to write plays for, Shakespeare turned to the older and more respected literary model of writing polished poetry for an aristocratic patron. *Venus and Adonis*, an erotic narrative poem retelling a myth from Ovid's *Metamorphoses*, was written during this period of theater closure and dedicated to Henry Wriothesley, the Earl of Southampton. It was a smash hit upon publication, going through multiple editions within the next few years and making Shakespeare's name as a serious poet.

In contrast, when Shakespeare's first published play appeared in 1594, the title page of *The Most Lamentable Roman Tragedy of Titus Andronicus* made no mention of its author whatsoever. Poems were literature, plays were entertainment; poets were authors and artists, playwrights were behind-the-scenes workmen. This dynamic changed notably over the ensuing decade, and a chronological comparison of title pages will show playwrights' names, and particularly Shakespeare's, first appearing out of nowhere and then steadily growing in size and prominence. Clearly, booksellers began to find that it was a worthwhile selling point to advertise a play's authorship, and professional playwriting thus took on qualities of respectability and literariness that had previously been afforded only to poetry.

As Shakespeare's public fame as a writer began to grow, his financial success in the industry grew as well. This success was largely attributable to his ability to become an equal shareholder in the Lord Chamberlain's Men company in 1595, a company that—in no small thanks to the quality of the plays Shakespeare wrote for it, of course—became one of the preeminent forces in the professional theater, particularly following their construction of the Globe Theatre in 1599. Their prominence almost got them in trouble in 1601 when the Earl of Essex commissioned a performance of Shakespeare's *Richard II*, a play dramatizing the successful deposition of a monarch, in an attempt to arouse public support in advance of his unsuccessful coup attempt upon Elizabeth. Happily, while Essex lost his head, Shakespeare and his company escaped punishment.

The political unrest occasioned by the childless Elizabeth's years of failing health and eventual death in 1603 culminated in the peaceful succession of her cousin James VI of Scotland, who initiated the Stuart dynasty as James I of England. James elevated Shakespeare and the Lord Chamberlain's Men to his personal service, and they became the King's Men. The accession of James and elevation of Shakespeare's company marked a dividing line in both the political life of England and the professional life of Shakespeare. At the height of his success and creative powers, Shakespeare wrote many of his most famous plays early in the Jacobean period, including *Macbeth* and *King Lear*. The witty comedies and nostalgic histories of his Elizabethan writing career became increasingly replaced by tragedies, and especially tragedies focused on the anxiety, isolation, and moral challenges accompanying power.

James I was, rather self-interestedly, a firm believer and defender of the absolute power of monarchs, asserting a divine right to rule in any way he saw fit. This absolutism led him to be intolerant of divergent views and strict in enforcing obedience among his subjects, which naturally led to backlash. The famous Gunpowder Plot of 1605 was an early attempt at disproving the infallibility of the king, and while Guy Fawkes and his coconspirators failed and James lived out his reign, James's son Charles I was beheaded by the people he claimed an unassailable divine right to rule. While outright revolution was a generation away, the fault lines of the traditional monarchical structure were beginning to show, and the drama of the period reflects a fascination with corruption.

While making the most of dramatizing the moral challenges of the powerful, Shakespeare was no stranger to moral challenges in his personal life: from what little evidence survives, we know he may not have always been a paragon in how he exerted his own economic power. Shakespeare used his success in London to build a substantial property portfolio in his native Stratford, and at one point was fined for hoarding grain during a time of famine. When Shakespeare dramatized exactly this situation in *Coriolanus*, is the hero's callous attitude toward the desperate, starving peasants a reflection of Shakespeare's own hard-nosed self-interest, or a reflective critique of it? This is the type of tantalizing question that our scant biographical knowledge, combined with a sensitive reading of the plays, can arouse but never fully answer.

Following his period of writing mainly dark tragedies, Shakespeare finished his career in the theater by returning to two of the hallmarks of his early career: comedy and collaboration. The late comedies, though, were so complicated by dark overtones and generic mixture that most scholars today put them in a genre of their own, the romances. With thematic interests including the passage of time, the transition of authority from one generation to the next, and the purgation of past moral failings, plays such as *The Winter's Tale* and *The Tempest* are frequently read as retrospective meditations on a complicated personal and creative life. While these interpretations of Shakespeare's late work as reflective and abstracted are often compelling, the late plays were also where Shakespeare performed the clearly practical work of training his successor. While Shakespeare's early collaborations, occurring as they did before the theater was considered truly literary and before playwrights regularly received recognition for their work, have required centuries of painstaking and controversial scholarship to identify the collaborators, two of Shakespeare's last works directly announce that John Fletcher, Shakespeare's successor as primary playwright for the King's Men, shared in the labor.

His labor done and the baton passed, Shakespeare retired from the theater and returned to Stratford in 1613. He died of illness three years later, and is buried in the same church where he was baptized, whence he hoped, according to his epitaph, never to be moved:

> Good friend, for Jesus' sake forbear,
> To dig the dust enclosèd here.
> Blest be the man that spares these stones,
> And cursed be he that moves my bones.

While his bones remain, his words and reputation have lived on, and the lines first spoken within the wooden "O" of the Globe Theatre have circled the planet for which it was named.

Works Cited and Consulted

Ackroyd, Peter. *Shakespeare: The Biography*. Anchor, 2006.

Archer, Jayne Elisabeth, Howard Thomas, and Richard Marggraf Turley. "Reading Shakespeare with the Grain: Sustainability and the Hunger Business." *Green Letters: Studies in Ecocriticism*, vol. 19, no. 1, 2015.

Baldwin, T. W. *William Shakespeare's Small Latine and Lesse Greeke*. U of Illinois P, 1944.

Erne, Lukas. *Shakespeare as Literary Dramatist*. Cambridge UP, 2003.

Greenblatt, Stephen. *Will in the World: How Shakespeare Became Shakespeare*. Norton, 2005.

Shapiro, James. *A Year in the Life of William Shakespeare: 1599*. Harper, 2005.

_____. *The Year of Lear: Shakespeare in 1606*. Simon, 2015.

Shoenbaum, Samuel. *Shakespeare: A Documentary Life*. Oxford UP, 1975.

CRITICAL CONTEXTS

Reading *Macbeth* from 1611 to Today_____

William W. Weber

Literary criticism provides invaluable insight, both into the literature it takes as its focus and into the interests, concerns, preoccupations, anxieties, and fascinations of the era in which it is written. The works of William Shakespeare, due to their sustained popularity across over four hundred years and countless cultures, provide especially fertile grounds for those interested in learning from the various ways that previous thinkers have approached a common text. What strikes some readers as brilliance can seem borderline obscene to others; details that entire generations overlook or take for granted can, when seen from a fresh perspective, provide rich new modes of thought. The story of Shakespearean criticism is the story of intellectual development itself, and *Macbeth* provides an excellent case study.

While *Macbeth* was not published until the First Folio of 1623, it was the subject of critical commentary even before then. Of course most of what original audiences thought of the play when it was first produced was never written down, and most of what was written down has been lost, but we do have two individual examples of people in Shakespeare's era responding to the play. First, and our only eyewitness account of a production of *Macbeth* during Shakespeare's lifetime, the astrologer Simon Foreman recounted his experience in the audience of a production in 1611. Foreman's concern was almost entirely with plot and spectacle, as an excerpt readily shows: "The next night being at supper with his noblemen, whom he had bid to a feast (to the which also Banquo should have come), he began to speak of noble Banquo and to wish that he were there. And as he thus did, standing up to drink a carouse to him, the ghost of Banquo came and sat down in his chair behind him" (fol.207v). Preserving both a general overview of the play's action as well as several insights into original staging, Foreman's summary helpfully illustrates how original audiences largely viewed the work of Shakespeare: as entertainment, pure and simple.

What worked well as entertainment in 1606 or 1611 could not be counted on to entertain audiences forever, though, and the history of Shakespeare criticism through the rest of the seventeenth century is largely that of theater professionals attempting to keep his plays relevant to evolving tastes. Even before *Macbeth*'s publication, we have good reason to believe that it had undergone a significant revision. The play's relative brevity, especially compared to the other tragedies Shakespeare wrote around the same time, such as *King Lear* and *Othello*, as well as its inclusion of cues for several songs probably written not by Shakespeare but by Thomas Middleton, suggest that text in the First Folio reflects a revival of the play by the King's Men, likely after Shakespeare's retirement, in which many lines of dialogue were cut and replaced with additional songs, dances, and spectacles from the witches in particular. The people wanted spectacle, and if Shakespeare's text needed to be altered in order to achieve it, then altered it was.

Such alterations to Shakespeare's original scripts became the norm in the Restoration period of the latter seventeenth century, as theater audiences at that time saw the work of Shakespeare and his contemporaries as woefully old-fashioned. William Davenant took it upon himself to produce an adapted version of the *Macbeth*, in which he added even more song and dance numbers for the Weird Sisters, simplified much of Shakespeare's dialogue to remove words already seen as archaic in the 1660s, and added new lines to provide the play with a clearer moral arc. Perhaps most (in)famously, Davenant had Macbeth die with a brand new line: "Farewell, vain World, and what's most vain in it, Ambition." More spectacle, more music, less challenging language. The Restoration stage was in many ways anticipating adaptation strategies now favored by Hollywood, and for precisely the same reason: because that was what audiences wanted. Where Shakespeare provided paradox, Davenant gave clarity: "To us fair weather's foul, and foul is fair," sing his witches at the play's opening, making their announcement an explanation of their own subjective preferences rather than the ominous declamation that ushered audiences into the complex world of Shakespeare's play.

When Shakespeare wasn't being adapted and simplified for changing theatrical tastes in the Restoration, he was often being attacked for lacking the refinement and decorum that literary critics of the period valued. The ethos of Neoclassicism looked back to the Roman poet Horace, one of the most polished writers of all time, as an exemplar compared to whom Shakespeare's more spontaneous style of writing seemed almost barbaric. John Dryden, perhaps the most accomplished of the Neoclassical poets and playwrights, alluded to Macbeth's "bombast speeches…which are not to be understood" (qtd. in Halliday 258). While Dryden may have disliked elements of *Macbeth*, though, he found great value in what he saw as Shakespeare's natural creative genius. While Shakespeare undoubtedly lacked the symmetry, poise, and elegance of ideal Neoclassical verse, Dryden saw his lack of learning as a source of power: "he was naturally learned; needed not the spectacles of Books to read Nature; he looked inwards, and found her there" (XV.344).

A generation or two later, in the first half of the eighteenth century, critical attention largely swung away from seeing Shakespeare as mere entertainment and began to consider his works as literature worthy of the same kind of careful study and consideration as had long been afforded the classic works of the Greeks and Romans. A host of erudite editors began to compete with one another to produce the best scholarly editions of Shakespeare's plays, and thinkers such as Samuel Johnson began to write extensive essays that, while very different in character from modern scholarship, are entirely recognizable as being part of the same critical genre. Criticism of this age was predominantly evaluative, explaining the critic's opinion about which features of a work of literature are particularly good or bad. When discussing Macbeth's soliloquy immediately before the murder of Duncan, for example, Johnson evocatively writes, "In this passage is exerted all the force of poetry; that force which calls new powers into being, which embodies sentiment, and animates matter" (204). High praise indeed.

In their robust appreciation for what they described as Shakespeare's natural creative genius, Johnson and Dryden in many ways anticipated the Romantic critics of the late eighteenth and early nineteenth centuries. Thanks largely to Schlegel's translation of Shakespeare's plays into German, early Romantics such as Johann Wolfgang van Goethe became enamored of the English playwright and found in him the example they had been seeking to help them demolish the strictures that Neoclassicism continued to impose upon much literary output of the century. The German Romantics in turn inspired their counterparts back in England, perhaps most notably the prolific essayist William Hazlitt. Along with other prominent figures like Coleridge and De Quincey, Hazlitt and the English Romantics ushered in a new focus on emotion as the most important feature of literature. Hazlitt beautifully sums up this kind of reaction to *Macbeth*:

> The lights and shades are laid on with a determined hand; the transitions from triumph to despair, from the height of terror to the repose of death, are sudden and startling; every passion brings its fellow-contrary, and the thoughts pitch and jostle against each other as in the dark. The whole play is an unruly chaos of strange and forbidden things, where the ground rocks under our feet. Shakespeare's genius here took its full swing, and trod upon the furthest bounds of nature and passion. (45)

The final coupling of "nature and passion" effectively distills the Romantic movement to its quintessential heart, and Hazlitt's focus on the play's interest in alternating extremes is most insightful.

The next major critic to discuss Macbeth was A. C. Bradley, whose influential early twentieth-century monograph *Shakespearean Tragedy* did much to cement today's common cultural assessment of Shakespeare's greatest achievements being his "big four" tragedies: *Hamlet*, *Othello*, *King Lear*, and *Macbeth*. While other critics had given these plays positions of prominence in their accounts, Bradley focused almost entirely on them and discussed them in greater detail than almost any critic before. Largely concentrating on characters' motivation and psychology, Bradley treated each of Shakespeare's tragedies like a fully formed Victorian novel, extrapolating tiny textual details into entire situations and narratives going beyond the onstage action. He spends a great deal of time attempting to find answers to questions like how much time passes within plays, how old characters are, and such. In fact, Bradley so industriously pursued such avenues of inquiry, attempting to make perfect logical sense of these works of imaginative fiction, that he became the subject of one of the most famous and influential scholarly jokes of all time.

In 1933, L. C. Knights published "How Many Children Had Lady Macbeth? An Essay in the Theory and Practice of Shakespeare Criticism." The question in its title is at no point taken up in the essay itself, but rather serves to illustrate the type of unanswerable and arguably irrelevant question that Knights believed critics like Bradley were wasting their time attempting to answer. Pushing back against the Bradleyan obsession with character and novelistic narrative, Knights argued passionately that critics should return to treating Shakespeare's plays as the examples of dramatic poetry that they were written to be, that critics should appreciate ambiguity rather than attempt to explain it away. Knights helped usher in a critical focus that privileged theme above character, which remains an influential trend in how Shakespeare is read and taught today.

It is impossible, of course, to claim truthfully that any one vein of Shakespearean criticism truly dominates the way we approach the plays in the twenty-first century. The dispute between Bradley and Knights was but one of countless methodological disputes that regularly punctuated the twentieth century, often with so much frequency and overlapping that any attempt to continue telling the story of *Macbeth*'s reception chronologically would risk being misleading. Additionally, no matter how many approaches are considered, *Macbeth* has elicited so much commentary in recent decades that it would be impossible to come close to a comprehensive account of how the play has been understood. Consider the following paragraphs illustrative of how some of the most prominent theoretical and methodological trends have affected our understanding of the play, but by no means exhaustive.

Another prominent way of reading that became popular early in the twentieth century is the psychoanalytic method. Inspired partly by Romantic attention to emotion, partly by Bradleyan focus on character, and largely by the hugely influential theories of Freud (and, in later years, Jung and Lacan), psychoanalytic criticism strives to explain literature as a reflection of the mind, as a concrete symbolic representation of inner mental strife. *Macbeth*, as deeply psychological as its action is, has naturally inspired more than its share of this type of reading. Freud himself famously speculated that Macbeth and Lady Macbeth were actually just fictive representations of two parts of a single mind.

One important way of reading was that supported by the so-called New Criticism that became dominant in the middle of the twentieth century. In some ways growing out of the thematic method of interpretation advocated by Knights and others like him, New Critics focused on *how* literature creates its thematic meanings, describing in great detail the organization and utilization of figures of speech—especially metaphors. By undertaking "close readings" of texts, New Critics like Cleanth Brooks described poems as highly structured, thoroughly organized systems of meaning-creation, explaining how specific word choices and uses of figurative language create the author's intended effect. Every detail, this reading style presumes, was carefully selected by the author to create the most powerful symbolic message possible. In an essay attempting to explain two particularly strange-seeming metaphors in *Macbeth* (namely one about the bloody daggers used to kill Duncan as wearing breeches of blood, and another comparing Duncan to a naked newborn baby), Brooks provides a characteristic example of the methodology he made famous:

> Yet I think that Shakespeare's daggers attired in their bloody breeches can be defended as poetry, and as characteristically Shakespearean poetry. Furthermore, both this passage and that about the newborn babe, it seems to me, are far more than excrescences, mere extravagances of detail: each, it seems to me, contains a central symbol of the play, and symbols which we must understand

if we are to understand either the detailed passage or the play as a whole. (204-05)

Brooks then goes on to trace the symbolic patterns of imagery that these metaphors evoke, suggesting that Shakespeare—whether consciously or not—created his play with the intricacy and balance of a perfectly structured, organic whole.

This method of close reading is both elegant and ingenious, and in many ways continues to be one of, if not the, dominant mode of interpretation taught to students today. Among professional scholars, however, New Criticism is old news, largely dismissed as detached and ahistorical. By focusing so heavily on internal patterns of symbols, images, and language, the New Critics' critics argue, practitioners of this methodology wind up considering texts in independent vacuums, neglecting the indisputable fact that every work of literature is written within a specific historical and cultural context, and that it is impossible for that context not to be intimately bound up in the text's meanings as they would have existed for the author and the original audience. The fact that no reader of *Macbeth* before Cleanth Brooks had managed to unearth the precise symbolic pattern that Brooks did suggests either that Brooks is uniquely perceptive or that he is so ingenious as to be creating his own unique new interpretations rather than truly discovering Shakespeare's own ingenious structuring of the text.

Such criticisms were leveled at the New Critics in their own time, of course, but as more traditional avenues of historically informed readings had been thoroughly exhausted by scholars of earlier centuries there was relatively little urgency to move away from such an exciting and rewarding interpretive revolution. While historicism may not have been able to reassert its influence over the ascendant New Criticism, New Historicism did. New Historicism, most frequently associated with the influential scholar Stephen Greenblatt, who pioneered it in his studies of Shakespeare, looks at literary texts not in relation to the major historical events in the context of which they had long been considered—the accession of James I—but rather by combing through archives for long-overlooked evidence of texts' embeddedness within the broader cultural moments at which they were created. By studying canonical works alongside books, treatises, pamphlets, and other artifacts, practitioners of New Historicism managed to provide myriad new ways of understanding texts whose meaning had long been debated in isolation, outside of meaningful contact with many relevant modes of discourse. Importantly, New Historicism does not generally contend that an author was necessarily familiar with the specific cultural artifacts brought into consideration; rather, New Historicists contend that gaining a fuller understanding of an author's cultural milieu, by any means, helps give a reader a fuller understanding of the literary text in question. For example, in a fascinating and provocative study of *Macbeth* and witchcraft, Greenblatt looks not just at the most famous early modern English book on the subject, Reginald Scot's *Discoverie of Witchcraft*, but also at the continental European texts on the subject to which Scot was indebted, but which Shakespeare likely never encountered. By getting a fuller sense of what he calls the "circulation of social energies," Greenblatt's New Historicist methodology provides nuanced ways to discuss texts as they relate to complicated systems of power, authority, gender, and other crucial cultural categories.

Through this focus on power structures, New Historicism often becomes intertwined and even indistinguishable from a number of other important recent critical schools of thought. Reflecting contemporary fascination with questions of identity, a great deal of scholarship is being produced that approaches texts through a particular identity-focused lens—for example, feminist, postcolonial, queer, Marxist, and/or disabilities studies. Through the increasingly crucial framework of intersectionality, scholars are demonstrating time and again how thoroughly the texts we've been reading in certain traditional ways for centuries are in many ways inseparable from their cultures' complicated and problematic histories of inequity.

As of today, no one critical school of thought appears to hold clear dominance. Many scholars increasingly disavow the rigidity of following any one philosophical or ideological system when approaching their scholarship, and hybrid methodologies are becoming more and more popular. Many of the best Shakespearean scholars, including those published below in this volume, freely incorporate elements of New Historicism and the New Criticism it so opposed; psychological readings are coexisting with feminist ones, and above all a willingness to experiment with how to look for new information about *Macbeth*, about Shakespeare, and always about ourselves.

Works Cited and Consulted

Brooks, Cleanth. "The Naked Babe and the Cloak of Manliness." *The Well Wrought Urn.* Harcourt, 1947. Reprinted in Macbeth *by William Shakespeare*. Edited by Sylvan Barnet. New American Library, 1963, pp. 196-221.

Bradley, A. C. *Shakespearean Tragedy.* Glasgow UP, 1904.

Dryden, John. "Essay of Dramatic Poesy." In *Essays of John Dryden.* Clarendon, 1926.

Foreman, Simon. *The Book of Plays and Notes Thereof.* Manuscript, 1611. www.shakespearedocumented.org/exhibition/document/formans-account-seeing-plays-globe-macbeth-cymbeline-winters-tale. Accessed 28 July 2017.

Freud, Sigmund. "Some Character-Types Met Within Psycho-Analytic Work," 1916. In *The Standard Edition of the Complete Psychological Work.* Edited by James Strachey, vol. 14, pp. 318-19.

Greenblatt, Stephen. "Shakespeare Bewitched." In *Shakespeare and Cultural Traditions.* Edited by Tetsuo Kishi, Roger Pringle, and Stanley Wells. U of Delaware P, 1994, pp. 17-42.

Halliday, F. E. *Shakespeare and His Critics.* Duckworth, 1958.

Hazlitt, William. *Characters of Shakespeare's Plays.* Hunter, 1817.

Knights, L. C. "How Many Children Had Lady Macbeth? An Essay in the Theory and Practice of Shakespeare Criticism." In *Explorations.* New York UP, 1964, pp. 15-54.

Johnson, Samuel. "Macbeth." In *Johnson on Shakespeare.* Edited by Humphrey Milford.Oxford UP, 1929.

Williams, Glenn. "A Very Brief Survey of the First Three Hundred Years of Commentary on Shakespeare's *Macbeth*." www2.cedarcrest.edu/academic/eng/lfletcher/macbeth/ papers/gwilliams.htm. Accessed 28 July 2017.

Drama in Context: The King's Evil, the Royal Touch, and Shakespeare's Deployment of History in *Macbeth*_____

Bryon Williams

When in 1603 King James VI of Scotland succeeded the recently deceased Elizabeth I as the English monarch and became King James I of England, interest in Scottish matters ascended across English society. Sometime in 1606, as patron of his King's Men acting company, James almost certainly saw the troupe perform William Shakespeare's latest tragedy *Macbeth*, a work occasioned by the Scottish king's accession to the English throne. While *Macbeth* is not considered one of Shakespeare's history plays, the playwright drew the story from the same sources he mined for his histories: Raphael Holinshed's *Chronicles of England, Scotland, and Ireland* (1587), a work that blended fact and legend into popular history. Shakespeare further modifies and adapts history to his own ends—some ends artistic, others decidedly topical and political. The putative performance of the play for James entailed an intersection of two distinct but related worlds: the world of Macbeth and the world of *Macbeth*. That is, on its face the play is about the Scotland and England of the eleventh century, and about a historical Macbeth who had ruled as King of Scotland almost 600 years before the play's composition. Yet the play is indirectly but just as forcefully "about" the living Scottish and English issues of Shakespeare's own day in the late sixteenth and early seventeenth centuries, issues often too controversial to be debated directly. One of Shakespeare's distinctive strategies as an artist is that of writing about a different era as a means of broaching the conflicts within his own contemporary society. This chapter presents an in-depth cultural history of one such controversy—the King's Evil malady and its Royal Touch remedy, described in *Macbeth* Act IV, Scene 3—as a microcosm of England's most pressing cultural issues in Shakespeare's own historical moment: the succession crisis (that is, who would assume the throne upon the death or removal of a sitting monarch), questions on the sources of a sovereign's legitimacy, attitudes toward magic and the supernatural, and Catholic-Protestant tensions in both theory and practice. I begin by placing the Royal Touch ritual in context with other notable intersections between the medieval world depicted onstage and the early modern world in which *Macbeth* was written, performed, and received.

History and Drama in Dialogue

While viewing *Macbeth*, King James midway through Act IV would have seen Malcolm (Duncan's elder son whom the king had named as his successor) and Macduff as they visit the English court of Edward the Confessor, the historical Macbeth's contemporary counterpart on the English throne. Malcolm asks if the king is nigh, and a doctor replies,

> Ay, sir: there are a crew of wretched souls
> That stay his cure: their malady convinces
> The great assay of art; but at his touch,
> Such sanctity hath heaven given his hand,
> They presently amend. (IV.3.141-45)

When Macduff inquires about the strange affliction, Malcolm describes the malady and its royal remedy:

> 'Tis called the evil:
> A most miraculous work in this good king...
> How he solicits heaven
> Himself best knows, but strangely visited people
> All swoll'n and ulcerous, pitiful to the eye,
> The mere despair of surgery, he cures,
> Hanging a golden stamp about their necks,
> Put on with holy prayers; and, 'tis spoken,
> To the succeeding royalty he leaves
> The healing benediction. With this strange virtue,
> He hath a heavenly gift of prophecy,

And sundry blessings hang about his throne
That speak him full of grace. (IV.3.168-181)

Onstage, the eleventh-century healer Edward, whose benevolence radiates in a halo of grace and virtue, serves as a thematic contrast to Macbeth, who has metastasized into the disease of Scotland, and whose crimes and tyranny are reflected in widespread disorders of nature and weather. In the larger viewing context of early seventeenth-century England, a more complicated dynamic was at work. In the audience, five and a half centuries after Edward, sat James, who was himself the "succeeding royalty" and who had inherited, for better or worse, "the healing benediction" of the Royal Touch. James himself performed the healing ritual for his subjects, but a complex of political, religious, and personal factors made the rite a royal prerogative about which the king was deeply conflicted.

Before examining the Royal Touch ritual in depth, however, it is crucial to note that the scene describing the King's Evil is only one among numerous intersections between the world depicted onstage in *Macbeth* and the world of the play's audience. Onstage is presented a plot to murder a king; in the audience sits James, a king who only the year before had been targeted for assassination in the foiled Gunpowder Plot of 1605. Onstage are depicted forces of magic, witchcraft, superstition, and the supernatural; in the audience is a king who not only wrote a book on necromancy and the dark arts (a work that may have even influenced Shakespeare's depiction of witchcraft in the play) but who believed himself to have been a victim of witches' conjuring (including storms at sea, much like the curse of tempests described by the witches in *Macbeth* I.3) and who on becoming the English king immediately enacted stricter laws against witchcraft. Onstage Macbeth is tormented by a vision of the future line of kings descending not from him but from his compatriot Banquo; the eighth and final king in this line is presumably James, who considered himself descended from the legendary Banquo (no doubt a major reason that Shakespeare fundamentally changed the role and character of Banquo, who in

Holinshed's *Chronicles* is presented as an accomplice to Duncan's murder but in the play is a loyal and virtuous foil to Macbeth). Onstage, among the gravest issues are questions of succession and sovereignty: Who should rightly take the throne upon the death or deposition of a sitting monarch? Who should decide, and how? What precisely constitutes the source and the nature of a monarch's power, legitimacy, and sovereignty? What is the proper relationship between the ruler and the ruled? And in the audience is James, whose own legitimacy had been challenged after the English succession crisis had reached a fever pitch in the 1590s as Elizabeth aged without an heir.

Such intersections reveal the unique role drama could play in public discourse and the uses for which Shakespeare could deploy history. So controversial were these topics in Shakespeare's time that open debate on such issues was often deemed dangerous, illegal, or treasonous. In 1571, Elizabeth ordered the Statute of Silence, which made any public discussion of the queen's successor punishable as treason (Carroll 185). In 1603, the newly coronated James' first acts included not only stronger laws against witchcraft but also an order that all copies of a popular book skeptical of the reality of magic be burned. But drama afforded Shakespeare a mode by which to obliquely address contemporary debates while technically writing about another and distant historical era altogether.

Succession, Sovereignty, and the Supernatural

Among the conflicts looming largest over England's political climate in the sixteenth and seventeenth centuries was the question of succession. While the issue had caused discord before, a series of succession crises in the sixteenth century precipitated some of the most momentous developments in England's political and religious history. Even a cursory overview shows the tumult to be dizzying. When Henry VIII (ruled 1509-1547) sought an annulment from his first marriage because Catherine of Aragon produced no succeeding male heir, Pope Clement VII denied the annulment, leading Henry to break from the Roman Catholic Church and declare himself supreme head of the Church of England. The instability carried on with the offspring who did eventually succeed Henry. During the short reign of the young Edward VI (ruled 1547-1553), church theology and liturgy became increasingly Protestant in nature. When Henry's Roman Catholic daughter Mary (ruled 1553-1558) assumed the throne, she reinstated papal authority and reversed the turn to Protestantism. Her half-sister Elizabeth (ruled 1558-1603) immediately restored Protestantism upon becoming queen, but struck for a moderate path to help quell long-brewing tensions. Elizabeth's reign in many ways fostered needed stability by sheer virtue of its long duration, but the queen kept succession anxieties very much alive by never marrying, having children, or naming a successor. As Elizabeth aged and began to decline in the 1590s, the issue of succession blistered in many quarters into full-fledged crisis.

In Shakespeare's play, Macbeth (much like Henry VIII) is tormented by an absence of successors in his line, and is spurred to take extreme and violent action in his unrest. The witches' prophecy that Banquo will produce kings leaves Macbeth dissatisfied with simply possessing the throne in the present: he seethes in a soliloquy that the Weird Sisters

> hailed [Banquo] father to a line of kings:
> Upon my head they placed a fruitless crown,
> And put a barren sceptre in my gripe,
> Thence to be wrenched with an unlineal hand,
> No son of mine succeeding. If't be so,
> For Banquo's issue have I filed my mind,
> For them the gracious Duncan have I murdered,
> Put rancours in the vessel of my peace
> Only for them, and mine eternal jewel
> Given to the common enemy of man,
> To make them kings, the seed of Banquo kings! (III.1.59-69)

For Macbeth, the costs he has incurred—the guilt of murdering a king benevolent toward him and all the country, and the subsequent loss of peace of mind and descent into existential despair and desperation—are far too great a price to pay for a "fruitless crown" and a "barren scepter," with Banquo's descendants innocently enjoying the fruits of Macbeth's misdeeds. Rather than leave behind a secure dynastic line, Macbeth leaves behind instead a legacy of shame, destruction, and disorder. In contrast to the scourge of Scotland stands the saint-like healer Edward, the English king who not only enjoys "sundry blessings [that] hang about his throne" (IV.3.180) but who bears the miraculous gift of the Royal Touch that he shall bequeath to his descendants: "To the succeeding royalty he leaves/ The healing benediction" (IV.3.155-56). The Royal Touch and its royal inheritance as depicted onstage—along with the related elements of succession, sovereignty, magic, and the role of miracles and the supernatural in liturgy and theology—reverberated throughout the reigns of the two English monarchs of Shakespeare's lifetime, and indeed throughout all of England's culture and society.

The King's Evil and the Royal Touch in English History

The "King's Evil" most commonly denoted scrofula, a tubercular swelling of the lymph glands in the neck, and the term came to refer to any of a number of swellings or lesions in the neck area, whether due to tuberculosis or not. The history of the "Royal Touch"—that is, the monarch's curing the disease by laying hands on the sick, accompanied by varying degrees of ceremony—in England is a long one, stretching from the practice's legendary origins with Edward the Confessor (ruled 1042-1066) into the eighteenth century. The healing ritual was performed for the last time on April 27, 1714, by Queen Anne, marking the end of a rite performed since ancient times.

The historical record on the actual origins of the ritual in England is relatively scant. While sixteenth-century clergyman William Tooker nominates the legendary King Lucius and even the biblical Joseph of Arimathea as initiators of the Royal Touch in England, the consensus tradition credits the saintly Edward the Confessor as the true founder of the practice. William of Malmesbury, writing during the reign of Henry I (1100-1135), saw the story of Edward as founder as a tale constructed and promoted by Henry to secure his own dynastic security and legitimacy. William is the first in a long line of skeptics on the nature of the king's power to heal: "In our day, some have used these miracles… to support a false idea. They have claimed that the king possessed the power to heal this illness, not by virtue of his holiness, but by hereditary title, as a privilege of the royal line" (in Bloch 23). William's objection highlights one of the most controversial aspects of the practice: the *source* of the king's curative powers. William seems to say that in Henry I's day, it makes sense that a holy person—a saint—could perform miracles, but for a king who is not a saint to work miracles by virtue of some inherited royal power is unthinkable. Eventually, English monarchs would assert that they were God's own anointed agents on earth, and that the performance of miracles therefore had political and theological justification. Henry I's original claim was a bold move down this path—and it worked. By 1587, Henry's version of history is firmly codified in Holinshed's *Chronicles*, Shakespeare's direct source for *Macbeth*:

> As hath beene thought, he [Edward] was inspired with the gift of prophesie, and also to haue had the gift of healing infirmities and diseases. He vsed to helpe those that were vexed with the disease, commonlie called the kings euill, and left that virtue as it were a portion of inheritance vnto his successors the kings of this realme. (Holinshed I.754)

The ritual grew in popularity until it had reached elaborate ceremonial status in the reign of Henry VII. By the time of Elizabeth's reign, as we shall see, the source of the monarch's miraculous power had become a hotly-debated matter indeed.

Elizabeth I: A Touch of Strategy

Explanations for the origins of the power claimed by the monarch were legion. Some thought that the power could come from the king's own goodness. Others saw it as "a personal gift from God to Edward the Confessor" handed down to subsequent rulers through royal blood (Thomas 196). Many argued that "the miraculous power sprang from the monarch's consecration with holy oil at his coronation"—a rather literal "anointing"—while others preferred the anointing to be symbolic and "regarded the power to cure the evil as an intrinsic quality pertaining to the sacred person of the monarch" (Thomas 195). The attempt to bring the practice into line with orthodox religious practice led many believers to see the monarch as a powerful intermediary whose prayers and intercession simply handed the sick over into God's power. Elizabeth's contemporary Reginald Scot, another skeptic concerning the supernatural, included a spectrum of explanations in a summary from his *The Discoverie of Witchcraft* (1584): "[The Royal Touch] is supposed to be a miraculous and a peculiar gift, & a speciall grace given to the kings and queenes of England. Which some referre to the proprietie of their persons, some to the peculiar gift of God, and some to the efficacie of words" (Scot 255). Not only was the source of the monarch's power debatable this late into Elizabeth's reign, but the very propriety of the ritual itself came into question. Why would Elizabeth so willingly embrace a practice that in many ways flew in the face of both Reformation attitudes and an emerging rational-scientific worldview?

In many ways, the opposition Elizabeth faced actually *encouraged* the queen to embrace and promote the healing ritual. Despite the potential hazards she faced in theological and scientific quarters, popular belief placed significant faith in all kinds of miraculous healers. If villagers were lining up for the services of traveling cunning-men and other miracle workers, the queen, as God's own anointed, saw fertile ground for reaffirming the crown's own established power to heal. Elizabeth had much to gain from performing the rite because the public perceived the Royal Touch as *effective*. The perception of efficacy had significant effects in realms ranging from the theological to the political: "Elizabeth's healings were cited as proof that the Papal Bull of Excommunication had failed to take effect; and were even claimed as justification for giving her ambassadors diplomatic precedence over those of Spain" (Thomas 195). In fact, the perceived effectiveness of miraculous healing, royal or not, often managed to defuse religious objections in fundamental ways, for "many theologians stressed the wickedness of magical cures, but not their futility" (Thomas 207). The increasing opposition from various quarters—mainly from rational skeptics like Reginald Scot, from Catholics, and from Puritans—thus led Elizabeth to forcefully secure and display the healing power that was coming under attack (Bloch 190). With the common people's readiness to believe already an advantage, the queen moved to further formalize the religious nature of the healing ceremony so she could capitalize on a ritual that would be seen as not only efficacious but as theologically legitimate as well.

As Elizabeth sought to increase the frequency and visibility of the royal healing power, she enlisted a series of apologists for the Royal Touch, especially clergy who could inculcate the public as they justified the practice—one often criticized as Papist—from their pulpits. This tactic was representative of the queen's fertile strategic mind, for "throughout her reign, Elizabeth had mastered the art of separating herself from Catholic images and rituals, while at the same time appropriating them for her own purposes," and the royal healing ceremony was just such an appropriation (Carroll 227). In denying miracles and questioning royal privilege in general, the Reformation had threatened on theological grounds to weaken beyond repair the monarch's claim to hold healing powers, but the testimony of Elizabeth's contemporary apologists reveals the extent to which the queen sought to frame the practice as above all a religious rite. William Tooker laid down a detailed description of the ceremony in 1597. After a reading from St. Mark affirming the healing power of laying on hands, the queen laid her bare hands upon the affected parts of each sick person. The sick then retired as a second reading from St. John was delivered, after which each person approached Elizabeth again so that she could place a gold coin ("bored and slung on a ribbon") around each neck, make the sign of the cross over the supplicant, and deliver a prayer and blessing over each person. As the ceremony ended, the queen and the entire congregation knelt in prayer, reciting not only common prayers but also "a special prayer…not found in the Book of daily Prayers." Tooker offers personal testimony that he saw Elizabeth "worn with fatigue, as when in one single day...she healed eight and thirty persons of the struma" (Tooker 72). The queen's own surgeon William Clowes issued in 1602 a treatise affirming the monarch's healing powers on the basis of medical success, theological justification, and personal testimony of individuals healed by Elizabeth. Through "the gift and power of Almightie God," says one man who had long sought a cure, "I am by her Maiesty perfectly cured and healed; and after her Grace had touched me, I never applyed any Medicine at all" (Clowes 50). The man then revealed the "Angell of golde" (a gold coin bearing the angel Michael on it) that the queen had placed upon him and that he still wore faithfully. Clowes's conclusion from such a testimonial is that we must "confidently affirme and steadfastly believe that...when all Artes and Sciences doe faile... her Highnesse is...peerlesse and without comparison" as an agent of healing (Clowes 50).

Such accounts make it easy to see why Elizabeth, already excommunicated by Rome, became the target of both rationalist thinkers and Protestant reformers; "as Protestantism inevitably became a screen for rationalism," denouncements of the Anglican Church's "magical ceremonial rites" became commonplace from both secular and religious critics (Thomas 69). The queen succeeded, however, in securing the faith of perhaps the most important parties concerned: the largely uneducated public who believed in magic and miracles of all kinds. Despite the scripture, signs of the cross, and prayers filling the ceremony, the congregation did not always see the atmosphere attending the rite as primarily religious in nature (Thomas 194). What the public did recognize in the ceremony was just what other authorities attacked it for: its elements of magic. The gold coin had ceased being the alms offering it had originally signified to being "commonly looked upon as a talisman possessing its own intrinsic medicinal power" (Bloch 182). The core elements of the ceremony under Elizabeth— the bearer of supernatural powers laying hands upon the afflicted, saying miraculous words and offering a curative and protective talisman—inspired public confidence primarily not because they were sanctified by the church but rather because they looked like the magic with which villagers were already familiar.

Thus by the time of her death, Elizabeth had shaped the practice of the Royal Touch into a ritual that proved the monarch's divine status; secured royal privileges for political gain; received thorough justification from some theological quarters and strident condemnation from others; and received widespread public support (and inspired high expectations from the people) because of its perceived effectiveness and its resemblance to magic. It was this version of the Royal Touch that James VI of Scotland inherited, along with the English crown, from his distant cousin Elizabeth in 1603.

James I: A Touch of Ambivalence

James's reluctance to embrace the seemingly divine power of the Royal Touch appears odd in someone who so ardently championed the theory of the divine right of kings. Yet James's conflicted attitude toward the monarch's power to heal the King's Evil was a natural extension of his complicated attitude toward the supernatural in general. On one hand, James believed that the powers of magic and witchcraft were real. Not only did he believe that he himself had been the victim of witches' conjuring (in 1590, mighty storms at sea delayed his return trip from Denmark, where he had gone to get his Anne, his new queen), but he also personally involved himself in witchcrafts interrogations and trials (Carroll 305). In 1598 James wrote his own *Daemonologie*, largely as an attack on the skepticism of Reginald Scot, and "[a]mong his first acts on becoming King James I of England in 1603 was the enactment of more stringent laws against witchcraft and the order that all copies of [Scot's] the *Discoverie [of Witchcraft]* were to be burnt" (Williamson 23).

On the other hand, James held his own genuine and deep-seated skepticism toward religious miracles. His upbringing in the more Calvinist climes of Scotland led him to view miracles as imposture on the part of practitioners and superstition on the part of believers

(Bloch 191). Therefore, James felt that his own performance of the Royal Touch ritual would place him in multiple binds. First, he would be leading a rite full of magical and miraculous elements at the same time he was officially spearheading a movement to banish many such practices in the kingdom at large; as one scholar put it, "It was a rather hard measure to put English rustics to their penance for relying on the charms operated by local healers, and at the same time to bid them trust the Royal Touch for the King's Evil" (Kittredge 151). Second, King James himself found it difficult to even *pretend* to believe in the supposedly divine nature of the rite. A letter from an Italian ambassador at James's court in 1603 says that "he [James] did not see how the patient could be healed without a miracle, and nowadays miracles had ceased and no longer happened: so he was afraid of committing a superstitious act" (Carroll 224-5). On this count James finds himself in unlikely company by being in full agreement with none other than Reginald Scot, who devotes his own chapter to establishing that "miracles are ceased...[and] such things as seeme miraculous, are cheeflie doone by deceipt, legierdemaine, or confederacie" (Scot 143). Thus James found himself faced with either a] performing a highly public, magical-superstitious act while simultaneously banning similar acts in his kingdom, or b] refusing to fulfill a royal function that his subjects not only desperately believed in but expected from their king. As James wrestled with this dilemma, lingering public doubts about his own legitimacy following the succession crisis of the previous decade surely weighed on his mind, since "[t]he ability to cure the Evil...[was] a touch-stone for any claimant to the English throne, on the assumption that only the legitimate king could heal the scrofulous" (Thomas 195). Personally and politically, James found himself deeply conflicted over an ancient rite that had profound contemporary implications.

In the end, James found it necessary to perform the ritual, but not without compromises in both form and content. To temper the miraculous nature of the ceremony (and his own role as a kind of wizard), he attempted to characterize the rite as "no more than a kind of prayer addressed to Heaven for the healing of the sick, a prayer in which he invited all those present to join him" (Bloch 191). While he eliminated the sign of the cross from the ceremony, he continued to bestow the gold coin upon the afflicted, but only after ordering that a cross and the word "miracle" be removed from the coin's design. Perhaps more important than the formal modifications he made to the ceremony were the personal reconciliations James made with his own role as both king and healer to his people. As the reluctant James gradually came to embrace the practice of the Royal Touch, the king also came to embrace his role as a healer, one whose rite worked not through the efficacy of miracles but through the power of the patient's own belief: "We know that he actually touched for the evil on various occasions, for reasons of state, knowing well that the ceremony could not harm the sufferers and might work beneficially upon them through the imagination" (Kittredge 316). Thus James may not have been simply a monarch who performed a royal and religious charade in the interests of his own security; the picture that emerges is of a king who resided over a rite that he did *not* believe in for the express reason that his subjects *did* believe so ardently. As Arthur Wilson's 1653 history of James's reign put it,

> He was a king in understanding and was content to have his Subjects ignorant in many things. As in curing the *Kings-Evil*, when *Miracles* were in fashion; but he let the World believe it, though he smiled at it, in his own *Reason*, finding the strength of the *Imagination* a more powerful *Agent* in the *Cure*, than the *Plasters* his *Chirurgions* prescribed for the *Sore* (Wilson 289).

Even James's reconciliation to the rite is decidedly ambivalent. While there is an element of cynicism in his conscious decision to administer a virtual placebo, such an action is more than just a rationalization for carrying out a politically beneficial charade. The intent to help and even heal his ailing subjects, especially in the absence of any other effective treatment, comes across as potentially sincere. Although he could not believe in the ritual as a miraculous, supernatural cure for the King's Evil, he could conceive of himself as a king who cured his afflicted subjects through the near-miraculous power of belief itself.

So as King James watched the legendary Edward the Confessor portrayed onstage, he saw a virtuous king with the heavenly power to cure the sick by a miraculous touch. Perhaps James had come to believe that he, too, could be a king with just such a beneficial effect on his subjects, not through the power of heaven but through the nature of the patient's own mind. Shakespeare is duly hailed for his psychological insight, fully on display in *Macbeth*'s study of ambition, deception, and conscience. The practice of the Royal Touch by Elizabeth and James sheds light on the psychological acumen of the two English monarchs who ruled during the playwright's lifetime and who navigated a minefield of political, theological, and philosophical firestorms during an era of reform and upheaval. In setting aside their own skepticism and unleashing the restorative powers of faith itself, Queen Elizabeth and King James may have realized that when an ailment exceeds the reach of both medicine and prayer, it may indeed be true that, as Lady Macbeth's attending physician says of the diseased mind, "[t]herein the patient/ Must minister to himself" (V.3.48-49).

Works Cited

Bloch, Marc. *The Royal Touch: Sacred Monarchy and Scrofula in England and France.* Routledge and Kegan Paul, 1973.

Carroll, William C., editor. *Macbeth: Texts and Contexts.* Bedford/St. Martin's, 1999.

Clowes, William. *A right frutefull and approoued treatise, for the artificiall cure of that malady called in Latin Struma, and in English, the evill, cured by kinges and queenes of England: Very necessary for all young practizers of chyrurgery.* Edward Allde, 1602.

Holinshed, Raphael. *The Chronicles of England, Scotland, and Ireland.* 1587. 6 vols. J. Johnson, etc., 1807-08.

Kittredge, George Lyman. *Witchcraft in Old and New England.* Harvard UP, 1929.

Scot, Reginald. *The Discoverie of Witchcraft.* 1584. Southern Illinois UP, 1964.

Shakespeare, William. *Macbeth*. 1606. Edited by Stephen Orgel. Penguin Books, 2016.

Thomas, Keith. *Religion and the Decline of Magic.* Scribner's, 1971.

Tooker, William. *Charisma sive donum sanationis (The King's Evil).* 1597. Raymond Crawfurd, translator. Clarendon P, 1911.

Williamson, Hugh Ross. Introduction. *The Discoverie of Witchcraft* by Reginald Scot. Southern Illinois UP, 1964.

Wilson, Arthur. *The History of Great Britain, Being the Life and Reign of King James the First*. London, 1653.

Mele's Self-Deception in *Macbeth*_____

Mohammad Shaaban Ahmad Deyab

Introduction

William Shakespeare's *Macbeth* has attracted the attention of many critics who attempt to study the psychology of its principal characters. For example, in "Phantasmagoric Macbeth" David Willbern provides a psychoanalytic reading of the play where he views the play as a scrambled dream, in which everything is representative of one or more inner desire or process. Michael Goldman's "Speaking Evil: Language and Action in *Macbeth*" refers to Macbeth's ambition as the main reason that leads him to do what he knows is morally wrong. Similarly, Lily B. Doren's "*Macbeth*: A Study in Fear" claims that although Macbeth and Lady Macbeth have different psychological makeups, they are similar in having the passion of ambition that motivates both to kill Duncan. Seth Shugar's "Knowing Is Not Enough" is another study that attempts to deals with Macbeth's psychology. According to Shugar, it is Macbeth's "akrasia" —his inability to perform an action he knows to be right—rather than his ambition that leads to his downfall.

Despite the variety of these critical approaches to Macbeth's psychology, this chapter attempts to provide a new critical interpretation of his behavior through the lens of self-deception theory that has gained an increasing popularity at the hands of Alfred Mele. Thus, taking this theory as a framework, this chapter attempts to explain how Macbeth goes through some of Mele's conditions to enter self-deception by following several mechanisms such as negative misinterpretation, selective focusing, and confirmation bias. The chapter begins by introducing Mele's self-deception and then provides a detailed discussion of two of Mele's conditions for a person to enter self-deception, which are perfectly apt for Macbeth.

Mele's Definition of Self-Deception

In his book *Self-Deception Unmasked,* Alfred Mele attempts to provide answers to such questions as how can a person deceive himself? What are the forms of self-deception? What are the conditions of self-deception? From Mele's perspective, self-deception happens when a person sustains some incorrect belief despite evidence to the contrary because of some motivation. As he puts it, "people enter self-deception in acquiring a belief that P if and only if P is false and they acquire the belief in a suitably biased way" (120). In this case, self-deception is a psychological state in which the subject is "motivated or has a motivated component" to believe in a specific proposition (Mele 5). It requires the person to commit his own action to a motivation and that on the basis of that incentive the individual endorses certain psychological strategies and behavioral patterns that persuade him of the truth of what he believes.

Moreover, Mele argues that there are two different forms of self-deception: "straight" vs. "twisted." Straight self-deception "involves an agent's being self-deceived about some proposition P is being true when she is motivationally biased in coming to believe that P is true" (25). In this type of self-deception, the self-deceptive belief matches the person's desire that causes him to discount data that should count against the desired outcome, and to see data as supporting the desired outcome when it really does not. In twisted self-deception, "the person is self-deceived in believing something that he wants to be false" (Mele 4). In this type of self-deception, the person's self-deceptive belief opposes his desire, and he ends up believing what he does not wish. In both forms, "our desiring something to be true sometimes exerts a biasing influence on what we believe" (Mele 11).

Mele's Conditions for Self-Deception

In *Self-Deception Unmasked,* Mele outlines four possible conditions for the subject (S) to enter self-deception:

1. S's belief that P is false.

2. S treats data relevant, or at least seemingly relevant, to the truth-value of P in a motivationally biased way.
3. This biased treatment is a nondeviant cause of S's acquiring the belief that P.
4. The body of the data possessed by S at the time provides greater warrant for not-P than for P (50-51).

To serve the objectives of this chapter, the following discussion deals extensively with the first two of these conditions, which the character of Macbeth perfectly meets.

S's (Macbeth's) Belief that P is False

From Mele's perspective, for anyone to be self-deceived, he must believe in something (proposition P) that he knows is untrue. This implies that the self-deceived person intentionally deceives himself into believing something that is false. As Mele puts it, "people enter self-deception in acquiring a belief that P if and only if P is false" (120). In this way, self-deception entails a blind or unexamined acceptance of a belief that can easily be "spurious if the person were to inspect the belief impartially or from the perspective of the generalized other" (Sahdra 213). Moreover, by being resigned to this false belief, the subject is unable to get out of his self-deception.

This is typically true of Macbeth, who believes in something that he knows is false, although "the body of the data possessed" by Macbeth when he meets the witches for the first time "provides greater warrant for not-P than for P" (Mele 51). For example, when Macbeth first receives the witches' prophecies, "All hail, Macbeth, that shalt be King hereafter!" (I.3.50), he is so much sure their prophecies are false that he questions their validity:

> I know I am Thane of Glamis,
> But how of Cawdor? The Thane of Cawdor lives,
> A prosperous gentleman; and to be king
> Stands not within the prospect of belief,
> No more than to be Cawdor. (I.3.71-75)

According to this quotation, Macbeth questions the truth of the witches' sayings, and he knows deep in his heart that their prophecies are false for many reasons. First, Macbeth knows "The Thane of Cawdor lives. Why do you dress me / In borrowed robes? (I.3.108-9). Second, Macbeth is aware that it is impossible for him to be the next in line for the throne because after the king's death, his eldest son, Malcolm, whom Duncan names "The Prince of Cumberland" (I.4.39), will be his heir. Third, the prophecies are told by witches, who are considered to have supernatural powers that none would trust. Macbeth himself once said "damn'd all those that trust them!" (IV.1.161), and Banquo emphasizes this idea when he said,

> But 'tis strange;
> And oftentimes, to win us to our harm,
> The instruments of darkness tell us truths,
> Win us with honest trifles, to betray [u]s. (I.3.122-125)

then, too, the witches' physical existence is so doubtful that neither Macbeth nor Banquo is sure of their reality. To use Macbeth's words regarding the existence of the witches: "There's no such thing. / It is the bloody business which informs / Thus to mine eyes" (II.1.48-50). Thus, these witches are, like Macbeth's dagger, "a false creation, / Proceeding from the heat-oppressèd brain?" (II.1.39-40).

Regardless of their dramatic role, the fact that the witches appear only to Macbeth and Banquo at the beginning of the play might find an explanation from a psychological point of view. Macbeth and Banquo are suffering from sleep deprivation because of the fatigue of the battle that runs for the whole day. Thus, one can argue that Macbeth's and Banquo's fatigue results in "the experiences of individual psychotic experiences such as delusions or hallucinations" (Reeve et al. 111). In other words, their physical fatigue and lack of sleep lead them to see things that do not exist. As Brandon Peters has precisely stated,

> Beginning to hallucinate is among the more common symptoms of sleep deprivation. A hallucination is the perception of something that is not really present in the environment ... sleep deprivation can

actually cause other symptoms that mimic mental illness, such as disorientation and paranoid thoughts... Though visual experiences predominate, some hallucinations may involve hearing things. These auditory hallucinations may range from voices to loud sounds or other stimuli.

In the light of Brandon's account, because of their lack of sleep, both Macbeth and Banquo experienced visual and auditory hallucinations causing them to be unable to differentiate between what is real and unreal. The way the witches appear to Banquo and Macbeth supports this argument. They appear and disappear like a visual hallucination, making it difficult for Macbeth and Banquo to distinguish between the hallucinatory and the real:

> You should be women,
> And yet your beards forbid me to interpret
> That you are so. (I.3.45-47)

Banquo here suggests that he is really confused about the nature of these witches and supports the argument that they are not likely real witches, but only hallucinatory ones. In another quotation, Banquo reiterates his doubts about the physical existence of the witches and suggests that he and Macbeth might be hallucinating:

> Were such things here as we do speak about?
> Or have we eaten on the insane root
> That takes the reason prisoner? (I.3.83-85)

Although Macbeth knows that the witches are unlikely to be real, and their prophecies thus might be false, the question remains: How does Macbeth deceive himself despite his belief in the falsehood of the witches' prophecies?

From the standpoint of Mele's theory, Macbeth tends to believe the witches' prophecies because he wants them to be true even when considering these prophecies later would show that they are probably false. Macbeth's burning desire to know where the witches got their information, "Stay, you imperfect speakers, tell me more" (I.3.71), implies his interest in the prophecies themselves. This explains how Macbeth starts the process of discounting any evidence that will contradict his desire to fulfill the most important of them all: to be a king. In this way, Macbeth's self-deception has a "doxastic conflict" between the false belief he acquires ("you might be the King hereafter") and the true belief he denies ("King Duncan is still alive").

After meeting the three witches, Macbeth has two contrasting beliefs, but is conscious of only one of them, because he wants to remain unconscious of the other. In other words, Macbeth deceives himself by believing in what the witches said and behaves in such a way as to motivate himself to believe the negation of that truth ("King Duncan should be dead") by arranging the murder with his wife. Thus, in his search for evidence of his belief that he is going to be a king, Macbeth engages in belief-misleading activities such as sending a letter to his wife to create an imaginary world where he is preparing himself to be a king. In other words, Macbeth engages in a form of "mental *simulation*, i.e. his motivation to avoid the recognition of ($\neg p$) leads him to mentally escape the real world and intermittently inhabit a 'p-world,' an imaginary environment which protects him from the inconvenient or undesired evidence" (Porcher).

After hearing Ross's greeting, Macbeth has evidence based on which he believes that the other witches' predictions are more likely to be true than to be false. This is called, in Mele's words, "positive misinterpretation" (26) where Macbeth misinterprets some evidence (being appointed as Thane of Cawdor) as favoring his desired proposition (I will be a king) "when that evidence, in absence of the biasing desire, would easily be recognized as counting against the desired proposition" (Mele 27). From the standpoint of Mele's theory, Macbeth's desire to be a king leads him to interpret any data to support this belief, whereas he would effortlessly decide to act against this belief in the desire's absence. Thus, Macbeth constructs Ross's message in a certain way so that it looks like evidence for P (I will be a king). This is very clear in Macbeth's first soliloquy: "Glamis, and Thane of Cawdor— /

The greatest is behind" (1.3.116-17). In this soliloquy, Macbeth deceives nobody but himself, and it marks the starting point of his self-deception because he convinces himself of something that he does not believe is right.

Thus, Macbeth convinces himself that he is destined to be a king, which reflects his mental state as a self-deceived person who is convinced that he has an obligation to do this by either fair means or foul. Macbeth's first step is to send a letter to his wife, waiting for positive confirmation from her to go ahead with his next move. By sending this letter, Macbeth, to use Mele's words, wants to reach a state of mind, that is, "the belief that P, which he likes, or wants, to believe, and he also wants reality to be exactly as he wants it to be, that is, P to be true" (25). The letter reads as follows:

> They met me in the day of success, and I have learned by the perfect'st report they have more in them than mortal knowledge. When I burned in desire to question them further, they made themselves air, into which they vanished. Whiles I stood rapt in the wonder of it, came missives from the King, who all-hailed me Thane of Cawdor, by which title, before, these weïrd sisters saluted me and referred me to the coming on of time with "Hail, king that shalt be!" This have I thought good to deliver thee, my dearest partner of greatness, that thou might'st not lose the dues of rejoicing by being ignorant of what greatness is promised thee. Lay it to thy heart, and farewell. (I.5.1-13)

By writing this letter, Macbeth has, from the standpoint of Mele's theory, a self-focused desire to believe these prophecies, and this would be the principal reason for his self-deception. The opening and closing sentences make it clear how he feels about the witches and their prophecies. His reiteration of the witches' prophecy in the letter, "Hail, king that shalt be!" (I.5.9-10), implies his endorsement of that prediction. Therefore, as he has been convinced, Macbeth is doing his best to convince his wife of the witches' prophecies. That is why he tells his wife every detail of what happened in a way to support his desire to be a king. For example, Macbeth informs Lady Macbeth about how he was told he was becoming

Thane of Cawdor, and then King. It is to be noted that Macbeth never mentioned anything in the letter related to Banquo's issue; an action that implies that he is trying to avoid anything that will destroy his happy belief and seeks, instead, to focus his attention on the person— "my dearest partner of greatness" (I.5.10-11)—who is ready to make it true: Lady Macbeth.

Moreover, Macbeth's concluding the letter by asking his wife to rejoice with him about the greatness that is promised to them is an obvious indication of his straight self-deception because he is clearly self-deceived about the witches' prophecies being true when he is motivationally biased to believe these predictions. Thus, Macbeth's letter could be explained as "part of an attempt to deceive oneself, or to cause oneself to believe something, or to make it easier for oneself to believe something (e.g., intentionally focusing on data of a certain kind as part of an attempt to deceive oneself into believing that P)" (18). From the standpoint of Mele's theory, Macbeth writes this letter as if he believed that he has already become a king, which suggests that he believes he is; and his saying "this have I thought good to deliver thee, my dearest partner of greatness" (I.5.10-11) refers to his absolute self-deception by focusing his attention on the only prophecy that refers to him as a future king. Moreover, "one could be motivated to self-deception by having a desire to believe what one's peers believe, while being indifferent to the truth or falsity of what is believed" (Funkhouser). In this regard, Macbeth needs someone to confirm what he desires and this could be achieved only by his wife. As William Ruddick has stated,

> We choose the company of those whose views coincide with our own. Hence, our projects come to be questionable only from a perspective we are unlikely or even unable to take ... our associates, out of sympathy or cowardice, tend to keep the lights turned down low. (383)

From Ruddick's point of view, since the person looks only to those who hold similar views, he is unlikely to find any help in recognizing his self-deception. This is true of Macbeth when looks to Lady

Macbeth as a confirming voice to carry out the ugly deed of killing his own king. As Maria L. Howell has observed,

> Lady Macbeth's triple greetings, "Great Glamis, worthy Cawdor / Greater than both, by the all-hail hereafter" (I.5.53-4), not only resonates with the witches' predictions at the beginning of the play, it leaves no doubt that Lady Macbeth sees the kingship as a reality which has already come into being. (6)

To conclude this part, by sending the letter to his wife, the self-deceived Macbeth wants to be in a state of mind of belief that P, which he knows is false. Despite his knowledge that these prophecies are false, Macbeth continues to ignore the facts, and instead holds onto this false belief because of his desire be king. This leads to our discussion of Mele's second condition for an individual to enter self-deception.

S (Macbeth) Treats Data Relevant, or at Least Seemingly Relevant, to the Truth-Value of P in a Motivationally Biased Way

From the perspective of Mele's second condition, one of the factors that cause a subject to be self-deceived is his treatment of the data provided to him at the time of his self-deception in a motivationally biased way, and his doing so is triggered by his desire concerning whether his acquired belief is true or not. As Mele puts it, "S's desiring that P leads S to manipulate data relevant or seemingly relevant to the truth value of P, this manipulation is a cause of S's acquiring the belief that P" (22). This is very pertinent to Macbeth, where his desire for the throne affects his reasoning in a way that leads to his self-deception.

In view of Mele's theory, what causes Macbeth to be self-deceived is that he "forms a false belief due to the causal influence of a motivational state (typically, a desire)" (Fernández 380). In other words, Macbeth's desiring P (being a king) leads him to misinterpret the witches' prophecies in a way that would never be if Macbeth lacked this desire. Throughout the play, Macbeth does not deny that he has "black and deep desires" (I.4.51) for the throne.

For example, he openly states that it is his "[v]aulting ambition" (I.7.27) that is behind his hidden desire to be king. Thus, Macbeth's "[v]aulting ambition" to get "the imperial theme" motivates him to fall into what is called "intentional misinterpretation" of the witches' prophecies. In Act I, Scene 3, Macbeth says in an aside:

> Two truths are told,
> As happy prologues to the swelling act
> Of the imperial theme. (I.3.127-8)

In these lines, Macbeth misinterprets the witches' prophecies and expresses his own desire that they might be true. Because of this desire, Macbeth is motivated to think about the prophecies in a biased way by regarding them as "happy prologues to the swelling act / Of the imperial theme," and his motivated desire causes him to deal with the evidence in a way at odds with its real implication. In Mele's theory, this is called motivated reasoning, which is defined as,

> the process of arriving at a conclusion on the basis of motivationally biased information processing. Thus, an agent who desires to believe p may interpret, misinterpret, seek and recall evidence in a way that supports p, even if the stock of available evidence supports ¬p. (Kopylov)

From Mele's standpoint, Macbeth's motivated reasoning leads him to be biased in his treatment of Ross's message "He bade me, from him, call thee Thane of Cawdor" (I.3.105) that might confirm his belief that he is going to be king. Without this motivated reasoning, self-deception would not occur in Macbeth's inner mind. According to Seth Shugar, "Macbeth is in the grip of an immense, self-deceiving want. He wants, wants deeply, to live up to Lady Macbeth's idealized image of him as a conquering warrior-king who fully deserves to rule" (69).

Macbeth's biased thinking leads him to believe everything that supports his desire for the throne; thus, he looks for evidence that backs up his original idea about "the imperial theme" rather than seeking out information that opposes it. He writes a letter to his wife to receive an affirmative answer that supports his desire to be a king. He looks for the outcomes that he would get if the witches' prophecies were true, rather than what would occur if they were untrue. Although Macbeth has formed a false belief, he has treated this belief in a motivationally biased way. The fact that Macbeth admits in his letter that the witches "have more in them than mortal knowledge" refers to his biased treatment of the data given him by the witches. Moreover, the letter is another example of two self-deception mechanisms that Macbeth endorses: "confirmation bias" and "selective focusing."

As a matter of fact, after hearing the witches' prophecies, Macbeth falls into what is called confirmation bias, "the tendency to search for, interpret, favor, and recall information in a way that confirms one's preexisting beliefs or hypotheses, while giving disproportionately less consideration to alternative possibilities" (Plous 233). By writing his letter, Macbeth creates his own "subjective social reality" from his perception of the information he has received, and this dictates his behavior in dealing with people around him. Thus, Macbeth's cognitive bias leads to "perceptual distortion, inaccurate judgment, illogical interpretation, or what is broadly called irrationality" (Kahneman and Tversky 431).

This is very clear in Macbeth's subsequent thinking and action: he does not perceive circumstances objectively. Rather he remembers information selectively, and interprets it in a biased way. For example, he starts to pick out those bits of data that make him believe he is going to be king. Accordingly, as he becomes more convinced of this belief, he tends to disregard information that contradicts that belief. Consequently, being influenced by his bias toward the throne, Macbeth decides to go ahead with his plan to do away with his king.

> I am settled, and bend up
> Each corporal agent to this terrible feat.
> Away, and mock the time with fairest show;
> False face must hide what the false heart doth know. (I.7.79-82)

At the same time, Macbeth's confirmation bias makes him engage in several rationalizations and confabulations of why he formed his belief of being a future king:

> This supernatural soliciting
> Cannot be ill, cannot be good. If ill,
> Why hath it given me earnest of success
> Commencing in a truth? I am Thane of Cawdor.
> If good, why do I yield to that suggestion
> Whose horrid image doth unfix my hair
> And make my seated heart knock at my ribs
> Against the use of nature? (I.3.130-37)

This quotation can be read as an explicit verbalization of Macbeth's self-deceiving inclination to believe propositions that he knows are false and that his judgments are colored by his motivation because the process of constructing justifications is biased by Macbeth's goals, where he is motivated to arrive at a conclusion. This motivation causes Macbeth to

> enact certain mental strategies and behavioral patterns that convince him or her of the truth of P, despite his or her exposure to information that tips the scales towards accepting the truth of the proposition (or state of facts) not-P. (Marcus 187)

In his attempt to get out of this confusion, Macbeth tries to apply reason. Unfortunately, his rationalization results in erroneous decision making because this biased information tends to affect his frame of reference, leaving him with an inadequate understanding of the situation:

> Present fears
> Are less than horrible imaginings:
> My thought, whose murder yet is but fantastical,
> Shakes so my single state of man that function
> Is smothered in surmise, and nothing is
> But what is not. (I.3.137-42)

In this quotation Macbeth loses his sense of objectivity and of rationality, and becomes somewhat delusional. He has a conflict between his wicked thoughts of killing his own king and not to proceed with them: "Present fears / Are less than horrible imaginings." Moreover, Macbeth becomes more disturbed about what might happen than about reality: " nothing is, but what is not."

In addition, there is another psychological mechanism that Macbeth unconsciously endorses, and that contributes to his self-deception: selective focusing. Under the influence of his desire to be king, Macbeth tends to focus on evidence that seems to confirm his claim and, contrariwise, to overlook the evidence that seems to disconfirm it. In his letter to his wife, Macbeth sets his mind on being a king and ignores all other possibilities that might help him make a more informed decision. Part of Macbeth's selective focusing is to make his attention focused exclusively on one aspect of things; that is, to start following up his thoughts with actions right now.

> From this moment
> The very firstlings of my heart shall be
> The firstlings of my hand. And even now,
> To crown my thoughts with acts, be it thought and done[.] (IV.1.168-71)

Unfortunately, focusing his actions to become King of Scotland brings out the worst in Macbeth and makes him unconscious to the truth of reality. Macbeth's biases and selective focusing distort his reasoning and judgment:

> If chance will have me King, why, chance may crown me
> Without my stir. (I.3.143-44)

However, after killing his own king, recognizing that he has violated one of his moral principles, Macbeth feels some sort of mental anguish:

> We will proceed no further in this business.
> He hath honored me of late, and I have bought

Golden opinions from all sorts of people,
Which would be worn now in their newest gloss,
Not cast aside so soon. (I.7.31-5)

In this case, Macbeth suffers from a radical dissociation between his deeds and his moral sense: "To know my deed, 'twere best not know myself" (II.2.76). In psychology, this is known as "cognitive dissonance" (Festinger 93). Resolving this dissonance requires Macbeth either to "change his behavior to align more closely with his beliefs, or to change his beliefs to align more closely with his behavior" (Festinger 93). Since it is easier to "change beliefs than it is to change behavior, he tends to resolve dissonance through changing his beliefs" (Cooper 15). The best way to do that is through the immoral act of killing. Once Macbeth gets into the mode of self-deception, it is very difficult for him to get out of the cycle:

I am in blood
Stepped in so far that, should I wade no more,
Returning were as tedious as go o'er. (III.4.137-39)

To sum up, from the perspective of Mele's second condition, Macbeth believes what the witches said because he *wishes* to believe these prophecies, and this desire has prompted him to deal with the evidence concerning their prophecies in a prejudiced way.

Conclusion

This chapter provides a new analysis of Macbeth's character in the light of Alfred Mele's theory of self-deception, which has been proved to be a fruitful approach to closely examine how Macbeth is predominantly a striking case of self-deception. From the viewpoint of Mele's theory, Macbeth deceives himself by his desire to be king, and this causes him to be biased in treating the witches' prophecies in "a motivationally biased way." Thus, the witches are not responsible for deceiving Macbeth, but rather they are "the internal workings of Macbeth's own mind in an imaginative form, which, however, he himself does not recognize as his own" (Snider 194). In other words, their prophetic sayings are just a reflection of his inner desire and feelings, and Macbeth has a case of "wishful thinking."

In the light of Mele's theory, if the witches' prophecies did not reflect Macbeth's inner and dark desires, he would not deal with them in a prejudiced way and would not remain firm in his belief that he is going to be king even though he knows that the witches are lying. Moreover, what makes Macbeth count as a typical Mele's self-deceived model is not merely that his belief that he will be king is sustained by a motivationally prejudiced handling of his evidence, but because holding this belief requires Macbeth's vigorous effort to escape believing that he is not. Were Macbeth able to rid himself of such self-deceit, he would be more skillful in making ethical decisions and living a moral life.

Works Cited

Cooper, J. *Cognitive Dissonance: 50 Years of a Classic Theory*. Sage, 2007.

Doren, Lily B. "*Macbeth*: A Study in Fear. " *Readings on Macbeth*. Edited by Clarice Swisher. Greenhaven, 1999, pp. 126-35.

Fernández, Jordi. "Self-deception and self-knowledge." *Philosophical Studies*, vol. 162, no. 2, 2013, pp. 379–400.

Festinger, Leon. "Cognitive dissonance." *Scientific American*, vol. 207, no. 4, 1962, pp. 93-107. https://www.nature.com/scientificamerican/journal/v207/n4/pdf/scientificamerican1062-93.pdf. Accessed May 25, 2017.

Funkhouser, Eric. "Do the Self-Deceived Get What They Want?" *Pacific Philosophical Quarterly*. vol. 86, no. 3, 2005, pp. 295-312, www.comp.uark.edu/~efunkho/selfdeception.pdf. Accessed April 4, 2016.

Goldman, Michael. "Speaking Evil: Language and Action in *Macbeth.*" *Acting and Action in Shakespearean Tragedy*. Princeton UP, 1985, pp. 94-111.

Howell, Maria L. *Manhood and Masculine Identity in William Shakespeare's* The Tragedy of Macbeth. UP of America, 2008.

Kahneman, D., and A. Tversky. "Subjective probability: A judgment of representativeness." *Cognitive Psychology*, vol. 3, no. 3, 1972, pp. 430-54.

Kopylov, Igor, and Jawwad Noor, (2010). "Self-deception and Choice," 1, 35, http://people.bu.edu/jnoor/research/Self-Deception.pdf. Accessed January 11, 2017.

Marcus, Amit. "The Self-Deceptive and the Other-Deceptive Narrating Character: The Case of Lolita." *Style. Dekalb*: vol. 39, no. 2, 2005, pp. 187-205.

Mele, Alfred. *Self-Deception Unmasked.* Princeton UP, 2001.

Peters, Brandon. "Can Sleep Deprivation Cause Hallucinations?" *Verywell* (2016), www.verywell.com/can-sleep-deprivation-cause-hallucinations-3014669. Accessed Dec. 14, 2016.

Plous, Scott. *The Psychology of Judgment and Decision Making.* McGraw-Hill, 1993.

Porcher, José Eduardo. "Is Self-Deception Pretense?" *Manuscrito Campinas*, vol. 37, no. 2, 2014, January 13, 2015.

Reeve, Sara, Bryony Sheaves, and Daniel Freeman. "The Role of Sleep Dysfunction in the Occurrence of Delusions and Hallucinations: A Systematic Review." *Clinical Psychology Review*, vol. 42, 2015, pp. 96-115. https://www.ncbi.nlm.nih.gov/pmc/articles/PMC4786636/. Accessed Oct. 15, 2016.

Ruddick, William. "Social Self-deceptions," in *Perspectives on Self-Deception.* Edited by B. McLaughlin and A. O. Rorty. U of California P, 1988, pp. 380-89.

Sahdra, Baljinder, and Paul Thagard. *Self-Deception and Emotional Coherence.* U of Waterloo, 2003.

Shakespeare, William. *Macbeth.* Edited by Stephen Orgel. Penguin, 2016.

Shugar, Seth. "Knowing is not enough: Akrasia and self-deception in Shakespeare's Macbeth." *MA Thesis.* Prod. McGill U, 2006.

Snider, Denton J. *System of Shakespeare's Dramas*, 2 vols. Jones, 1877.

Willbern, David. "Phantasmagoric *Macbeth.*" *English Literary Renaissance*, vol. 16, no. 2, 1986, pp. 520-49.

Between Heart and Hand: Desire, Thought, and Action in *Hamlet* and *Macbeth*_____

William W. Weber

On Comparing and Contrasting

The critical genre of the comparative analysis or, as it is often known to students and teachers, the compare/contrast essay, provides some very clear benefits to its practitioner. To write in this mode, one must possess thorough knowledge of the two texts in question as well as the discernment necessary to recognize how they relate to one another. In practice, however, it is far too common for someone working in this genre to end up with a piece of writing that can be summed up in a single sentence: here are a few ways these things are similar; here are a few ways they are different; the end. This is a thoroughly logical structure to give a compare/contrast essay, and yet following this structure virtually guarantees a boring result. What matters in a comparative analysis are not simply the points of commonality and dissimilarity but rather what we can learn from putting two complex texts in conversation with one another. How can reading one text with another in mind help us see it in a new way? How can bringing a second, related text into play help clarify an aspect of the first text that was initially confusing? What do we know about either text that we could not have known had we not read them in parallel?

This chapter takes as its subjects two of the most famous plays ever written, *Hamlet* and *Macbeth*. Both by William Shakespeare, both likely written between 1599 and 1606, both dealing with individual tragedies against backdrops of dynastic and international violence and upheaval, so that providing a full set of similarities and differences would be a project for multiple books and there would be no guarantee that any particular insights would ensue. Instead, let us attempt to identify an interpretive problem in one of the texts that could potentially be solved through the application of insights from the other.

Arguably the most significant, the most lasting, the most divisive challenge to interpretation found in either tragedy is right at the heart of the earlier play: why does Hamlet take such an incredibly long time to think and rethink the same decision that he appears to have made in the very first act? What reason, or reasons, could there be for his delay to keep prolonging itself? These questions can prompt any number of answers from within *Hamlet* itself—for example, that Hamlet has a conscientious aversion to murder (except when Rosencrantz, Guildenstern, and Polonius are concerned, apparently), that Hamlet does not trust the ghost's word (until he tests it with the Mousetrap, and then delays for two more acts, at least), or perhaps that Hamlet wants to spare his mother the grief of losing a second husband (he certainly fails to prioritize her feelings in other respects). Even the most nakedly pragmatic reason, that Shakespeare needed to prolong the action for the course of an entire play, fails to explain the sheer extent of the delay—the necessities of the dramatic form could explain a certain amount of dilation, but do not come close to justifying the length of Shakespeare's longest tragedy. Let us try looking for an answer instead in his shortest: *Macbeth*.

While Macbeth's situation is arguably more closely analogous to Claudius's than to Hamlet's, in that while all three faced the challenge of committing regicide, only Hamlet had the potential ethical justification of avenging a crime without any other possibility of being met with justice. Like Hamlet's target for vengeance, Macbeth kills out of personal self-interest rather than service to an external ideal, and yet even when faced with much more significant logical and moral arguments against enacting his intended violence he manages to overcome all impediments with relative ease. How does Macbeth succeed in achieving action while all Hamlet can do is keep thinking, keep talking, keep waiting? A careful examination of how characters in both plays conceptualize their own deliberations holds out the possibility of an answer: Macbeth acts on his desires not because he is any less naturally thoughtful or more naturally violent than Hamlet, but because he possesses a greater measure of self-control to go along with the self-understanding that sets both characters apart as giants of the tragic form. Ironically, what makes

Macbeth's increasingly impetuous acts of tyranny possible is not a loss of willpower but its increase via mindful practice. Conversely, Hamlet finally enacts his long-plotted revenge not when he finally builds up the necessary resolve but when he finally loses his ability to resist the inexorable pull of tragedy. Read as two sides of the same tragic coin, *Macbeth* and *Hamlet* show us Shakespeare at his darkest, where human reason can most effectively hasten our self-destruction but never fully avoid it.

Hamlet's tragic fate is sealed from the beginning; the only questions are how and when he will manage to meet it. The full title of the play, *The Tragical History of Hamlet, Prince of Denmark*, leaves no doubt about this, and Hamlet shows quite the opposite of what will become his axiomatic hesitance upon first hearing from old Hamlet's ghost that his death was no accident:

> Haste, haste me to know it, that with wings as swift
> As meditation or the thoughts of love
> May sweep to my revenge. (I.5.29-31)

It is telling here that, in the opening act, Hamlet conceives of "meditation," of considered thought as well as the passion of love, to be a fitting simile for rapid action, and equivalent to a metaphor of flight. The ghost approves of this initial enthusiasm, and underscores it with what will come to be seen as highly ironic foreshadowing of just how thoroughly Hamlet's resolution will change:

> I find thee apt,
> And duller shouldst thou be than the fat weed
> That rots itself in ease on Lethe wharf
> Wouldst thou not stir in this. (I.5.31-4)

The allusion to Lethe, the mythological river of forgetfulness in which all recollection of motivation would be washed away, fits perfectly with his famous admonition to his son: "Remember me" (I.5.91). Hamlet's response to this is similarly vehement to his initial statement of vengeful resolution:

Remember thee?
Ay, thou poor ghost, while memory holds a seat
In this distracted globe. Remember thee?
Yea, from the table of my memory
I'll wipe away all trivial fond records,
All saws of books, all forms, all pressures past
That youth and observation copied there,
And thy commandment all alone shall live
Within the book and volume of my brain[.] (I.5.95-103)

This insistent repetition of the verb "Remember" helps ensure that the audience does not forget the proposed trajectory of the play's action, and creates an initial expectation that memory and thought will serve as necessary prerequisites for effective action. As the play continues, though, Shakespeare repeatedly undermines this expectation.

When Hamlet does remember his quest, he increasingly does so with diminishing insistence on immediate action. In Act II, Scene 2, we find that, far from having erased "the table of [his] memory," Hamlet in fact remembers entire speeches from old plays— particularly "Aeneas' tale to Dido, and thereabout of it especially where he speaks of Priam's slaughter" (II.2.426-8). Hamlet proceeds to recite the beginning of this speech, describing how Achilles's son Pyrrhus went on a murderous rampage through Troy, killing all in his path indiscriminately on his way to King Priam's citadel. It is a horrid narrative, full of both blood and bombast, and it quite clearly provides an analogue for Hamlet's own situation as he sees it: like Hamlet, Pyrrhus is the son of a murdered father, intent upon revenge and unconcerned with the fact that it will cost the "blood of fathers, mothers, daughters, sons" to be achieved. Like Hamlet in this moment, too, Pyrrhus pauses in the course of his vengeance:

Then senseless Ilium,
Seeming to feel his blow, with flaming top
Stoops to his base, and with a hideous crash
Takes prisoner Pyrrhus' ear. For lo, his sword
Which was declining on the milky head

Of reverend Priam, seemed I'th'air to stick.
So, as a painted tyrant, Pyrrhus stood,
And, like a neutral to his will and matter,
Did nothing. (II.2.454-62)

Distracted in the course of action, Pyrrhus momentarily changes his imagined status from an actor in a play to the subject of a painting, frozen in time and space, "neutral." It is not difficult to see how Hamlet sees himself here, and how he might draw hope from the ensuing lines:

But as we often see against some storm
A silence in the heavens, the rack stand still,
The bold winds speechless, and the orb below
As hush as death, anon the dreadful thunder
Doth rend the region: so, after Pyrrhus' pause,
A rousèd vengeance sets him new a-work[.] (II.2.463-68)

Vengeance has merely slept for a moment, and now newly "rousèd" proceeds inevitably on its way. A force of nature, nothing can stand up against the storm. And yet Hamlet continues to delay, continues to occupy the painted stasis of "Pyrrhus' pause," and his self-contempt grows:

Why, what an ass am I! Ay, sure, this is most brave,
That I, the son of the dear murderèd,
Prompted to my revenge by heaven and hell
Must, like a whore, unpack my heart with words[.] (II.2.563)

Hamlet views his overabundance of "words," of thought, as evidence of an inversely proportionate lack of action.

The most famous enumeration of this prejudice against words comes in the following scene, late in Hamlet's most famously verbose soliloquy:

Who would fardels bear,
To grunt and sweat under a weary life,
But that the dread of something after death,

The undiscovered country from whose bourn
No traveller returns, puzzles the will,
And makes us rather bear those ills we have
Than fly to others that we know not of?
Thus conscience does make cowards of us all;
And thus the native hue of resolution
Is sicklied o'er with the pale cast of thought,
And enterprises of great pith and moment
With this regard their currents turn awry,
And lose the name of action. (II.3.78-90)

Gone are the "wings / as swift as meditation," replaced by the imagery of thought as illness, repressing the body's natural vigor. The length of Hamlet's soliloquies, the sheer amount of stage time they take up without directly advancing the "action," lend credence to what he says. Language, far from facilitating decisiveness, instead ushers in a never-ending succession of doubts, worries, and fears.

In *Macbeth*, we find some similar attitudes toward thought and language, but there Shakespeare deploys them to radically different effect. Macbeth and Lady Macbeth, like Hamlet, occupy a period of time between when they first aim to kill Duncan and when Macbeth strikes the fatal blow. Both of them think about thoughts, making explicit what will be a recurring theme in the play. Macbeth sounds much like Hamlet when he first considers how he might make the witches' prophecy of his kingship come true:

Present fears
Are less than horrible imaginings:
My thought, whose murder yet is but fantastical,
Shakes so my single state of man that function
Is smothered in surmise and nothing is
But what is not. (I.3.137-42)

"Imaginings," "thought," "fantastical," "surmise"—over and over the language of contemplation punctuates this very first mentioning of murder, and the idea that "function / Is smothered" closely echoes Hamlet's suggestion that "resolution / Is sicklied." And yet, without first thinking about his future act, without hatching a plan, would any action be possible?

Lady Macbeth, too, thinks about thinking almost immediately upon hearing the prophecy that prompted Macbeth to do so, saying,

> Come, you spirits
> That tend on mortal thoughts….
>   Make thick my blood;
> Stop up th' access and passage to remorse,
> That no compunctious visitings of nature
> Shake my fell purpose nor keep peace between
> Th' effect and it. (1.5.39-40, 42-6)

Here Lady Macbeth introduces a three-part sequence beginning with "purpose" and ending with "effect." In between the two is a space prone to "compunctious visitings of nature," where "remorse" could be introduced as a stumbling block. The fact that the spirits she invokes are ones that she imagines "tend on mortal thoughts" suggests that thoughts are requisite for the entire process of conceiving and effecting action, and indeed she is thinking through the logic that will drive her and her husband to murder right before our eyes. Only a certain kind of thinking, that which leads to remorse, must be excluded if one is to be truly efficacious.

Macbeth is somewhat less specific in his next evocation of this theme, just before he commits the murder. After an extended passage of highly stylized poetry describing his thorough self-consciousness of the evil he is about to enact, Macbeth thinks that it is time to stop soliloquizing, as "Whiles I threat, he lives; / Words to the head of deeds too cold breath gives. / I go, and it is done" (II.1.61-63). While Macbeth here suggests the very opposition between "words" and "deeds" that Hamlet bemoaned, he also demonstrates a pronounced shift in his diction: an extended section of poetry replete with imagery, metaphors, and classical allusions suddenly, following an aphoristic couplet, resolves into a series of declarative monosyllables: "I go, and it is done." The words here are not delaying the deed, but effecting it. All that was requisite was a shift from the language of compunctious contemplation to the language of action.

Macbeth further solidifies this way of conceptualizing the triune purpose/compunction/action thought process at two subsequent points in the play, pointing to it as a means of reinforcing his further progress into the role of an impetuous tyrant:

> Time, thou anticipat'st my dread exploits.
> The flighty purpose never is o'ertook
> Unless the deed go with it. From this moment
> The very firstlings of my heart shall be
> The firstlings of my hand. And even now,
> To crown my thoughts with acts, be it thought and done:
> The castle of Macduff I will surprise,
> Seize upon Fife, give to th' edge o' th' sword
> His wife, his babes, and all unfortunate souls
> That trace him in his line. (IV.1.166-75)

Cleverly, this speech does not single out the middle stage of words, even to claim that it will be eliminated. Effectively, it already has, unless the speech itself is read as an ironic commentary upon the impossibility of actually accomplishing what Macbeth asserts as his goal. For someone claiming to act purely on impulse, Macbeth here certainly provides an eloquent account of this plan, minimizing the importance of language through beautifully structured verse. The "heart…hand" pairing perfectly encapsulates the twin poles of desire and action through alliterative synechdoche, and the declarative "be it thought and done" clearly evokes his prior claim of action, "I go, and it is done."

Clearly, what Macbeth is doing his best to avoid is not language, but moral consideration. This narrowing of the focus on what the active ruler must avoid gets as clear a description as can be when he says, "Strange things I have in head, that will to hand, / Which must be acted ere they may be scanned" (III.4.140-1). This couplet, utilizing all the usual techniques of finely wrought poetry, draws a dinstinction between the thought process of intentionality— "things I have in head"—and that of consideration—"they may be scanned." This usage of "scanned" to mean ethically interrogated is an interesting one, for at least two reasons. First, the verb had its origins in the vocabulary of literary criticism, as scanning verse means analyzing its metrics. Only from the literary usage did the broader meaning "to analyze" come into being, and in Shakespeare's day it still held a decidedly poetic overtone—almost to the point where it could be considered a metaphor when applied to one's thoughts. Macbeth thus is suggesting that he needs to stop being so poetic, so precise, so metrical, and become more purely spontaneous and emotion-driven if he is to achieve his quest for power. The other reason "scanned" is worth attending to is that it is a direct echo of a line from *Hamlet* in which it does precisely what Macbeth fears: it prevents the hero from accomplishing his intentions.

After proving Claudius's guilt through the stratagem of the Mousetrap play-within-the-play, Hamlet comes upon his uncle alone in the chapel, down on his knees. Unaware of Hamlet's presence, Claudius is as vulnerable as can be and Hamlet sees his opportunity for vengeance:

> Now might I do it pat, now a is a praying,
> And now I'll do 't,
> > [*he draws his sword*]
> > > and so he goes to heaven,
> And so am I revenged. That would be scanned.
> A villain kills my father, and for that
> I , his sole son, do this same villain send
> To heaven.
> O, this is hire and salary, not revenge! (III.3.73-9)

This time, Hamlet's language-driven delay centers on an inverted sort of moral calculus, wherein he does not fear the punishment due his own soul for acting out against injustice, but rather fears the lack of punishment for his would-be victim. This is not the compunction that Lady Macbeth fears, nor the blunting of desire Macbeth seeks to avoid, but a kind of overly scrupulous insistence on complete control. Hamlet lets Claudius live, and immediately begins to lose the control he displays here in a kind of crazy overcompensation.

After leaving Claudius in the chapel, Hamlet proceeds to his mother's room where he rants at her, sees the ghost again, and then wildly kills Polonius by stabbing him through a curtain. Hamlet asserts that he thought it was the king, but no such thought should have been possible; the king, whom Hamlet had just left, was literally the one person in the world who Hamlet should have known could not have been hiding in the room. Instantaneously, then, we see Hamlet vacillate from planning and scanning to reacting with stabbing, eliminating any thought process whatsoever and effecting a bloody outcome. This type of thoughtless recourse to violence typifies the play's butchery in the final scene, where Hamlet stabs Claudius with a poisoned sword in immediate retribution for his own mortal wounding, then forces him to drink poison in immediate retribution for the accidental poisoning of Gertrude. Hamlet performs the act he had been planning all along, but without any apparent memory of that intentionality. As long as Hamlet retained his memory and his capacity for thought, he managed to avoid perpetuating the cycle of violence. Hamlet's delay is not his failure but his strength. And yet, as the example of the Macbeths shows, thought alone is no protection from evil. Even when disavowing the mediating process of moral thought between heart and hand, Macbeth is using his reason to discern the most effective way to transcend the ethical limitations upon his power. By looking at *Hamlet* through the instructive lens of *Macbeth*, we find Shakespeare exploring the way that the preternatural drive for domination within all of us can wreak havoc on society, whether or not we consciously choose to pursue it. Without both acknowledging and actively combating the darkness within, tragedy will never end.

Works Cited

Shakespeare, William. *Hamlet*. In *The Norton Shakespeare, 2nd Edition*. Edited by Gary Taylor and Stanley Wells. Norton, 2008, pp. 1696-784.

_____. *Macbeth*. Edited by Stephen Orgel, Penguin, 2016.

CRITICAL
READINGS

The Poetic Soundscape of *Macbeth*———————

David Currell

How Does *Macbeth* Sound?

In an age of silent reading, the words of *Macbeth* are most likely to be consumed soundlessly. The earliest audiences, however, would have received these words by listening to actors, taking them in through the ear. The argument of this chapter is that attention to that aural context—available to us as well when we see and hear *Macbeth* at the theatre or cinema—adds value to the silent readings of *Macbeth* we perform in the study, library, or classroom. *Macbeth* is at once a poem that rewards (and demands) close reading—the critical exploration of a text's significance through scrupulous analysis of its words, their semantic range, their relationships, and their effects, both locally and in the context of the entire work—and a play that moves us when heard spoken from stage or screen.

Shakespeare's own culture recognized that dramatic literature— texts written for theatrical performance—carried a dual identity: "the poem," or the script as written by the playwright (or playwrights), and "the play" as it was performed, which might abridge, augment, or otherwise adapt the playwrights' work. In the case of *Macbeth*, the earliest text, the 1623 First Folio from which all modern editions derive, is almost certainly of the second kind (Erne 190-91). That the text of *Macbeth* comes from a performance context does not at all invalidate the methods of close reading but it does give us a special reason to think about aural effects while doing that reading. In fact, the very first words we read in the printed text of the play are a stage direction calling for sound: "*Thunder and lightning*" (1.1.0). The sound effect "*Thunder*" (produced in Shakespeare's time by rolling a cannonball over a metal sheet offstage) was associated by theatrical convention with the supernatural, so this beginning already communicates meaningfully about the play-world the audience was about to enter (Dessen and Thomson 230). While, near the end of the play, Macbeth evokes "a tale / Told by an idiot, full of sound and fury, / Signifying nothing," in an image sequence that associates this with "the stage" (V.5.25-29), the most furious of theatrical stage-sounds has already signified something at the start of *Macbeth*, before a word was spoken. This thunder is not a one-off: think of the frequent renewal of this supernatural stage direction (especially when cueing the reappearance of the witches); the frequency of martial sound effects, including "*Drum*," "*Colors*," "*Alarum*"; the bell; the owl; and the famous, ominous "*Knock*." As Stephen Orgel notes, it is easy not to register how much greater a span of time and attention music would have occupied in early stagings, compared to the instant it takes to read the stage direction "*Music and a Song*" (159). *Macbeth* is full of noises. The nonverbal soundscape is extensive and important in itself, but the remainder of this chapter will concentrate on the verbal. Asking not only "How does *Macbeth* sound?" but also "How do sounds make meaning in *Macbeth*?" I am going to perform an experiment in closely reading *Macbeth* as a *poetic* soundscape.

"Things that do sound so fair": Analyzing Sound and Verbal Pattern

Critics and editors of *Macbeth* keep coming back to its language. Two related ideas are especially prevalent: that distinctive structures of sound and rhythm form patterns that seem to place this play and its characters in their own sonic universe, and that Shakespeare uses the repetition of thematic keywords to create the play's overall cognitive and emotional effect. In this section I will explore both ideas, patterns of sound and the effects of repetition; in the second section I will concentrate on a special subset of moments in *Macbeth* where Shakespeare uses puns, words that sound the same (or highly similar) but point to multiple meanings.

Here is how two distinguished Shakespeareans capture these effects:

> The paired consonantal sounds in "fair" and "foul" make a surprisingly sustained, complex alliterative pattern that runs across the whole play—a nonsignifying pattern in "far," "fear," "free,"

"file," "fail," "fall," "false"...a quietly sustaining pattern that is only literally *full* of sound and *fury* and that, though it signifies nothing, helps a sane human mind experience tragedy[.] (Booth 117-18)

It is surely impossible to deny that certain words – "time," "man," "done"—and certain themes—"blood," "darkness"—are the matrices of the language of *Macbeth*. (Kermode 215)

Both of these are concluding claims, made at the end of book chapters about *Macbeth*: they are the ends of arguments rather than the beginnings. Stephen Booth even seems to wish to shut down argumentation ("it signifies nothing"). Nevertheless, they are claims well suited to beginning critical arguments, and even the beginning critic can join the fray. Close reading is an accessible method, in that all one needs to practice it is the text of *Macbeth*, time, and a dictionary (the more time and dictionaries the better). Yet "accessible" is not the same as "easy": close reading may not call explicitly upon specialized historical or theoretical resources, but it does require a disciplined attentiveness and judicious creativity. Stephen Booth and Frank Kermode give us a foundation upon which to exercise these faculties.

Let's start with the famous line spoken by the witches that contains the keywords from which Booth generates his list:

Fair is foul, and foul is fair. (I.1.12)

This is a tightly structured line of verse. It is perfectly symmetrical, a word-palindrome (it reads the same if you pronounce the words in regular or reverse sequence). The *f* words that will prove so important to the soundscape of the play are all emphasized, in a rhythm of alternating stressed and unstressed syllables. The baseline verse of Shakespearean writing also alternates stresses, but with some significant differences: the characteristic number of stresses is five, not four, and lines typically begin with an unstressed, rather than a stressed syllable. In technical language, the metrical rhythm of the witches' line is a form of trochaic tetrameter, as against the more commonplace iambic pentameter, which can be illustrated by the first line Macbeth speaks:

So foul and fair a day I have not seen. (I.3.38)

Macbeth's words conform to a different meter, but also a different implicit attitude to meaning. Macbeth is commenting on a *mixture* of foul (bad weather) and fair (military victory), whereas the witches assert *identity*: foul *is* fair and fair *is* foul. The reversal of the terms "fair" and "foul" in the logically redundant repetition is another way of implying the asserted sameness (the syntactic position occupied by "foul" on one side of "is" is now occupied by "fair"— they are completely interchangeable). Trochaic rhythms (lines beginning with the stress) and shorter lines remain particular to the witches throughout *Macbeth*, setting them apart from the generally iambic rhythms of Macbeth and almost all other characters. Yet simultaneous with this rhythmic difference is an uncanny similarity: Macbeth has used and paired the witches' words "foul" and "fair"— still vividly in the short-term aural memory of the audience struck by the play's supernatural beginning—even though he has not yet met them.

David Kranz has argued that this arresting repetition, like the larger pattern that Booth records but declines to interpret, is a symptom of how the language of *Macbeth* unfolds in general: that ways of speaking introduced by the witches, and seemingly characteristic of them especially, spread across the whole cast of characters, becoming general, and implying on a close linguistic level that all the other characters live and act within the witches' weird and fatal world. There is a countercurrent within Kranz's argument, and his overall interpretation of the play finds a balance between cyclical fate and progressive providence; what is crucial for us is how often critics have been drawn to the idea that in *Macbeth* individual styles of speech exhibited by characters are less important than the total verbal texture of the play woven of all its speakers (Hope and Witmore 184). A way to test this for ourselves is to track the words Booth presents, and take up the invitation implied by his ellipsis to add to the list—watch for the word "fell," for example, or the suffix "-ful," and consider Banquo's cry "Fly, good Fleance, fly, fly, fly!" (III.3.21), or Macbeth's "My way of life / Is fall'n into the sere, the yellow leaf" (V.3.24-25).

This language shared by other characters more gradually binds the words "fair" and "foul" that the witches force together at the outset, forming a kind of phonological net trapping attractive appearances under a pall of evil. In Banquo's discourse, the word "fear" comes to mediate between "fair" and "foul," as illustrated in the following two speeches:

> Good Sir, why do you start and seem to fear
> Things that do sound so fair? (I.3.51-52)

> Thou hast it now—king, Cawdor, Glamis, all,
> As the weird women promised; and I fear
> Thou play'dst most foully for't. (III.1.1-3)

The first speech is Banquo's reaction as he watches Macbeth react wordlessly to the witches' prophetic hailing, soon after Macbeth's "So foul and fair a day I have not seen" (38). The noble and royal titles "Thane of Glamis," "Thane of Cawdor," and "king hereafter" *sound* fair indeed—why should *fair* give rise to *fear*? It is not the witches but Macbeth's reaction that makes Banquo wonder if he is seeing things—Macbeth must surely only "seem to fear"; his body language calls for speech that would explain it differently. Macbeth, of course, says nothing—the actor has only gesture and facial expression available until the text cues his own plea for more sound: "Stay, you imperfect speakers, tell me more...Speak, I charge you" (70-78).

The second speech quoted above is also Banquo's, and it marks the dramatic distance between I.3 and III.1. Banquo is using second-person address ("Thou"), but the addressee is absent, or imaginary: the fearfulness unleashed upon Scotland makes it impossible for Banquo to speak these words frankly to Macbeth. When the Macbeths do arrive the dialogue is stilted and menacing, and charged with more permutations of the key sounds ("Fail not our feast" [27]).

The break in shared experience and trust inaugurated by Macbeth's withdrawal upon the heath into unresponsive reverie and registered in Banquo's question, "why do you start and seem to fear / Things that do sound so fair," has become a permanent breach. By now, the fear is real, and it is Banquo feeling it: "I fear / Thou play'dst most foully for't." In the overall poetic soundscape of the play, Banquo's two speeches show how *fear* acts as both a thematic *and* an aural mediation between *fair* and *foul*.

The quotation from Kermode at the beginning of this section illustrates a method closely related to Booth's. Where Booth identifies an aural pattern created by similar-sounding syllables, Kermode isolates a handful of keywords that critics have felt to be both quantitatively overrepresented in *Macbeth* and qualitatively indicative of its dominant themes. In a fine essay on the language of *Macbeth* that also alludes to Kermode, Jonathan Hope and Michael Witmore have applied more rigorous quantitative methods to these perceptions—counting frequencies and measuring their statistical significance (a method facilitated by wide access to digital texts and tools). One of the most striking results of their study is that *Macbeth* contains an unusual preponderance of definite articles (*the*) over indefinite articles (*a* or *an*). This is the sort of result that is much easier for a computer to scan than for a human ear to detect, but Hope and Witmore also ratify the greater presence in *Macbeth* (relative to other Shakespearean plays) of the kinds of semantically rich words, such as *time*, mentioned by Kermode. *Fear* turns out to be such a word; another is *deed* (196-97).

Deed is a noun that derives from the verb *do*. English tends to reserve *deed* for a significant action, something that constitutes an achievement, but *do* is about as protean a verb as exists: *to do* can denote just about any action at all, and in its most basic sense of something done, something someone did, a deed can be just as protean. This is what makes the witches' reply when Macbeth seeks them out in IV.1 so unnerving:

MACBETH How now, you secret, black, and midnight hags,
What is 't you do?
ALL   A deed without a name. (70-71)

What is *it* you are doing? Macbeth expects a reply that will give definition to the scene by naming an action. The reply he hears— "A deed without a name"—suggests the unspoken deed must be something unspeakable. This trick of leaving the verb "do" without specification is initiated by the First Witch very early in the play: "I'll do, I'll do, and I'll do" (I.3.10). Consistent with an interpretation of the soundscape that sees the witches' language setting the style of *Macbeth*, these moments appear to seed a much more generally observable speech habit where the words *deed*, *do*, and *done* are being constantly spoken, but seemingly in a way that withholds definition.

But only seemingly:

If it were done when 'tis done, then 'twere well
It were done quickly. (I.7.1-2)

We know what Macbeth means by "it." He means "th' assassination," (and immediately comes out and says so), yet this speech begins a pattern where "do it" functions as a cloaking euphemism that covers up direct references to murder (see Palfrey 66-70 for an especially rich discussion of how euphemistic repetition works poetically at I.7.1-2). It is still early in the play—the assassination is not yet done—and Macbeth is speaking in soliloquy. When Lady Macbeth enters and joins the dialogue their vocabulary turns allusive: "I dare *do all* that may become a man; / Who dares *do more* is none" (46-47); "When you durst *do it*, then you were a man" (49). At the end of Macbeth's next soliloquy, his diction seems vaguely to intuit the play's poetics: "Words to the heat of deeds too cold breath gives" (II.1.62). This both expresses a commonplace contrast of speech (as enervating) and action (as energized), and hints at the fact that Macbeth occupies a verbal space of deeds without names: "I go, and *it* is *done*" (63).

As their dialogue in I.7 indicates, Lady Macbeth has independently adopted the same norms of discreet indefinition:

> Thou'dst have, great Glamis,
> That which cries "Thus thou must do" if thou have it;
> And that which rather thou dost fear to do
> Than wishest should be undone. (I.5.21-24)

This care with words cannot protect Lady Macbeth from the effects of the deeds. When, during her final scene, she says "What's done is done" (V.1.67), the phrase in itself may have a proverbial and abstract flavor, but in the context of *Macbeth* it shows how she is haunted by the concrete deed of killing denoted by *to do* in Acts I and II. Moreover (and here again the idea of a style or soundscape characterizing the entire play is relevant), the association of doing and killing is not confined to the principals. When Ross takes responsibility for the execution of the former Thane of Cawdor, he says "I'll see it done" (I.2.67). On a poetic level this can be seen as distantly setting in train Macbeth's own "I go, and it is done."

To round out this section on the analysis of sound and verbal pattern, I offer a brief observation on a third poetic effect reliant on sound: rhyme. Successive end-rhymed lines—rhyming couplets—are another acoustic phenomenon first audible in the witches' speech:

> Fair is foul, and foul is fair.
> Hover through the fog and filthy air. (I.1.12-13)

These lines conclude the first scene of *Macbeth*. Shakespeare uses couplets at the end of a scene often enough that it can be heard as a poetic convention: a summative judgment, resolution, or mood is underlined by rhyme and hangs in the audience's ears as one set of actors make their exits and another their entrances for the next scene. In *Macbeth*, this convention is very heavily used: scenes I.1, I.2, I.7, II.1, II.3, II.4, III.1, III.5, IV.3, V.3, V.5, V.6, and V.8 all end in couplets, while scenes III.2, III.4, IV.1, V.2, and V.4 end with a version of the couplet convention that tacks on a small extra bit of speech after a couplet, such as "So prithee go with me" (III.2.57).

Of twenty-eight scenes, eighteen (nearly two thirds) end in couplets: a notably high incidence. Couplets also abound within scenes: the witches are frequent rhymers, as is Macbeth himself. Macbeth uses couplets in complex ways when speaking alone. They contribute an incantatory quality that conveys something like self-hypnosis. When he uses couplets in dialogue with his wife, it therefore introduces an impression of self-absorption and unshared reverie into even their most conspiratorial conversations (see Palfrey and Stern 476-88). Macbeth's couplets signal a privacy, a mental and emotional separation. This dramatic effect is augmented by Macbeth's use of couplets near the end of a scene: he speaks a couplet such as "Come what come may, / Time and the hour runs through the roughest day" (I.3.146-47) or "yet let that be / Which the eye fears, when it is done, to see" (I.4.52-53), and it is as if the scene is over *for him*—in the latter instance he does in fact exit after the heavy line containing the keywords "fears" and "done." Duncan formally concludes the scene in addressing the other thanes, but the initiative has left with Macbeth; Duncan is done for.

"To th' selfsame tune and words": Equivocation and Uncomic Puns

These kinds of metrical, rhythmic, and rhyming effects are not accidental: the literary culture of Shakespeare's age placed self-conscious emphasis on these aural dimensions of poetry, and the desire for systematic knowledge concerning literary effects is reflected in the popularity of rhetorical handbooks such as George Puttenham's *The Art of English Poesy*, published in 1589, as Shakespeare's career writing for the public theatre was just beginning. The prosodic part of rhetorical discourse went hand in hand—and in Puttenham's treatise sits side by side—with the study of diction: how a poet's selection and combination of words in figures of speech further multiply and deepen poetic effects ("poetics" is itself a more general term encompassing prosody, diction, and their interactions). One aspect of *Macbeth* that has attracted attention is the presence of ambiguous diction: the play's concentration of words that support a double meaning or of paired words that are aurally very close yet create semantic complexity or tension instead of clarity or reinforcement.

Puttenham's remarks on *amphibologia* (ambiguous speech, or words of double meaning: the specialist terms of rhetorical study, like the field itself, derive from Greek and Latin sources) form part of Steven Mullaney's analysis of *equivocation* in *Macbeth* (39). Mullaney connects Puttenham's discussion to a legal and political controversy that absorbed England while *Macbeth* was being composed. As the editor of the Pelican *Macbeth*, Stephen Orgel, explains, when the Porter uses the word "equivocator" Shakespeare's first audiences would have heard the word as "alluding to the equivocating testimony given by Jesuit conspirators in the Gunpowder Plot, 1605" (note to II.3.8). An "equivocator" gave testimony according to a juridicotheological theory that countenanced noncommittal responses, reserving the truth for the private conscience. That the equivocator who "could not equivocate to heaven" (10) is an especially important part of the Porter's fantasy is confirmed by the recurrence of "equivocation" when Macbeth is shaken by understanding the witches' Birnam Wood prophecy:

> I pull in resolution, and begin
> To doubt th' equivocation of the fiend
> That lies like truth. (V.5.42-44)

Macbeth's doubt becomes anger when the ambiguity of "of woman born" is likewise exposed: "And be these juggling fiends no more believed, / That palter with us in a double sense" (V.8.19-20). But doubleness is an inescapable feature of the poetic soundscape of *Macbeth*. We might think of the witches with their "Double, double toil and trouble" (IV.1.10) as the metaphysical root of this doubleness, but many speakers join in: "As cannons overcharged with double cracks, / So they doubly redoubled strokes upon the foe" (I.2.37-38); "All our service / In every point done twice, and then done double" (I.6.16-17); "He's here in double trust" (I.7.12); "But yet I'll make assurance double sure" (IV.1.105).

For Macbeth, "double sense" creates "doubt"—and the verbal likeness of *doubt* and *double* tightens the connection. Equivocation compressed into a single word can become a pun, where one sound diverges into more than one sense. An example is the Porter's toying with different meanings of the word "lie" at II.3.33-39. This is an important rhetorical technique in *Macbeth*, which I will end this chapter by discussing in parallel with the related technique wherein two senses converge by virtue of common sounds.

Here is an example of this convergent effect:

> True, worthy Banquo: he is full so valiant,
> And in his commendations I am fed;
> It is a banquet to me. (I.4.54-56)

In the moment, Duncan's quibble with "Banquo" and "banquet" sounds like a throwaway quip (we can imagine the courtier thanes straining to perform polite amusement). In the wider context of *Macbeth*, however, the play on *Banquo* and *banquet* anticipates the sensational appearance of Banquo's ghost at the Macbeths' own feast (they do not use the term "banquet"—a telling avoidance, as their consciences suppress the sound of the murder victim's name?)

As that later feast begins, Lady Macbeth welcomes the company with another pun:

> To feed were best at home;
> From thence, the sauce to meat is ceremony:
> Meeting were bare without it. (III.4.35-37)

Her remark about where it is best for her guests to *feed* is subjected to its own irony thanks to Macbeth's later revelation "There's not one of them but in his house / I keep a servant *fee'd*," that is, a hired spy (III.4.132-33). This irony is inaccessible to the assembly onstage, but all can follow Lady Macbeth's wordplay: to *meet* away from home is made more palatable by courtesies ("ceremony"), as *meat* is made more palatable by "sauce." The manner of expression is an effort to practice what is being preached: the hostess's rhetorical turn is an example of "ceremony," but the gap between the affected mirth (the presumed purpose of punning) and the terrors of this table yawns unbreachably.

The entire play of *Macbeth* challenges that presumptive association of wordplay and comedy. The way in which similar-sounding words are deployed *un*comically has been felt to be one of the play's most distinctive and provocative features. Critics have coined terms such as "uncomic pun" (Muir) and "mirthless pun" (Palfrey 132) to try and capture the oxymoron: puns are expected to be humorous or frivolous, comedic and mirthful. Uncomic puns in *Macbeth* sound as rhetorical disturbances.

In the cases of Banquo/banquet and meat/meeting, Duncan's and Lady Macbeth's wordplay is situationally plausible. Uncomic puns proper emerge incongruously, seemingly without the conscious design of their speakers. These cases have a poetic rationale instead of a dramatic one. Lady Macbeth is responsible for perhaps the most famous:

> If he do bleed,
> I'll gild the faces of the grooms withal,
> For it must seem their *guilt*. (II.2.58-60)

Gilt is a thin layer of gold, applied to give an object a superficial richness. The superficiality is the key quality conveyed in metaphorical uses of the verb "to gild," as here, where Lady Macbeth's suggestion is to *gild* (thinly coat) the grooms' skin with blood. The word choice explodes in the next line: "For it must seem their *guilt*." (In the Folio text the spelling "gilt" makes the pun even clearer visually.) Lady Macbeth's plan is that those who find the grooms will interpret the blood not as *gilt* (falsified ornamental surface) but as *guilt* (culpability for murder). So in fact this guilt must *not* "seem…gilt," lest their cover be blown. From her perspective as one of the true murderers, however, the pun and its image of guilt as superficial and easily put on may betray the hope that guilt is just as easily taken off—a moral error that sets up the couple's horror at the perception of real, hallucinated, and metaphorical stains upon their hands and souls that cannot be washed away. Another example of "convergence" invites a similar interpretation:

> If th'assassination
> Could trammel up the consequence and catch
> With his surcease success[.] (I.7.2-4)

The phrasing captures Macbeth's wishful thinking, his will to believe that Duncan's foul "surcease" could give way to his own fair "success" (but see further Empson 71).

Let's conclude by wading one step deeper into the muddy semantic terrain Shakespeare creates in *Macbeth* by merging senses through sound. John Hollander has noted how the phrasing of the line "And sigh the lack of many a thing I sought" (from Shakespeare's sonnet 30) is enriched by the way that the words *sigh* and *sought* can be (mis)heard as even more tightly bound than they already are because they mimic the forms of an irregular English tense-pattern (compare *buy* and *bought*): it is as if the seeking already implied, provoked, or was coincident with the sighing of unfulfilled desire (133). This highly refined artistry creates a virtuous circle of semantic enrichment. You can test for the strength of the poetic effect by substituting an alternative for one of the words: "And rue the lack of many a thing I sought" keeps only the superficial sense of the Shakespearean version—the poetic sense is diluted.

Sensitized by Hollander's example, consider part of Macbeth's speech in which he pulls himself together following the feast at which Banquo's ghost appeared:

> For mine own good
> All causes shall give way. I am in blood
> Stepped in so far that, should I wade no more,
> Returning were as tedious as go o'er. (III.4.136-39)

Macbeth resolves to make his "own good" the only reason or rationale (*cause*) for his actions: all (other) causes shall be put aside, shall "give way." Perhaps "give way" creates an image of obstacles retiring in the face of Macbeth's singular purpose as it progresses along an unimpeded path. "Give way" can mean more than just making way or getting out of the way, however; it is also what a structure or barrier may do under excessive weight or pressure. What sort of structure? Macbeth's imagery becomes much more concrete in the next sentence: he is envisioning his space of action not as a cleared pathway but as a flood or river. It is a version of Macbeth's preoccupying image of a "multitudinous sea incarnadine" (II.2.65)—the blood he has shed becomes a world-swallowing ocean. An aurally sensitive inspection of Macbeth's speech may now suggest an answer to the question "What sort of structure?" Macbeth's desire to move through this bloody topography suggests the want of a *causeway*: an elevated road giving passage across a piece of water or wetland, or a landing pier running into the sea or a river. "All causes shall give way": but in fact *the causeway* gave way, leaving Macbeth to *wade* (and here is the echo of Hollander's insight: as part of the same poetic soundscape, *way* and *wade* seem to share a spectral relation, as if they were different tenses of the same verb as well as marking different phases of a developing image). In summary, the sound of Macbeth's words emerges into a new layer upon the poetic image those words express: pressure (of a moral kind?) has *weighed* on a *causeway*, *causing* it to *give way*, compelling Macbeth to *wade* through blood to make his *way*.

The interest of these lines is not yet exhausted. Simon Palfrey and Tiffany Stern have commented on another feature, namely the way in which the formation of a rhyming couplet compresses the words "go over" into the elided form "go o'er" (*elision* is the omission of letters or syllables to ease or shorten pronunciation; here the apostrophe in "o'er" signals the elision of *v*). They note that this still leaves a line with more syllables than a regular iambic pentameter, creating a pressure on the actor to slide the last sounds even more tightly together—perhaps so that "go o'er" is heard as *gore* (485-86). The suggestion gains some more strength from the way the elision is printed in the Folio text (i.e. as "go o're"). Being stepped so far in blood (and do we perhaps begin to hear an under-echo of the stronger soaking word "steeped" in "stepped"?) puts the idea of "gore" in the audience's mind—and Macbeth has put the sound in the audience's ear earlier in the same scene, telling Banquo's apparition "Never shake / Thy *gory* locks at me" (III.4.51-52). Macbeth's lines contrast returning with going over; returning is simultaneously contrasted with goriness, the material taint of wading further into blood. Within the image of the crossing of a bloody body of water, backtracking would indeed foul the wader to the same extent as advancing. So Macbeth has created a poetic logic for his resolution to press on: it is the same tedious passage in either direction. At the same time, that final syllable embeds the poetic refutation of Macbeth's self-serving image: "returning" (repentance, or at least an end to murder) is different from a decision to "go o'er" because the latter (and only the latter) is precisely synonymous with yet more gore.

"Keep the word of promise to our ear": Listening to *Macbeth*

There is a memorable line from Alexander Pope's *An Essay on Criticism*, a poem about reading poetry: "The *Sound* must seem an *Echo* to the *Sense*" (line 365). This line is itself a celebrated bit of verbal mimesis: the sounds of the words *Sound* and *Sense* are made to seem to echo because of the way the sounds of the very words "seem" and "echo" fill the space between them with the sounds of *s*, *e*, and *o*. This chapter has sought to suggest how in *Macbeth* the sense can seem an echo to the sound: that meaning in the dramatic universe of Shakespeare's Scottish play partly emerges as an effect of verbal patterns, repetition, keywords, puns, and equivocations. Some of these suggestions may seem excessively ingenious, too much of a stretch. Aural close reading reaches after subtleties, and sometimes, like Macbeth, a critic may begin "to doubt th' equivocation" that she strains to hear (cf. V.5.43). But poetic meaning does not recognize any principle of economy: "to sound" can also mean to test the depths or find the bottom of something, and every ripple from the plumb line cast into the oceanic plenty of the Shakespearean text is worth attending to, as enrichment of the experience of silent reading, or as material that multiplies options for spoken performance. What's heard cannot be unheard. The play of *Macbeth* is "full of sound," and those sounds signify. Careful analysis of the poetic qualities of the play's soundscape is an indispensable part of entering into its sense and significance.

Works Cited

Booth, Stephen. *King Lear, Macbeth, Indefinition and Tragedy*. Yale UP, 1983.

Dessen, Alan C., and Leslie Thomson. *A Dictionary of Stage Directions in English Drama, 1580-1642*. Cambridge UP, 1999.

Empson, William. *Seven Types of Ambiguity*. 1930. Penguin, 1995.

Erne, Lukas. *Shakespeare as Literary Dramatist*. Cambridge UP, 2003.

Hollander, John. *Rhyme's Reason: A Guide to English Verse*. 3rd ed. Yale UP, 2000.

Hope, Jonathan, and Michael Witmore. "The Language of *Macbeth*." *Macbeth: The State of Play*. Edited by Ann Thompson. Bloomsbury, 2014, pp.183-208.

Kermode, Frank. *Shakespeare's Language*. Penguin, 2000.

Kranz, David L. "The Sounds of Supernatural Soliciting in *Macbeth*." *Studies in Philology*, vol. 100, no. 3, 2003, pp. 346-83.

Muir, Kenneth. "The Uncomic Pun." *The Cambridge Journal*, vol. 3, 1950, pp. 472-85.

Mullaney, Steven. "Lying Like Truth: Riddle, Representation and Treason in Renaissance England," *ELH*, vol. 47, 1980, pp. 32-47.

Orgel, Stephen. *The Authentic Shakespeare: And Other Problems of the Early Modern Stage*. Routledge, 2002.

Palfrey, Simon. *Doing Shakespeare*. Thomson Learning, 2005.

_____, and Tiffany Stern. *Shakespeare in Parts*. Oxford UP, 2007.

Pope, Alexander. *The Poems of Alexander Pope*. Edited by John Butt. Yale UP, 1963.

Shakespeare, William. *Macbeth*. Edited by Stephen Orgel. Penguin, 2016.

Adapting *Macbeth* to the Screen: Between Faithfulness and *Joe Macbeth* (1955)_____

Fernando Gabriel Pagnoni Berns

Introduction: A Brief Sketch of Adaptation Studies

The purpose of this chapter is twofold. First it will offer a brief sketch on the critical literature on adaptation studies regarding the transposition between printed words—novels, short stories, plays, –and so on—and film. Rather than fixed, the critical studies on adaptation have been lively in recent years. Second, the chapter offers a reading of the particularities of adapting William Shakespeare's works, concretely, his play *Macbeth* to the big screen. I will give particular attention to the film *Joe Macbeth* (Ken Hughes, 1955), a case study that proposes new readings on the play while engaging with the aesthetics and narrative devices of the canonical Hollywood film noir and gangster film of the era. What makes this film particularly interesting is the fact that it moves away from the printed world to create its own story.

Adaptation theory, the study of films based on literary works, is one of the oldest areas in film studies and, as such, it has changed substantially through the years. As James Welsh argues, "adaptation has always been central to the process of filmmaking" (xiii) since many of the movies made through the silent period and the classic era were based on a literary source. In fact, D. W. Griffith, the American father of narrative cinema, used literature as the basis of many of his films and, most importantly, adopted the logic of literature, especially the literary dramatic ideas developed by Dickens—different point of views, complicated storylines, parallel plots, –and so on—to his films (Leitch 67). With adaptation, however, came issues about the problem of how a literary work should be changed to fit the big screen.

The most basic and commonplace focus in evaluating adaptations is the issue of *fidelity*. How faithful is a film to its literary source? The different levels of "faithfulness" were taken as measures of evaluation, usually leading to the notion of hierarchies: the film, according this view that predominated in academia some time ago, was just an "illustration," a passive "reflection" of the literary work, and as such, a "minor" work. It was "good" only if the movie closely followed the story and themes of the adapted literary work. This complemented the idea that literature was "high" art while film was "minor." "Notions of anteriority and seniority assume that'older arts are necessarily better ones" (Welsh and Lev 110).

After the 1970s, luckily, academia slowly gave space to other approaches, in which film holds merits of its own. Rather than being just colorful illustration—a book in images—a movie was not second to the literary work but another work entirely among a long chain of interpretations. In this framework, there were not originals—source materials—but interpretations. In his text *Nietzsche, Freud, Marx* (1990), Michel Foucault describes these three thinkers as "masters of suspicion." What he is suggesting is that they all approach cultural discourse with suspicion, viewing it as distorted by a concealed motive: the "will to power" (Nietzsche), sexual desire (Freud), and class interest (Marx). Foucault builds on this premise, arguing that "language does not say exactly what it means. The meaning that one grasps … is perhaps in reality only a lesser meaning that shields … the meaning underneath it" (59). This idea became central to adaptation studies.

Interpretation becomes an endless task, never able to access a true point of origin; as Foucault explains, "the further one goes in interpretation, the closer one approaches at the same time an absolutely dangerous region where interpretation is not only going to find its point of no return but where it is going to disappear itself as interpretation" (63). There is *no original source*, but interpretation of other texts. Even the primary text—the so-called source—is related to previous texts that precede it chronologically. Thus, when a given text is interpreted, what the interpreter finds under it is just another interpretation. Shakespeare's *Macbeth* was not born in a vacuum, but it connects, in themes and narrative devices, with other texts of the era. In fact, *Macbeth* is a *tragedy* about fate, a genre and a topic that can both be traced to Greek roots.

As a result, interpretation is inexhaustible and never finished. There is no original meaning; there is nothing to interpret but interpretations (for example, *Macbeth* is an interpretation of other texts). In this scenario, each artistic work answers to the politics of readership and interpretation, mediated, in turn, by social and cultural contexts. In other words, a movie is a rewriting that speaks about itself and the society and culture that produced it rather than solely of the literary work on which it is based. In its most fundamental form, the premise "is one of ceaseless interpretation, in which the reader has to complete a meaning that the text leaves underdetermined" (MacCabe 2). Currently, little space is given to issues of fidelity anymore, as the idea of "original source" is replaced by the idea that a film based on a novel is not an illustration but, rather, another story (an interpretation) entirely. Rather than the fixed dyad of original and illustration, there is an infinite semiosis in which each text is connected to others in some way.

Fearing the Bard: Fidelity and the Adaptations of *Macbeth*

As mentioned, the issues of fidelity are outmoded in contemporary criticism. At least, until William Shakespeare is brought to the screen. Shakespeare is a special case, appealing, on the one hand, to an academic audience due to his status as the pinnacle of literature and, on the other, to a far wider readership drawn to Shakespeare for reasons having to do with "classroom exploitation" (Welsh and Lev 106). Shakespeare is "school material" and as such, it must be "adapted" right so it can teach valuable lessons to students and to people well aware of Shakespeare's themes, poetics, and world-view. As Emma French argues, each Shakespeare adaptation "prompts cultural anxiety about high-culture adaptation" (1) arising from issues of veneration. Adapting Shakespeare is not the same thing as adapting other authors. Directors, producers, and screenwriters become anxious when adapting a work as immensely recognizable as the works of Shakespeare because they know audiences worldwide will look closely to the result to find "faults" within the adaptation.

This could be the reason behind the fact that many of the adaptations of Shakespeare's *Macbeth* follow the play so closely. Indeed, both Orson Welles's adaptation (1948) and Roman Polanski's *Macbeth* (1971) lift entire dialogues almost verbatim from the play. The last adaptation, made by Justin Kurzel in 2015, also follows this path. Even with some minor changes, these films mostly "illustrate" Shakespeare's work. It is interesting to note that some of these films were made by directors considered to be *auteurs*. Authorship theory means that some directors are elevated to the category of *auteurs* if they have a distinctive voice running through their entire output, thus creating personal, distinctive, and "authored" films. Welles and Polanski were recognized as more than mere film directors: they are authors. Still, their *Macbeth* adaptations do not add much to what was already in the text, preferring to remain faithful to the printed word.

The need to keep the verse as it was written in the seventeenth century may owe to the fact that criticism regards the literary rhythm of the play to be essential in Shakespeare. Discussing Racine, Shakespeare, and Molière, André Bazin notes that what is specifically theatrical about these tragedies "is not their action so much as the human, that is to say the verbal, priority given to their dramatic structure" (106). For his part, Welsh argues that "Shakespeare's prime achievement was his poetry. He should not be valued for his *borrowed* plots. What a Shakespeare film looks like is of secondary importance; what it sounds like is of primary importance. If it doesn't sound right, then it probably was not worth doing" (112, my emphasis).

From all adaptators of Shakespeare's *Macbeth*, it can be argued that Welles, Polanski (both as *auteurs*), and Kurzel (as the latest) are the more widely known. All three keep the structure of the play and the sequence of actions: Macbeth meets three witches as he returns from battle. The witches tell him he will become king. He tells their prediction to his wife, and together they plot to murder King Duncan. In this new world, one of predestination, evil is inevitable. Soon enough, Macbeth is facing tragedy, triggered by his own ambition. All three directors add little to the play briefly sketched above, and keep the action firmly situated, chronologically and spatially, in the same location and historical time described by Shakespeare.

Thus, there is little deviation from the play. Kurzel make good use of the natural landscapes so he can give some "breath" to a theatrical play. Since nature is essential to the play—which opens with the evocation of thunder, lightning, and rain—the decision enhances the "awesome atmospheric phenomena traditionally associated with the power of male, uranic gods, and in the context of the play with masculine, endodynamic violence and power struggle (Sadowski 151). With a big budget and contemporary FX to his favor, Kurzel chooses to emphasize the importance of the natural environment and its association with masculinity. It is interesting to note that the three witches seem particularly fragile in the film, pale and seminaked as they are—thus highlighting the heavy contrast between their (supposed) feminine inferiority and warlike masculinity.

Orson Welles's bias, on the other hand, was to the idea of altering the play, at least in theater. In 1936, in Harlem, New York, Orson Welles directed for theater what came to be known later as his "Voodoo" *Macbeth*. Welles directed the play for the Negro People's Theatre, a unit within the US Federal Theatre Project that employed African Americans. "The tragedy was adapted to a Caribbean setting, where witchcraft could seem an accepted cultural fact" (Moschovakis 27). However, Welles mostly ditches any potential rewriting in his cinematic rendition of the play. Welles's *Macbeth* differs from his earlier staging, lacking both its Caribbean locale and its African-American cast. The film maintains the theatricality of the play, as the scenarios and landscapes certainly look artificial. Welles made his *Macbeth* for Republic Pictures, considered a "poverty row" studio because of its tiny budgets and short schedules for filming. Welles used this lack of resources to his advantage, giving the film some expressionist style—highly stylized, artificial backgrounds, skewed camera angles—which can be seen as "an externalization of Macbeth's mind" (Jorgens 151–52). As Moschovakis argues, Welles's adaptation of a play centered in the influence of evil can be linked to the social and cultural context of the postwar era, "reflecting the danger associated with moral dissolution in postwar minds" (27). Further, the play has been read as the internal moral fight between good and evil, a battle celebrated in the inner recesses of Macbeth's mind. The use of nonrealistic scenarios and expressionist-infused sets refers to a poetic based in the plastic and material manifestations of the psychology of the characters. When Welles uses artifice to construct his vision of *Macbeth*, he is re-creating in a visual way the conflict of good and evil using dark castles, eternally clouded skies, and swirls of fog. Visually, Orson Welles's *Macbeth* exteriorizes the somber thoughts haunting the main character.

Polanski, for his part, made his version shortly after the murder of his wife, Sharon Tate, at the hands of the Charles Manson family. The bleak nature of humanity is central in the play and, arguably, in the daily life of Polanski after the killings. "Polanski makes Macbeth himself not a tragic figure but a typical product of a brutalized and brutalizing society" (Moschovakis 33). In this sense, the play speaks about themes that the director probably wanted to paint onto the screen as a form of personal exorcism.

All this, however, it is not enough to explain the lack of interest in creating something new from Shakespeare's play. Arguably, both Welles and Polanski were highly regarded directors and, as such, their work will be carefully evaluated by critics and audiences alike. Maybe only a B-director such as Ken Hughes could tackle Shakespeare in a nonreverent way. If Welles's film is influenced by postwar anxieties, Hughes's take on *Macbeth* fully embraces the mindset of both, the era *and* the play, through the aesthetics and narratives of the film noir.

Joe Macbeth updates Shakespeare's Scottish play to a twentieth-century gangster/noir setting. The film revolves around Joe Macbeth (Paul Douglas) who, following the premonitions of a Tarot card reader, chooses the dark path of treason. The film takes many liberties with the play, and that is what makes it interesting. In the core of the film lives Macbeth's wife (Ruth Roman), who, faithful to the predominance of femme fatales in the 1950s, practically pushes her husband to murder. Thus, the film speaks about Shakespeare but also about anxieties concerning gender roles in the 1950s, thus making it relevant for its era.

Shakespeare and Postwar 1950s in *Joe Macbeth*

Joe Macbeth is a respected strong-arm man for crime boss Lennie (Bonar Colleano) in 1950s America. He is the number two man in the mob and is more than happy with his situation. His wife, Lily, is ambitious, however, and she begins to push Joe around about moving on up—which would entail removing Lennie. Joe vacillates but Lily remains resolute.

It is Lily who sets the film firmly within film noir territory. Film historians usually concur that the classic period of film noir lasted roughly from 1940 to 1960, years in which the American screens were populated with films that reflected the dark underside of American life. The characteristics were located around the generic regime of the crime film including a shift toward a chiaroscuro as main stylization—a metaphor of the dark corners of the human mind—a critique of the values of postwar American society, a psychological trend in the representation of the different characters and emphasis in unruly sexuality (Krutnik x). This aesthetic and narrative were perfect frames to narrate Macbeth's path to self-destruction.

There are subtle links connecting the film with Shakespeare's play: Banquo becomes "Banky" (Sid James) and Macduff is called "Duffy." One of the most intelligent transformations of the play can be found in the image of the three witches, now downsized to one, Tarot card reader Rosie (Minerva Pious), whose prophecies of Joe becoming the new kingpin set the story in motion. To emphasize the relationship of Rosie with her literary counterpart, the Tarot reader is seen in a scene preparing "red hot chestnuts" to sell in the streets: she is framed revolving a cauldron supposedly containing the treat. The scene plays with the imagery commonly associated to witchcraft and contained within the play *Macbeth*.

The main themes underlining the play are present in the film. Scholars presented *Macbeth*'s design as a dualistic one, invoking stark moral oppositions: Macbeth begins as a hero but once greed bores into his head, he deviates from the good, creating his own fatal fate—a well-known trope of classic tragedies. As noted by Moschovakis, three main ethical issues arise from the main plot (4-5): Was it ambition *Macbeth* chiefly warned against? Maybe the play—and the film—asks people to conform with the position that they have in life, rather than being constantly pushed higher in the social ladder. Or was it the corruption of male honor by female evil? Might it be, perhaps, the danger of tyranny?

These ethical questions belong not only to *Macbeth*, but also to film noir's mindset. What the film ultimately does is build on the basis of these moral questions while constructing a story that does not faithfully follow the play but reflects on the different themes of Shakespeare's work. Film noir, as Paul Duncan argues, is sustained on the poles of trust and betrayal, thus creating scenarios of paranoia where people can rely on no one. As the play begins, Macbeth ascends into a new role and is soon battling to climb up even higher. Arguably, ambition and desire for elevated social positions are integral to the universe of the gangster film. The majority of gangster/noir films make explicit commentary on the nature of human greed. Decisions based on ambition become of immense moral and psychological importance because they truly make a difference. One can always move on someone else and take his place. In the gangster film, "the world belongs to whoever's got what it takes to conquer it and hold on" (Shadoian 38). The play tackles this issue through battles and internal monologues, but it is a part of the dialogue that best exemplifies the mobility of positions within *Macbeth*: in the opening, when a new status is offered to Macbeth, the latter says: "The thane of Cawdor lives. Why do you dress me / in borrowed robes?" (I.3.108-9). The phrase points to the speed in which a position is filled by another man to keep the status quo unaffected. Thus, a position such as kingship is "not innate, predestined, and god-given, but merely a political distinction that can be conferred upon mortals—and stripped away just as quickly" (Kaaber 156). *Joe Macbeth*, a film that chose to discard original dialogues, finds a visual motif to say the same thing. The film begins with the camera tracking closer to the neon-lit front of Tommy's, the restaurant that serves as façade for criminal operations. The place belongs to the gangsters—Joe Macbeth among them—running the city. As the film progresses, however, and the treasons pile up, the place changes its name to parallel the person leading the gang (it is first changed to Luca's and ends the film called Mac's).

As mentioned, Moschovakis points to the cruelties of tyranny as another important theme within the play. *Joe Macbeth* replaces tyranny with a vision of a city living under the grip of gangsters occupying a symbolic throne. Ken Hughes, the director, recognizes the many similarities between tyranny as a political form based on social oppression and its mirrorlike regime, gangsterism. There is no more law than that of the gangsters—there is little presence of cops or sanctioned forms of law within the film—and nobody can raise a finger against those leading the gang.

The most important aspect of *Macbeth*, however, is that of how to make choices in life, where the morality of our actions resides. In the play, Macbeth and his wife have many chances to change their path, but every decision only exacerbates their doom. This is the main deviation of the film from the play, a deviation that answers to the politics of film noir and that shapes *Joe Macbeth* as something new.

Gender roles are important within the play. Macbeth does consider simply letting destiny happen to him. "But his wife convinces him, by appealing to his manhood, to take the initiative" (Snyder 82). Not only will the promised crown render him more man than he is, but taking positive action to reach that crown will in itself make him "so much more the man" (I.7.51). Even so, it is clear in the play that both Macbeth and his wife decide, together, to end the life of the king. Macbeth may have his doubts, but he is guilty. Joe Macbeth is also guilty but, faithful to the misogynistic image of the femme fatale dominating noir cinema, Lily, standing for Lady Macbeth, has a more prominent, malicious role. For example, after the killing of the king, Lady Macbeth recedes into the background in the play. In the film, however, Lily remains center stage.

The figure of the femme fatale was a sort of condensation of social anxieties with explicitly gendered sources, condensed on film into the criminal shenanigans of evil albeit beautiful women. Film noir encapsulated anxieties about female empowerment in the postwar era and the femme fatale was "a projection of postwar male anxiety about changing or ambiguous gender roles" (Grossman 2). Indeed, after the end of World War II, men returning from the battle front found their jobs and their position as breadwinners "stolen" by women. During the war, sisters, daughters, and wives had to access the public sphere and get a job to keep the economy of the household afloat. Men returning from the war experienced, thus, a series of gender shifts in which women were more independent and willful, creating anxieties about the role that men would occupy from that point on. Many felt "castrated" by all these empowered women. The image of the femme fatale, in turn, negotiated with gender anxieties creating a figure of a woman so powerful, mischievous, and beautiful that her existence was men's doom. In brief, the femme fatale crystallized a misogynistic world-view of women competing for power transformed into monsters.

In this scenario, Lily is even more assertive and evil than her literary counterpart, while Joe is more doubtful. The weakness of Joe Macbeth is compensated by the cold soul of Lily, the real brain behind the crimes. Like Lady Macbeth, she pushes her husband to kill the kingpin so he can assume that position. Unlike Lady Macbeth, Lily actually has a more active role in the killing, as she pushes her husband twice to kill the kingpin. Further, Lily seems at times exasperated by her husband's lack of drive, which obliges her to take a more active role. Lily only awakes to remorse when she sees a child murdered because of her plans. Still, it is too late for her and she follows the path of any evil woman in noir. Rather than kill herself jumping from a window or dying in bed, she is accidently shot by her own husband, a moral punishment in which she is killed by the monster she has created.

The intimate moral struggles framing *Macbeth* are separated into halves in *Joe Macbeth*. Since internal monologues can be seen as tiresome and antirealistic in film, the internal struggles (that the other adaptations resolve by lifting entire soliloquies from the play) are here reconfigured as two poles: weak-willed Joe Macbeth is practically pushed to madness by his cold, calculating, and ambitious wife. With this shift, the film makes a double movement. On one hand, it pushes Lady Macbeth/Lily, one of Shakespeare's most interesting female creations, to the forefront. On the other, it directly engages with the narratives of the film noir and its preoccupations with gender anxieties.

Conclusion

From the outset, more than a specific precursor, each book-to-film adaptation has been adapting an idea or interpretation of the universe of the book, generated by social and contextual categories of equivalences, relations, codes of interpretation, and ideologies that mediate between readings, emphasizing minor characters or situations to lead audiences to particular meanings.

In this particular, it is striking how faithful and close to the play the majority of *Macbeth*'s adaptations are, thus revealing particularities at the moment of adapting William Shakespeare, a "sacred" author whose words should be kept intact. Within this universe of fidelity, *Joe Macbeth* arises among the others, a work that creates something new from Shakespeare's play. Still, the important themes framing the play slips within the film, now reconfigured to fit the era's mindset. The ethics delineating the play that separate right from wrong are here shaped into a dichotomy that separates Macbeth from Lily, the real villain within the film. This dichotomy basically works visually to replace the play's internal ethical struggles, while fitting within the schemes of the film noir and the construct of the femme fatale.

Undoubtedly, William Shakespeare's *Macbeth* is a classic, and part of what makes it such an immortal piece is its potentiality of being written and rewritten constantly though time to speak to the new eras. Thus, the world should welcome more unfaithful adaptations of *Macbeth*.

Works Cited

Bazin, André. *What Is Cinema?* Translated by Hugh Gray. U of California P, 1967.

Duncan, Paul. *Film Noir: Films of Trust and Betrayal.* Pocket Essential, 2006.

Foucault, Michel. "Nietzsche, Freud, Marx." *Transforming the Hermeneutic Context: From Nietzsche to Nancy.* Edited by Gayle Ormiston and Alan Schrift. SUNY Press, 1990, pp. 59-68.

French, Emma. *Selling Shakespeare to Hollywood: The Marketing of Filmed Shakespeare Adaptations from 1989 into the New Millennium.* U of Hertfordshire P, 2006.

Grossman, Julie. *Rethinking the Femme Fatale in Film Noir: Ready for Her Close-Up.* Palgrave Macmillan, 2009.

Jorgens, Jack J. *Shakespeare on Film.* Indiana UP, 1977.

Kaaber, Lars. *Murdering Ministers: A Close Look at Shakespeare's Macbeth in Text, Context and Performance.* Cambridge Scholars, 2016.

Krutnik, Frank. *In a Lonely Street: Film Noir, Genre, Masculinity.* Routledge, 1991.

Leitch, Thomas. *Film Adaptation and Its Discontents. From* Gone with the Wind *to* The Passion of the Christ. Johns Hopkins UP, 2007.

MacCabe, Colin. *Perpetual Carnival: Essays on Film and Literature.* Oxford UP, 2017.

Moschovakis, Nick. "Dualistic *Macbeth*? Problematic *Macbeth*?" *Macbeth: New Critical Essays.* Edited by Nick Moschovakis. Routledge, 2008, pp. 1-72.

Sadowski, Piotr. "Macbeth." *William Shakespeare's Macbeth.* Edited by Harold Bloom. Infobase, 2010, pp. 165-78.

Shadoian, Jack. *Dreams and Dead Ends: The American Gangster Film.* Oxford UP, 2003.

Shakespeare, William. *Macbeth.* Edited by Stephen Orgel. Penguin, 2016.

Snyder, Susan. "Theology as Tragedy in *Macbeth*." *William Shakespeare's Macbeth.* Edited by Harold Bloom. Infobase, 2010, pp. 73-84.

Welsh, James. "Introduction: Issues of Screen Adaptation: What Is Truth?" *The Literature/Film Reader: Issues of Adaptation.* Edited by James M. Welsh and Peter Lev. Scarecrow, 2007, pp. xiii-xxviii.

_____, and Peter Lev, editors. "What Is a "Shakespeare Film,"
Anyway?" *The Literature/Film Reader: Issues of Adaptation.* Edited
by James M. Welsh. Scarecrow, 2007, pp. 105-14.

Interpreting the Weird Sisters: Page, Stage, and Screen_____

Pamela Royston Macfie

William Shakespeare initiates us to the rough energies of *Macbeth* with a scene controlled by characters the First Folio calls the "weyward" sisters. Unfolded in singsong repetitions and reversals, the scene is mysterious. This essay will explore the Weird Sisters' complex identity as it inhabits textual details that tend toward contradiction and unsettled interpretation. We will consider representative analyses of their nature within their critical history and devote special attention to interpretations of their power realized in several recent stage and cinematic productions. This work will substantiate two important propositions: (1) Shakespeare creates the Weird Sisters in such a way that they slip the noose of stable definition; and (2) it is this slippage, rather than their affiliation with Fate, witchcraft, or the demonic, that accounts for their haunting power.

Stretching from the first recorded comment upon their nature—penned in 1611 by Simon Forman, a fashionable London physician and devoted playgoer—to more recent textual, cultural, and feminist criticism, the Weird Sisters shift in shape and meaning. Commentary variously casts them as Anglo-Saxon reembodiments of the classical Fates (Tolman, Knight), recreations of the classical Furies (McGee), demons who have assumed human form (Curry, Harris, Hampton), phantasmagoric projections (Wilbern, Favila, Roychoudhury), sources of social disorder (Eagleton) or contagion (Callaghan, Levin, Purkiss), and local crones who merit suspicion but control neither Macbeth's nor the play's destiny (Frye, Willis). Reckonings of the Weird Sisters swerve from notions of supernatural agency to those of social victimization. By one account, the Weird Sisters are all-powerful; by another, they are all too human. Contradiction marks not only the sisters' interpretive history, but also single works of criticism. Certain scholars argue that these characters are one thing in the play's first act and another in its fourth (West, Kranz), others measure the Weird Sisters' significance within one scene with words that are incongruous.

The Weird Sisters' provocation of contradictory reactions inhabits the first comment upon their appearance on Shakespeare's stage. Writing about a 1611 performance at London's Globe in his *Booke of Plays*, Simon Forman describes the trio as "three women fairies, or nymphs" (qtd. in Schoenbaum 7). These words name the sisters as otherworldly, but refuse (given the alternative force of "or") to specify the supernatural identity that might account for their power. The word *nymphs* casts them as attendant spirits of forest or flood. *Fairies* ties them to the marvelous and metamorphic, associations that might recall Puck from *A Midsummer Night's Dream*. Forman's subtly different terms suggest the Weird Sisters' indeterminacy. Are they fairies or nymphs, of village or wood, makers of mischief or guardians of nature?

Scholarly analyses of the signal word applied to these characters also traffic in inconsistency. We have only one text of *Macbeth*: that of the First Folio, which we have noted uses the word *weyward* (rather than *weird*) in naming the sisters in I.3.30, III.1.2, and III.4.132. *Weyward* and *weird* are closely similar in etymology and sound. Both derive from the Middle English; both trace back to the Anglo-Saxon proper noun for the goddess of Fate (*Wyrd*, *OED*). Most editors, however, argue that *weyward* makes its way into the Folio because of a scribe's error (an idea reaching back to Lewis Theobold's 1726 *Shakespeare Restored*) and use the word *weird* because its spelling closely approximates *Wyrd*. Yet the *Oxford English Dictionary* ascribes the meaning of Fate, of "having the power to control the fate or destiny of human beings," to *weyward* and *weird* alike. Is it possible that modern editions print *weird* rather than *weyward* in order to suggest those ominous meanings—of the eerie and uncanny, the terrifying and strange, even the ghoulish and grotesque—that accrue to the sisters over the course of Shakespeare's play and its performance history? If this might be so, the Weird Sisters would seem nearly to dictate their own meaning.

Modern editorial preference for *weird* over *weyward* obscures several denotations pertinent to the sisters' forbidding effects upon Macbeth (their crucial audience onstage) and us (their audience in the larger theatre). In early modern usage, *weyward* signified that which is "intractable, self-willed, perverse," "contrary to what is expected," or "conforming to no fixed rule or principle of conduct" (*OED*). These meanings, which Shakespeare applies in other plays (*The Comedy of Errors* IV.4.4; *Pericles* xviii.10), speak to the Weird Sisters' behavior at several key turns. Intractable before authority, they deny Macbeth's several commands to explain their "strange intelligence" (I.3.76). Overturning the customs of cookery, they stir together "witch's mummy" (IV.1.23), "liver of blaspheming Jew" (IV.1.26), and "finger of birth-strangled babe" (IV.1.30). By unpredictable turns, their malevolence serves different purposes: when they devise punishments for a sailor whose wife has insulted one of them (I.3.4-29), they fulfill their own whim; when Hecate, the goddess of witchcraft, appears in III.5, they answer her bidding.

These characters accrue complex meaning not only through their repeated naming as *weird* but also through descriptions unfolded in the play's dialogue. Calling themselves *weird* (I.3.32) immediately before Macbeth and Banquo encounter them on the heath and receive their prophecies, they function as fateful seers, but are described by Banquo as ugly, aged, and infirm. Banquo fixes upon their being "so withered and so wild in their attire" that they "look not like th' inhabitants o' th' earth" (I.3.40-41). The adjective *withered* (applied by Macbeth in II.1.53 to a creeping personification of murder) yields more than an image of shriveled limbs and shrunken posture. The word's derivation from the Old English *wederian,* which denotes something exposed to and shaped by the weather (*OED*), suggests the Weird Sisters have been written by the elements. When at the close of this scene they disappear like "bubbles" or "breath into the wind" (I.3.79, 82), they return to the restless energy from which their appearance and meaning would seem to originate. The several layers of Banquo's lines (I.3.40-41) vacillate in meaning. The literal sense denotes that the Weird Sisters have been battered, weakened, and diminished by harsh conditions; the poetic sense, manifest in the rolling alliteration that fuses *withered* and *wild*, connotes the sisters are party—rather than victim—to the play's vertiginous weather.

An important strand of scholarship takes the Weird Sisters' associations with weather as evidence that they are witches. In the play's opening scene, the sisters consider whether "thunder, lightning, or . . . rain" (I.1.1) might determine their next meeting and command one another to "hover through the fog and filthy air" (I.1.13). In I.3, they materialize upon a wind-wrecked, "blasted" heath and vanish into its air. When Macbeth seeks their soothsaying in the cauldron scene, he suggests they have the power to "untie the winds and let them fight" (IV.1.74). King James's 1597 *Daemonologie*, a work Shakespeare consulted, states that witches raise storms and fill them with signs. Raphael Holinshed's 1577 *Chronicles of England, Scotland, and Ireland*, a direct source for *Macbeth*, identifies witches with pestilent wind, weather, and air. Brenda Gardenour Walters maintains that Shakespeare's Jacobean audience would have understood the Weird Sisters' hovering in fog (I.1.13; III.5.67) through "the longstanding cultural association between the witch and 'foul and filthy air'—whether she be riding upon it, directing it, or poisoning it with her own corrupt breath" (Walters 2). Studied in terms of its history, this association yields contradictory explanations of the Weird Sisters' power. Early modern theories of weather valorized witches, identifying them as a supernatural force that drives the winds and makes them revelatory; contemporaneous medical theory submitted witches to be "powerless except for [their] toxicity" of breath and person (Walters 5).

Feminist explorations of the Weird Sisters as witches through the lens of social discourse similarly privilege the sisters' agency on the one hand and demystify it on the other. Certain studies argue that the play presents the Weird Sisters as figures of subversion in order that the patriarchal order may explain away its failures (Adelman, Eagleton). In this, the Weird Sisters appear as the objects of an elaborate form of scapegoating. Others, reading *Macbeth* against early modern texts like Edward Jorden's 1603 *Briefe Discourse of the Disease Called the Suffocation of the Mother*, which diagnoses witches as suffering from hysteria, propose the Weird Sisters' power would have been understood in terms of a pathology (Callaghan, Levin). Considered in these contexts, the Weird Sisters' witchcraft seems less of the otherworld and more of the human.

What do contemporary stage and film productions of *Macbeth* make of the complicated contexts from which Shakespeare summons these characters? Do we glimpse in these productions something of fairy and nymph or recoil from diseased crones? Are we compelled by figures of fateful authority? Do the Weird Sisters clamor from the trapdoor in the stage as if they emanate from that part of the theatre Shakespeare and his contemporaries understood to represent hell? Do they make their entrances and exits from disparate places as if they are omnipresent? Do they move through the stalls as if they belong to our company?

Two stagings of *Macbeth* in the past ten years exemplify the Weird Sisters' potential to call upon our sympathies: Michael Boyd's 2011 production for the Royal Shakespeare Theatre on the main stage in Stratford and Iqbal Khan's 2016 production at The Globe. Boyd's production, taking liberties with Shakespeare's text, presented the Weird Sisters as children; Khan's version, equally determined to make the Weird Sisters new, cast them as veiled widows who never speak. Both of these interpretations depart from the idea (manifest, for instance, in Orson Welles's famous 1936 "Voodoo" *Macbeth* at Harlem's Lafayette Theatre, which included an actual Haitian witch doctor) that the Weird Sisters can compel awe in performance only through ghoulish props, loud noise, and over-the-top special effects. Though their casting and directing of the sisters differed, Boyd's and Khan's productions sounded similar chords. Both engaged their audiences with the Weird Sisters as characters who have suffered loss. Both considered that the Weird Sisters' prophetic power might derive from traumatic witness.

Boyd's casting of the Weird Sisters as children, even in its initial shock, served to explain their reach and relevance in the play. The shock was immediate. Before the houselights had fully dimmed, as the audience listened to three cellists playing among the elevated church ruins that formed the stage's backdrop, three children dropped from the fly space with such speed and clatter that some observers jumped in their seats. Invisible before their harnessed descent, the girls seemed initially to be puppets. Their limbs flapped as though they belonged to rag dolls; their heads bounced, then lolled, as if disjointed. For the handful of minutes in which they remained suspended midair, Boyd's Weird Sisters sustained the impression they were lifeless. Their eyes appeared flat as glass. Their hands seemed those of an effigy. Then, each as pale as her smock, the children began to speak: "When shall we three meet again? / In thunder, lightning, or in rain? / When the hurly-burly's done, / When the battle's lost and won" (I.3.1-4). The words sifted from above in eerie monotone.

When, lowered to the level of the stage, Boyd's child players removed their harnesses and scrambled away, they left the audience with several original explanations of their characters' prophetic authority. Through spatial metaphor, Boyd invited his audience to consider that the Weird Sisters and their powers descend from that part of the theatre that represented the heavens to Shakespeare and his contemporaries. In a decisive stroke, Boyd overturned the convention whereby the Weird Sisters rise from the theatre's cellarage and thus from hell. Boyd also canceled the precedent by which the Weird Sisters take the stage shrieking and howling. Except for the sudden thud as they fell into view, his Weird Sisters were one with an atmosphere of hush. Gentling his actors' speech, making it consonant with the cello's bowing melancholy, Boyd offered a second explanation of the Weird Sisters' truth-telling authority: it comes from their haunted (even, perhaps, their martyred) witness of sorrow. Boyd's whispering children compelled the audience to receive the play's famous formula, "fair is foul, and foul is fair" (I.1.12), as though they had never heard (and mouthed) the line before. The delicate timbre of the Weird Sisters' voices made their pronouncement a thing of awestruck discovery.

If Boyd's use of space suggested the Weird Sisters come to earth from heaven, his child actors' close-shouldered sidling across the floor suggested they were victims of trauma. Their self-defensive movement implied they had been conditioned to expect blows. This effect, compounded by the slightness of their physical presence, might have diminished the audience's sense of the Weird Sisters' power. Strangely, however, their vulnerability suggested they possessed an agency beyond their years. Even as they appeared as children, they also seemed as ghosts, an effect enhanced by the shifting of their filmy gowns. This doubling of identity seemed true to the Weird Sisters' ineluctable mystery in Shakespeare's text. At the same time, it linked the Weird Sisters' sorrowful prophesying to the grim ends ascribed to children in the play: the wholesale slaughter of Lady Macduff's "pretty ones" (IV.3.216) and the attempted murder of Fleance, who escapes when his father is dispatched to death suddenly and unprepared. The Weird Sisters' soothsaying in Boyd's production did not merely gain authority as their hailing of Macbeth as "Thane of Glamis," "Thane of Cawdor," and "king hereafter" (I.3.48-50) came to be fulfilled in later events. Their truth telling acquired special resonance in relation to the play's widening witness of loss, including that suffered by children. Boyd reinforced this resonance by having his child actors play not only the Weird Sisters but also Macduff's hapless children, who are killed onstage.

Iqbal Khan's production at London's Globe also suggested that trauma inhabits the Weird Sisters and their knowledge. Khan dressed his Weird Sisters in black gowns streaked with a rusty color suggesting bloodstains. At the opening of the play, Khan's sisters emerged from a heap of corpses and grisly body parts; pale faced and bruised, they seemed one with the dead. To unfold their "strange intelligence" (I.3.76) to Banquo and Macbeth, they wielded severed arms and legs, using them to lift in the air an inky shroud into which Banquo and Macbeth peered. Standing behind this cloth, the Weird Sisters shrouded themselves in widows' veils but did not speak the soldiers' doom. Khan ascribed their words to singers who chanted their lines, in minor key, from the stage balcony. Later, in IV.1, the scene of the apparitions, the soprano Melanie Pappenheim sang their parts, her haunting voice, accompanied by cello and oboe, also floating from above. Like Boyd, Khan insisted that his audience hear the Weird Sisters as though for the first time. He also multiplied all sense of their influence: onstage, the Weird Sisters' prophecies unfolded through primitive pantomime; from the theatre's heavens, they emanated from touches of harmony.

Khan increased his audience's perception of the sisters' influence by including them in a number of scenes in which Shakespeare neither stipulates nor suggests their presence. In I.2, Khan's Weird Sisters resuscitated from death the bloody captain who must speak to Duncan of the "damnèd quarrel" (I.2.14) through which Macbeth has defeated the rebel Macdonwald. Here Khan did not merely associate the sisters with a power that mediates death and life; he also suggested they determine messages beyond the words assigned them by Shakespeare. In III.4, the scene in which Banquo's ghost appears before Macbeth, Khan presented his Weird Sisters as supernatural midwives. In the banquet hall, they unfurled again the shroud into which Macbeth and Banquo had earlier peered together. Beneath this cloth, they smuggled Banquo onto the stage; with it, they controlled his appearance. Banquo's writhing under the surface of the voluminous fabric suggested he would be born from his winding sheet. In one instant, his hands and feet pummeled the cloth; in another, his face stretched its elastic surface into a distorted grimace. In the end, the Weird Sisters' portentous shroud appeared as both a gravecloth and the outer muscular layer of a supernatural womb.

In IV.1, Khan compelled the Weird Sisters' puppetry to come even more to the fore. Here the apparition of a king with a glass in his hands towered above its conjurers. That of the bloody babe, tossed upon the sisters' shroud (which purpled under a strange light), sickened the audience as it tumbled in the air. That of Birnam wood, forged from disparate body parts, metal screens, and leaves, seemed both a monstrous hybrid and a canny prediction of the ways in which Malcolm's soldiers would use the woods' limbs for defensive camouflage. Puppetry was not merely practiced by Khan's weird ones. In several ways, they seemed puppets themselves. This impression derived in part from their silence, in part from their almost Kabuki-style movement. Sometimes the Weird Sisters seemed about to lose practical control of the gigantic effigies they raised above the stage. In the end, however, they danced ahead of disaster.

Fleet of foot, Khan's Weird Sisters seemed to be everywhere. In his production, they did not merely appear on the heath or in their cave; they inhabited scenes of battle and state, watching Macbeth, for example, when he is crowned king. Their claim to omnipresence is closely related to that of a character Khan added to the play: a small boy, who strayed about the stage, attentive to the actions and words of Macbeth and his wife, though the actors playing these characters seldom looked upon him. Like the Weird Sisters, whom he sometimes followed, the boy functioned as a ghostly marker of past, present, and future. His signifying, like that of Khan's silent weird ones, depended on gestures of hand. As the play drew near its close, he cupped the candles and blew out the light Lady Macbeth had kept by her side.

Boyd's and Khan's suggestions that the Weird Sisters might be understood through the traumatic experience of children resonate with a recent filmic interpretation of the play: the 2015 *Macbeth* starring Michael Fassbender and Marion Cotillard directed by Justin Kurzel. Kurzel's association of the Weird Sisters with children is emphatic and persistent. When the camera pans across a barren landscape, bringing within view the three sisters standing atop an uneven hill, it also draws within its focus a child and a baby. A tiny, wide-eyed girl leans against the first weird sister, who clasps the child's shoulders as if to lend comfort and support. The second sister cradles in her arms a baby swaddled in grey. The third witch, herself little more than a girl, toys with a primitive doll made from bones. With these details, Kurzel humanizes the sisters, suggesting that, as they wander wrecked fields, they are widows and orphans of war. Simultaneously, he overturns his audience's initial impression of the sisters through a still shot that casts them as impassive Titans silhouetted against the sky.

Kurzel also linked his Weird Sisters with children through the visual prologue that opens his film. His opening shot, revising Shakespeare's text, does not present the Weird Sisters at all; it sustains a close-up of a baby, wrapped in a fringed shawl, resting among winter grass and heather. The baby is the Macbeths' dead child. In this scene, which Kurzel superimposes on Shakespeare's text (which leaves mysterious the identity of the infant Lady Macbeth claims once to have nursed), a grim-faced Macbeth covers the baby's eyes with two flat stones, as if he would protect it from the terrors of the afterworld. The hooded father scatters earth upon the little corpse and then sets the bier ablaze. When the camera carries us from the burning infant to the Weird Sisters and their sorrowful faces, they seem to mourn the baby. This impression is strengthened by the timbre of their voices. Kurzel's sisters produce a sense of hush. They do not shrill and cackle; they speak as one might croon to a child or to one who suffers.

When Kurzel's Macbeth and Banquo encounter the Weird Sisters on the heath, their wonder reacts not merely to the sisters' sudden appearance but also to their gentle calm. Before they speak, the Weird Sisters, together with the bonneted girl who leads them, touch the war-weary soldiers. The first draws a talisman from Macbeth's leather breastplate. The second traces a finger across his dirtied face as though she would read its wounds. The third cups Macbeth's face in her hands, resting his chin upon her palm, while the youngest hails him in prophetic terms. In sympathy and knowing, Kurzel's Weird Sisters seem to discern Macbeth's future through his injuries. Succor rather than malevolence characterizes their gestures; sympathy seems one with their scrutiny, which focuses on scars on Macbeth's visage that duplicate the ravages of their own.

Kurzel does not imply that Macbeth merits such care. The scene of battle that prefaces the hero's encounter with the Weird Sisters presents him in ignoble terms. The soldiers Macbeth leads against Macdonwald are frightened boys so unready for combat and so untrained that Macbeth must lash their weapons to their arms. Kurzel's camera provides a torturous view of the boys' faces as they look to the charge. At the end of the battle, whose slow motion sequences mire us in viscera and mud, the camera, together with the Weird Sisters, watches Macbeth abandon burying the dead. Though some of latter shots in this sequence track Macbeth carrying a dead boy, the final shots show him heaving the boy's corpse to the ground.

Like Boyd and Khan, Kurzel expands the presence of the Weird Sisters in Shakespeare's scenes. Simultaneously, he expands the presence of the hapless children with whom his sisters are associated. Kurzel's sisters do more than witness the battle (to which Shakespeare fails to make them party). Kurzel also adds them to the scene in which Macbeth, steeling himself to murder Duncan, asks, "Is this a dagger which I see before me?" (II.1.39). Here, at the sisters' apparent bidding, one of the boy soldiers sacrificed on the battlefield stands at Macbeth's threshold and hears his metaphysical question. When this spectral child, still speckled with the mud of battle, starts, as if the living may terrify the dead, the scene dissolves within a flashback that returns to the moment of the boy's slaughter. Again the Weird Sisters come into view, their gaze moving from the battle (and the past) to Macbeth in his present torture.

Kurzel's Weird Sisters haunt later scenes as well. In the scene in which Macbeth's henchmen set upon Banquo, one sister watches Fleance's pell-mell escape. In the scene in which Macduff avows he may dispatch Macbeth to his deserved death because "Macduff was from his mother's womb / Untimely ripped" (V.8.15-16), all three turn their eyes upon Macbeth. In the scene that culminates in Macbeth's slaughter, they stand as obdurate witness beneath a sky flaked with fire. They depart the audience's sight only when Macbeth is dead. Walking toward the horizon, they are accompanied by the child soldier whose ghost had recoiled from Macbeth's murderous soliloquy.

Kurzel's persistent return to the boy whom Macbeth abandons on death's field, like his persistent return to the Weird Sisters, confounds our precise understanding of the source from which revelatory significance would seem to derive. In II.1, Macbeth's conscience summons haunted memory through the boy, though the Weird Sisters, to be sure, look upon their encounter. In IV.1, the sisters' intelligence reanimates the boy; his ghost, which assumes the prophetic role of the bloody apparition, returns Macbeth to the field of death where Macbeth had left him: "Be bloody, bold, and resolute" (IV.1.101). Though the boy's presence seems consistently portentous, it invokes different realms of meaning. One of those realms, Macbeth's guilty conscience, seems fully human; the other, the Weird Sisters' revivifying power, seems fully supernatural.

All three of the productions we have surveyed present Shakespeare's Weird Sisters as the pained witness to death. This witness, even when it would seem to have muted Khan's weird widows, is never self-enclosed. Reaching outward, it compels others to look at the play's incessant reproductions of "another Golgotha" (I.2.40), the site of the crucifixion, which in Hebrew means "the place of the skull." Adding the Weird Sisters to scenes, especially those of death, from which Shakespeare excludes them, Boyd, Khan, and Kurzel lend their characters the authority of a tragic chorus. In voices that are largely undifferentiated, their wisdom speaks through and of our collective ruin.

What might this survey of interpretations attached to the Weird Sisters convey about the play they inhabit? We have seen how the Weird Sisters assume different meanings in different works of criticism and performance. Boyd, Khan, and Kurzel engage us with ghostly characters that are somehow sympathetic. Other directors offer Weird Sisters who arouse revulsion. Rupert Goold's 2007 Chichester staging and 2010 film cast the sisters as dead-eyed military nurses who eviscerate the wounded soldiers in their charge. Geoffrey Wright's 2006 film introduces a trio of squealing schoolgirls who in I.1 desecrate a graveyard and in IV.1 engage Macbeth in a drug-fueled orgy. Eve Best's 2013 *Macbeth* at the Globe summoned cackling grotesques that some audiences laughed to scorn. The Weird Sisters, it would seem, defy augury. As they introduce the play through a burst of doubletalk that insists, "fair is foul and foul is fair," so they take possession of their history. Shape-shifted in the extreme, that history energizes a play whose mystery cannot be contained.

Works Cited

Adelman, Janet. *Suffocating Mothers: Fantasies of Maternal Origin in Shakespeare's Plays*. Routledge, 1992.

Callaghan, Dympna. "Wicked Women in *Macbeth*: A Study of Power, Ideology, and the Production of Motherhood." *Reconsidering the Renaissance: Papers from the Twenty-First Annual Conference.*

Edited by Mario A. Di Cesare. Medieval and Renaissance Texts and Studies, 1992, pp. 355-69.

Curry, Walter Clyde. *Shakespeare's Philosophical Patterns*. Louisiana State UP, 1937.

Eagleton, Terry. *William Shakespeare*. Oxford UP, 1986.

Favila, Marina. "'Mortal Thoughts' and Magical Thinking in *Macbeth*." *Modern Philology*, vol. 99, 2001, pp. 1-25.

Frye, Roland Mushat. "Launching the Tragedy of *Macbeth*: Temptation, Deliberation, and Consent in Act 1." *Huntington Library Quarterly*, vol. 50, 1987, pp. 249-61.

Hampton, Bryan Adams. "Purgation, Exorcism, and the Civilizing Process in *Macbeth*." *Studies in English Literature*, vol. 51, 2011, pp. 327-47.

Harris, Anthony. *Night's Black Agents: Witchcraft and Magic in Seventeenth-Century Drama*. Manchester UP, 1980.

Knight, G. Wilson. *The Wheel of Fire: Interpretations of Shakespearian Tragedy*. Routledge, 1930.

Kranz, David L. "The Sounds of Supernatural Soliciting in *Macbeth*." *Studies in Philology*, vol. 100, 2003, pp. 346-83.

Levin, Joanna. "Lady Macbeth and the Daemonologie of Hysteria." *English Literary History*, vol. 69, 2002, pp. 21-55.

McGee, Arthur R. "Macbeth and the Furies." *Shakespeare Survey*, vol. 19, 1966, pp. 55-67.

Purkiss, Diane. "Body Crimes: The Witches, Lady Macbeth, and the Relics." *Female Transgression in Early Modern Britain: Literary and Historical Explorations*. Edited by Richard Hillman and Pauline Ruberry-Blanc. Ashgate, 2014, pp. 29-50.

Roychoudhury, Suparna. "Melancholy, Ecstasy, Phantasma: The Pathologies of *Macbeth*." *Modern Philology*, vol. 111, 2013, pp. 205-30.

Schoenbaum, Samuel. *William Shakespeare: Records and Images*. Scolar, 1981.

Shakespeare, William. *Macbeth*. Edited by Stephen Orgel. Penguin, 2016.

Tolman, Albert H. Notes on *Macbeth*," *Publications of the Modern Language Association*, vol. 11, 1896, pp. 200-19.

Walters, Brenda Gardenour. "Corrupt Air, Poisonous Places, and the Toxic Breath of Witches in Late Medieval Medicine and Theology." *Toxic Airs: Body, Place, Planet in Historical Perspective*. Edited by James Rodger Fleming and Ann Johnson. U of Pittsburgh P, 2014, pp. 1-22.

"Weird." *Oxford English Dictionary*. Oxford UP, 1986.

West, Robert. *Shakespeare and the Outer Mystery*. U of Kentucky P, 1968.

"Weyward." *Oxford English Dictionary*. Oxford UP, 1986.

Wilbern, David. "Phantasmagoric *Macbeth*." *English Literary Renaissance*, vol. 16, 1986, pp. 520-49.

Willis, Deborah L. *Malevolent Nature: Witch-Hunting and Maternal Power in Early Modern England*. Cornell UP, 1995.

"Withered." *Oxford English Dictionary*. Oxford UP, 1986.

"Wyrd." *Oxford English Dictionary*. Oxford UP, 1986.

Lady Macbeth and Trauma: Filmed Versions of the Sleepwalking Scene_____

Robert C. Evans

Psychological trauma, which has been so often studied in connection with numerous major authors and works, has been surprisingly little studied in connection with Shakespeare. In a series of recent articles, I have been exploring this issue by examining manifestations of trauma in such works as *Romeo and Juliet*, *Othello*, *King Lear*, and *Macbeth*. In the latter essay, I focused particularly on the trauma Macbeth experiences in the last act of the tragedy. In the present chapter, I wish to study how Lady Macbeth can seem clinically traumatized in the famous "sleepwalking scene" that opens Act V. I especially want to show that recent research has demonstrated a strong connection between trauma, stress, and the phenomenon of sleepwalking. Finally, and most importantly, I want to examine how Lady Macbeth's trauma has been depicted in various filmed versions of the play. In some of these versions, her trauma seems relatively understated; in others, however, her trauma is emphasized so forcefully that the sleepwalking scene can seem almost literally traumatizing to viewers themselves. Three performances in particular—by Jeanette Nolan, Judi Dench, and Kate Fleet—are in fact so horribly traumatic and traumatizing that they are almost impossible to forget, even if one wanted to erase them from one's memory.

Trauma and Sleepwalking

Perhaps the most helpful single-volume study of trauma, at least for nonspecialists, is still Ronnie Janoff-Bulman's book *Shattered Assumptions*. As its title suggests, this book argues that psychological trauma results when one's most basic assumptions about life, the world, other people, and/or oneself are broken down. One's "conceptual system" is threatened or destroyed (5); standard assumptions that the world is benevolent and meaningful and that the self is worthy are undermined (5); the common expectations that the world is just and controllable and that we ourselves are secure if not invulnerable are subverted (8, 10, 19); and unusual, unexpected, dramatic, traumatic changes suddenly destroy beliefs we have long taken for granted, so that our very survival can seem endangered (42, 53, 53). Mortality suddenly seems a real prospect (57); our individual symbolic worlds disintegrate (60); and the traumatized person suffers from such symptoms as intense fear and anxiety (64-65), hyperarousal (65), hypersensitivity (67), adrenaline-fed terror and stress (68), and an abrupt loss of psychological security, trust, and comforting illusions (69, 71, 78). Traumatized persons are likely to feel humiliated, powerless, sullied, tarnished, emotionally numb, and sometimes full of self-blame, self-contempt, and/or guilt (78, 80, 100, 118, 123-26). Many of these symptoms can be seen in persons suffering from PTSD (posttraumatic stress disorder), a condition so often discussed recently that there seems little point in examining it in any detail here.

My basic claims are that Lady Macbeth, in the sleepwalking scene, can be viewed as a deeply traumatized person, and also that that scene can sometimes be staged in ways that can at least metaphorically traumatize viewers. However, as will later be seen, presenting Lady Macbeth as thoroughly traumatized is not the *only* way the scene can be (or has been) staged. Some directors and actresses have sometimes chosen more subtle approaches. Such approaches, though, can often seem far less memorable than stagings emphasizing wholesale, outright trauma. The latter kinds of performance are the kinds most likely to stick in many viewers' minds.

Before examining various stagings of the scene, however, I want to comment briefly on connections between trauma and sleepwalking. The idea that Lady Macbeth sleepwalks *because* she is traumatized might seem obvious, but links between trauma and sleepwalking have sometimes been questioned. This is especially true in a 2001 article by D. Hartman et al., who reported that they had discovered a relatively low correlation between sleepwalking and trauma. Of 22 adult sleepwalkers they had examined, only six had experienced trauma. They concluded, therefore, that "a history of major psychological trauma exists in only a minority of adult patients presenting with sleepwalking/night terror syndrome." This conclusion, however, is open to debate. Although sleepwalking can have many, many different causes (including a genetic predisposition), numerous studies have repeatedly suggested at least *some* correlation between trauma and *some* instances of sleepwalking (see especially Pruitt). In fact, even Hartman et al. showed that trauma could be related to sleepwalking in 27.27 percent of the cases they examined.

Other reports and sources, meanwhile, have suggested significant connections between trauma and somnambulism (the technical term for sleepwalking). Sleepwalking is almost always mentioned as one of many possible symptoms of PTSD. A study by R. C. Calogeras saw sleepwalking as one of many ways to try to control trauma, noting the "repetitive-compulsive" nature of sleepwalking and "its similarity to the hypnotic state." A brief essay by Rick Nauert listed "stressful events" among possible causes of somnambulism, while an especially helpful (but unsigned) article by the National Sleep Foundation strongly emphasized the link between trauma and various problems with sleeping. A peer-reviewed article by John Mersh mentioned "excessive stress or anxiety" as common causes of sleepwalking, while the Sleep Health Foundation warned victims of PTSD that they might "experience . . . problems with how you sleep such as sleep terrors, sleep walking, sleep talking, upsetting dreams and night sweats." An especially detailed study by Silvia G. Conway et al. cited much support for the finding that sleepwalking can be "a manifestation of anxiety and emotions experienced in connection to anger-inciting events and overt hostility during the day"—a particularly interesting comment since Lady Macbeth, in the sleepwalking scene, is so often depicted as angry at her husband. Conway et al. suggested that "sleepwalking episodes are [often] triggered by emotional misalignment, which may be due to constant stress," and they also cited numerous other studies to support their claim that it is "possible that unreleased internal tensions during the day, …psychological conflicts,…and trauma…play important roles in precipitating and perpetuating sleepwalking events. The reduction of sleepwalking prevalence rates in adulthood reinforces the theory that genetics constitute only one important predisposing factor to sleepwalking manifestation." Numerous similar sources could easily be mentioned (see the Works Cited or Consulted section), including many suggesting a strong link between sleepwalking and PTSD (such as Pruitt), but the link will in any case seem obvious to most people. Citing multiple sources in this case would be like citing multiple sources to prove that the earth is round. Few people would doubt the commonsense idea that Lady Macbeth's sleepwalking is rooted, at least in part, in deep psychological trauma.

If we turn, however, to various filmed versions of the sleepwalking scene that have been produced over the years, we can see just how variously this scene has been imagined. Sometimes trauma has been thoroughly stressed (so to speak); sometimes trauma—or at least hysteria—has been somewhat minimized. The different filmed versions of the sleepwalking scene suggest just how variously words on the page can be interpreted on stage.

1948 (Jeanette Nolan)
In the 1948 production starring Orson Welles and Jeanette Nolan, the most immediately striking feature is the heavy, authentic Scottish accents used by all the characters. The doctor and the gentlewoman stand in gloomy darkness next to huge black boulders outside a massive castle. Lady Macbeth appears from a distance, at the top left of the screen, dressed in white and holding her candle. She proceeds slowly down some long stone steps. Her gradual pace makes her first sudden scream all the more shocking, both to viewers and to the other characters. During her abrupt outburst, she symbolically drops her light-giving candle. Her opening scream is the first indication of her trauma. Its suddenness catches viewers completely and frighteningly off guard.

As Lady Macbeth becomes more and more visible, she almost wrestles with her own arms, strongly jerking herself back and forth as she grips and rubs her hands. Nolan looks older than many later actresses playing this role—a fact befitting someone childless and long-married. As she descends the steps, she also descends ever deeper into trauma and madness, constantly staring at her hands, which are tightly clasped. She regards them as much with anger as with horror. Nolan superbly suggests Lady Macbeth's many distinct mental and emotional phases. She shifts abruptly from one mood and tone to another. Her mind, quite literally, seems to have broken down; it lacks any coherence. This is especially evident when, once again, she catches viewers completely off guard by first staring into the sky and then suddenly falling forward, as she both cries and then almost maniacally laughs. Nolan's shifting moods, attitudes, expressions, and glances all memorably imply a woman who lacks any psychological coherence and or emotional stability. She seems clearly traumatized.

She shifts, for instance, from guilt when referring to Duncan's blood to a strange, literally musical, almost perverse nursery rhyme as she sings about about Fife's wife (V.1.42), and then she shifts back to anger as she grips her hands once more. She then turns her anger against an imagined Macbeth, addressing him contemptuously as if he were actually there. This is the Lady Macbeth of the opening act—forceful, commanding, disdainful. She is reliving her moment of power in this later moment of psychological powerlessness. Nolan nearly retches in disgust when she imagines the smell of Duncan's blood on her hands, but then her voice soon becomes a kind of prolonged, painful howl that in turn becomes a whining, subdued, and agonized scream. As the Doctor and the Gentlewoman comment on her behavior, it is as if she can *almost* hear them. To her, they must sound like voices from within her own head and conscience. Again, any sense of mental and emotional stability seems to have broken down; Lady Macbeth seems truly traumatized, and nothing suggests that her condition is merely temporary.

Especially effective is the moment when Lady Macbeth, seemingly echoing the angry, disgusted words and tone of her husband, exclaims "Wash your hands, put on your nightgown," and so on (V.1.61-62). It is as if she has suddenly become a contemptuous Macbeth, who addresses her with the same disdain she had earlier shown for him. Whereas in some productions the claim that Banquo is buried and cannot come out of his grave (V.1.62-63) sounds like words spoken by Lady Macbeth herself, in this production the words—delivered at full volume and with real violence—seem to recollect words previously spoken by Macbeth.

This makes the sudden, completely unexpected appearance of Macbeth himself seem all the more shocking. His presence in this scene, of course, is not scripted by Shakespeare but is a brilliant invention by Welles. Macbeth grabs his lady and looks with embarrassment at the Doctor and the Gentlewoman (who, he realizes, have heard and witnessed everything). In another very effective innovation, when Lady Macbeth speaks her words "To bed, to bed . . ." (V.1.65-67) she speaks not to herself but to Macbeth, whom she grasps almost erotically and who seems stunned by her behavior. He keeps looking from her to the Doctor and the Gentlewoman. The fact that they have seen and heard it all makes Macbeth even more vulnerable. Finally, when Lady Macbeth insists again that they should go "to bed, to bed," he forcefully and lengthily kisses her—perhaps out of love, perhaps out of pity, perhaps merely to shut her up.

But Welles has one more surprise in store: just when we might assume that the couple will indeed go quietly off to bed, Lady Macbeth suddenly pushes herself away, stares Macbeth in the face, seems disgusted, and then runs off in the opposite direction, screaming more loudly than perhaps at any other point in this totally memorable scene. The abrupt and, in some cases, completely unpredictable shifts (no one could have predicted Macbeth's appearance here) catch viewers totally by surprise. The shifts help make the scene, in a sense, almost as traumatizing to us as it is to the characters. The Welles *Macbeth* offers a sleepwalking scene that is literally impossible to forget. Nolan is utterly convincing as a traumatized woman who has lost any hint of mental and emotional stability.

The sleepwalking scene in the 1961 television production starring Sean Connery and Zoe Caldwell will strike many viewers as much less memorable, as well as much less traumatic or traumatizing. Caldwell seems far more subdued than Nolan, often merely quietly moaning when Nolan had literally screamed. One interesting feature of this version is that Caldwell at one point comes very close to the camera, almost staring directly at viewers. But the sleepwalking scene seems to end very quickly, and Caldwell seems far less truly traumatized than Nolan had seemed. Many viewers will feel that the director (Paul Almond) missed a real chance to give his production a strong emotional punch. Caldwell's sleepwalking scene is notable mainly for seeming understated to the point of being somewhat boring.

In contrast, the sleepwalking scene in Roman Polankski's 1971 film is certainly memorable in its own odd way (a way typical of its era). Francesca Annis, Polanski's Lady Macbeth, was roughly twenty-five when the film was shot; she looks significantly younger than either Nolan or Caldwell (even though Caldwell was not much older when she played the role). Polanki's production (funded in part by *Playboy* magazine!) features Annis totally naked, although her long, flowing, reddish-blond hair does provide a bit of tactical covering. Her sleepwalking scene takes place indoors, in a large, furnished, well-lit room within the castle. (Since she's naked, Polanski wants to make sure that we can see her clearly.) Annis sits, rather than stands and walks, as she washes her hands (Polanski makes sure to give a full view of her bottom). In general, she (like Caldwell) seems much less manic at first than Nolan had seemed. The fact that she is nude means that she cannot address the camera until it moves discreetly toward her after another character first blocks any full-frontal glimpse of her breasts. Often her voice is just above the sound of a whisper; her "Oh, oh, oh!" (V.1.52) is not a long, extended howl but a brief single-syllable cry, and even that cry is not emphatic. The doctor and the nurse soon hustle her off to a big nearby bed (providing strategic camouflage of her naked breasts and other parts), and then the scene is over quickly. Polanski's Lady

Macbeth, far from seeming either traumatized or traumatizing, instead seems badly depressed. Polanksi avoids melodrama, but in the process he provides little excitement (except, of course, to any readers of *Playboy* who may have watched this film).

1978 (Judi Dench)

The sleepwalking scene in Philip Casson's 1979 television production (based on a stage version directed by Trevor Nunn) is one of the most traumatic and traumatizing imaginable. Judi Dench's performance is at the opposite end of the emotional and psychological spectrum from the performance of Annis in Polanski's film. Casson sets the scene in almost complete darkness—darker even than in Welles's production and perhaps the darkest in any major filmed version of the play. The Gentlewoman, who seems to be a nun, is dressed almost entirely in black, as is the doctor (whose hair is also dark). Immediately, then, the visual tone seems literally gloomy. When Lady Macbeth appears, holding a small, single candle, she too is dressed in dark colors and wears a dark covering over her head. She is already slightly moaning; already she seems terrified and holds her fingers to her mouth, her eyes brimming with tears. Dench effectively conveys the internal psychological pain her character feels; her tone is immediately intense and will eventually build to a stunning crescendo of trauma and horror.

Dench walks right between the Gentlewoman and the Doctor as if she doesn't see them. Barely visible, she then kneels, as if she lacks the strength to stand. She relentlessly rubs her hands while still quietly moaning, as if on the verge of crying. Only the single candle illuminates her frantic handwashing and her glistening eyes. A sudden close-up reveals that her eyes are wet with shining tears. Interestingly and ironically, her gleaming gold wedding ring is one of the few other sources of light. Lady Macbeth stares off into the distance, her mouth hanging open, as if all she can mentally see and ponder are her guilty deeds (and possibly her potential future as a damned soul). In an especially effective moment, after "washing" her hands continually, she holds one hand up behind the candle to examine whether it is really clean. Casson, wisely, lets the sleepwalking scene unfold at a leisurely pace. Unlike Polanski, he seems in no rush to get it over with. Instead, he forces viewers to witness the sheer terror Lady Macbeth is suffering. It is hard not to feel sympathy for her; she is obviously in enormous pain. Dench is already the most memorable Lady Macbeth on film since Jeanette Nolan, and her performance still has minutes to go. Her costume helps: in a production anachronistically full of turtlenecks and other modern clothing, her style of dress in this scene seems authentically medieval.

After holding one hand up to the candle, Dench now also examines the other. She finds a remaining spot. Her voice is quiet, subdued, frightened (in ironic contrast with what is to come). Rather than being angry at the "damned spot," she seems terrified of its implications. Only when she declares (while looking down) that "Hell is murky" (V.1.36) does her voice become louder. Thinking that she addresses Macbeth, she actually stares the Doctor in the face, her eyes again full of tears that are now also visible on her cheeks. Rather than being angry at Macbeth, she seems astonished by his fear. She begins to rub the front of her body, as if to soothe her own fears by smoothing her clothes. When she refers to how much "blood" Duncan had in him, she strains to say the word (V.1.38-40); she stares off to the side as if she cannot bear the memory. Instead of singing the "Fife/wife" passage (V.1.42) as if it were a nursery rhyme (as Nolan had effectively done), Dench speaks the words in terror, especially when she asks, of the wife, "where is she now?" Obviously Dench's Lady Macbeth is thinking of her own present and potential fate and is horrified. She seems tormented by fear and guilt. Her handwashing at one point looks and sounds like a desperate prayer ("What, will these hands ne'er be clean?" [V.1.43]). Again one is struck by the sheer amount of time Casson is willing to devote to this crucial scene, which is surely one of the most powerful in his entire production. It is hard to imagine a performer who brings more to—and gets more out of—this scene in emotional and psychological terms than Judi Dench. If any Lady Macbeth has ever seemed truly traumatized, it is she.

At one point, Dench, continuing to wash her hands furiously, brings one of them up near her nose and seems startled (rather than immediately disgusted, as Nolan had been) by the imagined "smell of the blood still" (V.1.50). But instead of speaking "still" in the same way as the other words, she pauses dramatically and then spits out the word in a stunned, unsettling, high-pitched squeak: "STILL!!!" Then she immediately modulates to a much softer, more introspective tone when mentioning "all the perfumes of Arabia" (V.1.50-51). Nothing, however, could prepare viewers for what happens next. Dench begins with a relatively quiet, high-pitched, but as-yet-subdued cry which then slowly builds to an ear-piercing, animalistic howl as she throws her head back in agony. When she finally recovers enough self-control to mention that Banquo cannot come out of his grave (V.1.62-63), it isn't clear whether she is quoting Macbeth (as in the Welles production) or is simply speaking, by herself, *to* herself.

In a final effective twist, when Dench hears "knocking at the gate" (V.1.65-6) she walks right between the Doctor and the Gentlewoman and comes directly up to the camera lens, as though looking directly at viewers—a technique already used in the Sean Connery film. But the effect is far more striking here. When Dench slowly, painfully, utters the phrase "What's done cannot be undone" (V.1.65-66), her words do not seem merely self-reflective and self-reflexive. Instead, they also uncomfortably indict any viewer who has ever "done" anything inspiring guilt. Then Dench, fairly quickly, exits the stage, quietly but constantly uttering "To bed" as she disappears into the darkness, until only a tiny candle flame is still visible (V.1.65-67). This is a searing staging and performance— arguably the best committed to film up to that time, and perhaps ever. Dench "sleepwalks" onscreen for roughly five minutes in the Nunn/Casson production. By contrast, the nude Lady Macbeth in Polanksi's version sleepwalks for a little over two minutes. Macbeth's wife is onstage for three minutes in the 1961 film, and in the Welles film the Lady's sleepwalking takes less than five minutes altogether. When compared with the Dench performance, Nolan's performance still seems powerful but also somewhat melodramatic.

1981 (Piper Laurie)

A 1981 television production, directed by Arthur Allan Seidelman and starring Jeremy Brett and Piper Laurie, unfortunately *looks* like a television production from the early 'eighties. The set (obviously a set) is well-lit when Lady Macbeth appears. She is dressed in a long white gown and holds a single candle. Laurie moves slowly, then notices a spot on her hands, then puts the candle down and begins to flutter her hands, as if in water. So far she is completely silent. She seems to splash imaginary water on her face, still completely silent and more obviously asleep than some earlier Lady Macbeths on film. This is a surprisingly subdued performance; it lacks much emotional energy (although Laurie does almost smack one hand with another to remove the stubborn spot). She seems more puzzled by the spot than traumatized. Only when shouting "Fie, my lord, fie" (V.1.36-37) does she seem especially agitated, and that agitation springs more from anger at Macbeth than from any sense of remorse or disgust with herself. Initially, she seems more bitter than traumatized. At one point, in fact, she even seems somewhat maniacally joyous, lifting her arms into the air and smiling broadly. The inappropriateness of these expressions perhaps implies her mental instability. In any case, Laurie's handling of this scene differs radically from any previous onscreen performance. It is the opposite of Dench's or Nolan's, with their frantic, frightened, terrifying sense of psychological horror.

At one point, Laurie lies down on the floor, nonchalantly sweeps her hands in Duncan's imaginary blood, and seems more amused than disgusted when she ponders how much the old king bled. Laurie seems briefly—*very* briefly—terrified when she mentions Fife's wife, but she soon returns to anger, first at her still-bloody hands and then (especially) at an imagined Macbeth. In fact, the keynote of Laurie's performance is anger, not intense fear. For the most part, no tears or terror (which pervaded the Dench performance) are really visible until close to the end of the scene. Only now, finally, does Laurie show any tormented remorse, but her performance here seems a bit theatrical: she cries out but does not weep; no tears fill her eyes or flow down her cheeks. Many viewers will feel conscious of watching a *performance* rather than eavesdropping on the thrashings of a genuinely tormented soul.

1983 (Jane Lapotaire)

Another televised production, for the BBC and directed by Jack Gold, starred Nicol Williamson and Jane Lapotaire. The relative darkness of the sleepwalking scene means that Lady Macbeth appears from out of the shadows, dressed in a flowing tan-brown gown and holding a flaming lamp. She walks in front of a gray, fog-filled background, puts the lamp on the ground, and then vigorously rubs her hands together. Already her mood and actions are entirely different from those in the Laurie performance. We see Lapotaire at first from a distance, but the view moves closer when she first begins to speak. She clearly seems agitated and disturbed, shifting from one mood to another. When she recalls the murder of Duncan, she seems almost joyous (as she moves, appropriately, toward the fog). But her mood quickly turns to anguish when she acknowledges that "hell is murky." Her tone turns again, however, to frustration when she remembers Macbeth's own fear. When she then mentions Duncan's blood, her tone is one of mystification and quiet disbelief. Lapotaire, then, is certainly showing many standard signs of trauma, especially instability of mood. Mentioning Fife's wife, she lapses into a kind of singing, but the tone is melancholy, not nursery-rhymish (as in the Nolan performance). Lapotaire never lingers on any emotion for very long, nor are her eyes consistently (if ever) wet with tears, as Dench's had been. Sometimes, when she is not washing her hands, she seems to hold them aloft in silent prayer, but then she soon seems repulsed by the blood's imagined smell. There has been, as yet, no screaming, crying, or intense moaning. Only after she continually sniffs her hands does she really raise her voice to exclaim "Oh, oh, oh!" (V.1.52). Only now does she seem truly frantic. She sniffs her hands again and again before suddenly clasping them over her ears when the Gentlewoman mentions "God" (V.1.57). Grabbing her flaming lamp, Lapotaire then walks right up to the camera (but stares off to the side) and speaks the words about Banquo as if she is saying them *to* Macbeth rather than hearing them *from* him. But Lapotaire's most innovative behavior in this scene occurs toward the very end, when she struggles manfully almost to *pull* and then to *push* an imaginary Macbeth off to bed. There is nothing erotic here, as in the Nolan performance. When we last see her, this Lady Macbeth is practically shoving her imaginary, reluctant husband off "to bed" (V.1.65-67). Lapotaire, although far more emotional and unstable that Laurie had seemed, does not appear nearly as traumatized as Dench, who so far is the most traumatized of all Lady Macbeths on screen (with Nolan a very close second).

1997 (Helen Baxendale)

In the 1997 film directed by Jeremy Freeston and starring Helen Baxendale and Jason Connery (son of Sean), darkness is heavily emphasized. When Lady Macbeth appears in period costume, her small candle is almost the only source of light, and the ominous visual tone is underlined by quietly ominous music. (Many earlier productions had lacked music altogether, at least in this scene.) Baxendale is a young Lady Macbeth and is observed from a distance by the Doctor and the Gentlewoman (who were often quite close to her in previous productions). She rubs her hands less vigorously than in some previous stagings, but she keeps examining them closely with her eyes, trying to wipe off the spot visible only to her. She is frustrated when it will not disappear. But her affect is surprisingly subdued, and when she remarks that "Hell is murky" (V.1.36), her tone is almost humorous. Even when she rebukes an imagined Macbeth, she seems gently mocking rather than bitterly angry. At one point, conspiring with him in her imagination, she whispers her words. Only when she mentions Duncan's blood does she begin to become quietly upset, and she speaks with some real anger when telling Macbeth "No more o'that" (V.1-43-44). Smelling the blood on her hands, she seems slightly disgusted but more obviously distressed, even kissing her palms and licking her fingers to remove the smell. She catches us by surprise when she suddenly but quietly cries out, as if she has stumbled over something, apparently an imagined Macbeth. She seems to speak in her own voice (not his) when announcing that Banquo is dead and buried, and in general her performance seems remarkably understated. The Doctor seems more genuinely and deeply agitated than Lady Macbeth, who seems more mystified than traumatized.[1]

2010 (Kate Fleet)

The 2010 televised production, directed by Rupert Goold and starring Patrick Stuart and Kate Fleet, offers a significantly different version of the sleepwalking scene than the one just discussed. Fleet and the other actors appear in modern costuming on a modern set, which even features a porcelain sink with two working metal faucets. When Lady Macbeth first appears, in a thin white slip and a thin blue sweater, she is carrying a large battery-powered flashlight (almost literally a "torch," in British parlance), which she quickly puts down. In addition to washing her hands in familiar ways, she also scratches the palm of one hand with the nails of the other. She already appears far more agitated than Baxendale had been. Walking rapidly toward the camera, she seems thoroughly disgusted when she pronounces that "Hell is murky" (V.1.36). She speaks contemptuously to the imagined Macbeth, accusing him of being fearful, but she actually begins sucking her thumb when remembering how much blood drained from Duncan. Already her moods seem precariously unstable. Mentioning Fife's wife, she seems pitying and disbelieving rather than singing the words (as Nolan and Lapotaire had done). She wrenches and almost collapses in pain when she realizes that her hands, which she now shakes, will never again be clean, and she is frankly furious when she scolds Macbeth, shouting "No more o' that, my lord" (V.1.43-44). In close-up, we can see the veins of her neck and the muscles of her cheeks straining in anger.

In a staging that is certainly innovative, Lady Macbeth now pulls a plastic bottle of some kind of detergent from beneath the porcelain sink. She struggles to remove the cap (even biting it at one point), before finally pouring it over one hand and wincing in pain. The Gentlewoman's shocked reaction suggests that the liquid may be some kind of strong, acid-based product. In any case, Lady Macbeth rubs it thoroughly over both hands, lifts her hands briefly to her nose, but then seems deeply anguished when she can still smell the blood. (A small tear is visible beneath one eye—different from the tear-flooded eyes of Judi Dench.) The keynote of Fleet's performance, perhaps, is anger: anger at herself, anger at her husband, and anger at the stubbornness of the blood and its unappealing smell. She stares at her fingernails with disgust, alternately weeping and screaming in psychological pain until she clenches her fists and lets loose with a long, piercing, tortured howl that reminds one of Dench's earlier prolonged outburst. But she soon returns to her agitated washing, looking almost crazed, with her mouth hanging open and her head down, over the sink. Abruptly, as the Doctor talks, Fleet looks up, shifts into another tone altogether, and sternly commands herself (mimicking Macbeth) to wash her hands, put on her nightgown, and cease to worry about Banquo. In a particularly pathetic moment, she stretches her arm out toward the Doctor as she repeatedly says, "Come, come, come, come" (V.1.66). She seems desperate for human contact, but the Doctor seems mystified. Then, in another highly innovative twist, she turns the lever of one of the sink's faucets. Astonishingly, it begins to run red with blood. Lady Macbeth is shocked and horrified and rushes forward to shut off the flow. Fleet often shifts suddenly from one mood to another, and the close-ups of her face communicate many subtleties of her alternating emotions. Although her Lady Macbeth differs from Dench's in some ways, it resembles it in others, especially in its sheer emotional force. Of the Lady Macbeths studied so far, Nolan, Dench, and Fleet seem the most clearly tortured and undeniably traumatized.

Different Kinds of Trauma

Trauma, of course, can manifest itself in different ways, and so the emotions of all the Lady Macbeths just reviewed can be described as traumatic in one sense or another. Stunned silence can be just as much a sign of trauma as screeching screaming. A distant, icy stare can symbolize trauma just as much as tear-filled eyes. If the performances of Nolan, Dench, and Fleet somehow seem *especially* traumatic, it is partly because they are so terrifying and traumatizing to the films' viewers. Dench's performance, once seen, cannot be put from one's mind. In that sense it resembles the blood and stench that she and all other Lady Macbeths try to rub from their hands. Viewers watching Dench, or Fleet, or Nolan performing this role are likely, in a sense, to feel stained for life. In their own small ways, such performances can *create* trauma as much as depict it.

Note

1.   Limitations of space prevent me from dealing with every single filmed *Macbeth*.

Works Cited or Consulted

Calogeras, R. C. "Sleepwalking and the Traumatic Experience." *International Journal of Psychoanalysis*, vol. 63, 1982, pp. 483-89.

Conway, Silvia G., et al. "Psychological Treatment for Sleepwalking: Two Case Reports." *Clinics*, vol. 66, no. 3, 2011, np.

Evans, Robert C. "The Blinding of Gloucester: Trauma and Morality in Some Films of Shakespeare's *King Lear*." *Critical Approaches to Literature: Moral*. Edited by Robert C. Evans. Salem, 2017, pp. 99-116.

_____. "Trance, Trauma, PNES, and Epileptic Seizures in Shakespeare's *Othello*." *Approaches to Criticism: Multicultural*. Edited by Robert C. Evans. Salem, pp. 63-77.

_____. "Trauma in *Romeo and Juliet*." *Critical Insights: Romeo and Juliet*. Edited by Robert C. Evans. Salem, 2017, pp. 163-80.

_____. "Trauma in Shakespeare's *Macbeth*." *Critical Approaches to Literature: Psychological*. Edited by Robert C. Evans. Salem, 2017, pp. 101-18.

Janoff-Bulman, Ronnie. *Shattered Assumptions: Toward a New Psychology of Trauma*. Free Press, 1992.

Hartman, D., et al. "Is There a Dissociative Process in Sleepwalking and Night Terrors?" *Postgraduate Medical Journal*, vol. 77, no. 906, Apr. 2001, pp. 244-49.

Macbeth. Directed by Orson Welles, Mercury Productions, 1948.

Macbeth. Directed by Paul Almond, Canadian Broadcasting Corporation, Jan. 22, 1961.

Macbeth. Directed by Roman Polanski, Caliban Films and Playboy Productions, Dec. 25, 1971.

Macbeth. Directed by Philip Casson, Thames Television, Jan. 4, 1979.

Macbeth. Directed by Arthur Allen Seidelman, Century Home Video, 1981.

Macbeth. Directed by Jack Gold, British Broadcasting Corporation, Nov. 5, 1983.

Macbeth. Directed by Jeremy Freeston, Cromwell Productions, May 16, 1997.

Macbeth. Directed by Rupert Goold, Illuminations, KQED, et al., Oct. 6, 2010.

Mersh, John. "Sleepwalking." Medicinenet.com. Mar. 2, 2016. www.medicinenet.com/sleepwalking/article.htm. Accessed 22 Oct. 2017.

National Sleep Foundation. "Sleepwalking: Why It Happens." www.sleep.org/articles/why-people-sleep-walk. Accessed 22 Oct. 2017.

_____. "Trauma and Sleep." www.sleepfoundation.org/sleep-disorders-problems/trauma-and-sleep. Accessed 22 Oct. 2017.

Nauert, Rick. "Sleepwalking Linked to Serious Mental Health Issues." The American Academy of Sleep Medicine. Psychcentral. Mar. 3, 2013, www.psychcentral.com/news/2013/03/01/sleepwalking-linked-to-serious-mental-health-issues/52081.html. Accessed 22 Oct. 2017.

Pruitt, Bill. "PTSD's Impact on Sleep and Sleep Disorders." April 2015. www.rtmagazine.com/2015/04/ptsd-impact-on-sleep-and-sleep-disorders. Accessed 22 Oct. 2017.

Schuder, Kirsten. "Sleepwalking in Adults." Lovetoknow.com. https://sleep.lovetoknow.com/Sleepwalking_in_Adults. Accessed 22 Oct. 2017.

Shakespeare, William. *Macbeth*. Edited by Stephen Orgel. Penguin, 2016.

Sleep Health Foundation. "Post Traumatic Stress Disorder (PTSD) and Sleep." SHF. www.sleephealthfoundation.org.au/pdfs/Post-Traumatic-Stress-Disorder.pdf. Accessed 22 Oct. 2017.

Zadra, Antonio, and Jacques Montplaisir. "Sleepwalking." *The Parasomnias and Other Sleep-Related Movement Disorders*. Edited by Michael J. Thorpy and Giuseppe Plazzi. Cambridge UP, pp. 111-18.

Blood and Milk: The Masculinity of Motherhood in Shakespeare's *Macbeth*_____

Savannah Xaver

Critics of Shakespeare's tragedy *Macbeth* classify it as a play fueled by masculinity, with a focus on male characters immersed in war and motivated by relationships involving other men. But the main female character of this play, Lady Macbeth, challenges the stability of masculinity and, more broadly, of gender itself, suggesting through her words that it is perhaps mutable. Although Lady Macbeth speaks of her feminine physical traits, such as the ability to breastfeed, she surprisingly includes images of violence and gore to such speeches, adding to the feminine category of nursing more masculine qualities. Lady Macbeth, in other words, adopts a masculine nature in order to be noticed and make a difference in her marriage. Shakespeare designed Lady Macbeth as a strong, nontraditional woman to create more conflict within the tragedy; rather than supporting the tragic hero through her speeches and actions, she challenges Macbeth, thus causing dramatic changes to the plot. This chapter will investigate the speeches made by Lady Macbeth along with the overall themes of *Macbeth*. The theme of defeating women and what it means for the men who do so will be applied to the conflicts that women are able to create. In addition, the allusions that Lady Macbeth makes to breastfeeding will be discussed with the role that milk plays in *Macbeth*. The role of milk coincides with the role of blood, each playing a crucial role in character development and conflicts between Macbeth and his wife.

A woman's role in *Macbeth* becomes supporting the man by any means necessary and this is seen in both Lady Macbeth and Lady Macduff. These women invest themselves completely in the lives of Macbeth and Macduff; however, Lady Macbeth's support appears to be overbearing. Madelon Sprengnether suggests that, above all else, Shakespeare's tragedies are about the many ways that love can kill (89). This claim, when applied to *Macbeth*, illustrates that the tragic hero suffers from the woman in his life becoming too powerful because of the love she feels. Lady Macbeth takes great pride in her husband's accomplishments. This pride comes from the investment she has placed in the war Macbeth has taken part in. Mary Beth Rose expands on Sprengnether's claim by suggesting that the mother's potential threat originates in her love, then becomes exposed as "an overindulgence of love" (Rose 301). I agree with Sprengnether and Rose that Lady Macbeth seems to become a strong-willed, nontraditional, outrageous woman in the name of love. Lady Macbeth alludes to infanticide to convince her husband not to break a promise he made to her out of love. Janet Adelman declares that tragic "protagonists die in terrible isolation, still in flight from the contamination that relationship to the female would bring" and therefore "figure maternal presence as devastating to the masculine identity of the son" (163). Within *Macbeth*, the tragic hero does not exist without female forces in his life. In Shakespeare's tragedies, "to talk about Shakespeare's women is to talk about his men, because he refused to separate their worlds physically, intellectually, or spiritually" (Adelman 185). With the overindulgence of female love comes the absence of Macbeth's ability to establish his own identity. Sprengnether, Rose, and Adelman agree that a combination of too much love and strong women causes disaster for Shakespeare's tragic heroes.

It is possible that Shakespeare crafted Lady Macbeth, and his other female characters, to parody the sense of gender that he understood. Margaret L. King explores the ideas of gender, specifically of female gender roles, during Shakespeare's time. The English Renaissance signaled major changes and opportunities for gender roles. Families became defined as a unit: two parents and their children. Women, although they were already defined as bearers and therefore caretakers of the children, ran the home. They were expected to raise the children during the early years of development while men worked outside of the home and often took on the role of training sons for their future careers. Men were also responsible for making decisions for the family, including for the wives, who had little to say in these decisions. A wife and mother was expected to obey and follow gender guidelines that were predetermined by her husband and society that specifically defined the ways she should act (King 1-12). King describes this phenomenon that occurred during the English Renaissance as a wife needing to "develop a relationship with her husband negotiated between contradictory injunctions" (35). Wives were expected to act as companion to their husbands; specifically, to bear his children, raise his children, maintain his house, and yet also be viewed as no more than a secondary partner in the marriage. Lady Macbeth and Macbeth begin the play as a happily married couple. In a letter to his wife, Macbeth refers to her as "my dearest partner of greatness" (I.5.10-11). The word *partner* refers to part of a whole; therefore, Macbeth views his wife as a part of himself and a part of what he has achieved. However, it can be determined through the events of the play that Macbeth and Lady Macbeth have no children. Lady Macbeth mentions that she had nursed a child, but there is no child character in the play. The cause of this is unknown, but the fact stands that Macbeth has no heir when he ascends to royalty. Lady Macbeth has not completed a basic task of an English Renaissance wife; despite this, Macbeth still regards her as his partner. This shows that there is more to their marriage than only the basic expectations of a Renaissance marriage. Lady Macbeth is forced to prove herself as an exceptional wife during the play because she has no chance to prove herself as a mother.

Of course, during the English Renaissance there were thousands of wives who did not receive the chance to define themselves as mothers at all. Rose points out that, due to the high risk of birth complications, a great many women did not survive their first pregnancy (294). Maternal mortality was prevalent for a variety of issues. Lower class women did not have access to midwives or nutrition. Even upper class women who did have access to healthcare were still difficult to protect during childbirth. The danger of childbirth, though, is what gives women power over men and sets the genders apart, especially in *Macbeth*. The character of Macduff symbolizes the act of overpowering women. During the play, Macbeth receives a prophecy, an image of a bloody child stating, "Be bloody, bold, and resolute. Laugh to scorn / The power of man, for none of woman born / Shall harm Macbeth!" (IV.1.101-03). Macbeth interprets this prophecy to mean that no man will ever be able to defeat him because all men in existence are born of women. Later, Macbeth relays this feeling to Macduff during their final meeting, explaining "I live a charmed life, which must not yield / To one of woman born" (V.8.12-13). Birth is a two-part action: a mother gives birth and a child is born. However, Macduff presents a loophole not only to the prophecy but to the act of being born. Macduff admits that he "… was from his mother's womb / Untimely ripped" (V.8.15-6). In order to be born, the fetus must pass through a woman's body. Technically speaking, Macduff was not born from a woman, but taken from one. Because Macduff presents this loophole, Macbeth dies by Macduff's sword. Indeed, Macduff, or rather Macduff's mother, is an instance of the woman who did not survive childbirth. The inclusion of this tragic event, and the importance of it in this play, illustrates the power dynamics between genders that exists in *Macbeth*.

Macduff's victory over Macbeth is not just a matter of sword fighting skills. Jonathan Goldberg interprets Macduff's success as a triumph over Macbeth's vulnerability to women. Macbeth is overpowered by Macduff, Goldberg argues, because he is a man who has twice defeated women by abandoning his wife and "triumph[ing] over his mother's womb" (174). Macduff has succeeded in the one area where Macbeth has failed by conquering women; therefore, he gains more power than Macbeth. Goldberg summarizes the conclusion of *Macbeth* as the "seizure of defeat of woman [as] a bid for immortality, for a power that will never fade" (174). For Macbeth, immortality was already within his grasp. He believes that no man born of a woman will ever defeat him, which rules out every living man. Macbeth believes that he has beaten natural law by defeating birth. He has not, however, conquered women in the ways that Macduff has. For example, the character of Lady Macduff, who is nearly the opposite of Lady Macbeth, is conquered by her husband's neglect. She does not cause conflict for her husband, rather she is targeted because of her femininity; she is a victim of the societal expectations of women. When Lady Macduff is faced with impending danger and forced to vacate her home, she does not know where to go, claims that she has done nothing wrong and states "Why then, alas / Do I put up that womanly defense, / To say I have done no harm?" (IV.2.78-80). Cristina León Alfar suggests that Lady Macduff's plea shows that she is completely aware of the masculine world in which she lives and her realization is that she is far too feminine to defend herself (118). Unlike Lady Macbeth, Lady Macduff embraces femininity. Alfar states that both Lady Macbeth and Lady Macduff are "deserted by [their] husband's driven masculinist honor to act out the play's violence" (118). Both women are left to fend for themselves in the absence of their husbands; Lady Macbeth must struggle with her developing madness and Lady Macduff is left alone, defenseless, with her children.

Although Lady Macduff insists that she has done nothing wrong, that does not protect her from danger. Alfar makes a connection between Lady Macduff's statements and Goldberg's argument that views "masculinity in the play as an assaultive attempt to secure power, to maintain success and succession, at the expense of women" (qtd. in Alfar 118). Lady Macduff becomes a victim of masculinity more so than does Lady Macbeth. Throughout the play, Lady Macbeth embraces masculinity and uses it to her advantage. Lady Macduff, however, is not as strong-willed and relies instead on her femininity. She is a conquerable woman; thus, she supports her husband by allowing him to overpower another woman and giving him the power to defeat Macbeth. Goldberg states "Birth and death are. . . man's downfall, the limits of beginning and end; they survive his success, unlimited limits" (174). Macduff succeeds at the end of the play because he has defeated his mother, the ultimate woman in his life.

Lady Macbeth's extreme personality creates conflict by challenging the tragic hero. The role she plays to Macbeth is obviously wife, but can also be categorized as mother. Lady Macbeth's role as a mother to Macbeth combined with her insistence on being masculine creates conflict for Macbeth within the plot of the play. Is it the role of the masculine wife or the masculine mother that causes more issues? Mary Beth Rose suggests that the role of mother is a dangerous one and perhaps the best kind of mother for the tragic character is an absent or dead mother (301). To investigate this, a large amount of hypothesizing must be done. In the case of *Macbeth*, not having a mother becomes an advantage. Macduff outlives his mother in the sense that he actually had to be removed from her, killing her in the process. As previously mentioned, this is crucial to defeating Macbeth. Rather than being about mothers in general—especially since Macbeth's own mother is of no importance in the play—the play is about conquering women. Unable to overpower his own wife, who takes on the dual role of wife and mother in the events of the play, Macbeth dies at the hand of a man who has overpowered both of those figures in his own life. Clearly, having the strong maternal influence in his life acts as a disadvantage for Macbeth. Rose's claim has much to do with the love that mothers give to their babies. Of course, all human life begins with the mother giving birth, but what a mother does for the child after it is born is unique for each situation.

Women give life to their babies not only by giving birth to them but also by giving them sustenance. During the Renaissance, babies were generally breastfed. King states that "those babies who survived were fed by breast, commonly for eighteen to twenty-four months" and this was obviously a woman's specific task (12). This practice was viewed as the only way to properly nourish a baby and, therefore, when a mother was unable to complete this task, the family would hire a wet nurse to ensure the baby's survival. With this being common practice, English Renaissance writers often included it in their work and developed the concept of weaning into a symbol of lost childhood innocence (King 13-18). In addition, breastfeeding generated a large amount of superstition. As only women could breastfeed, it was believed that all babies, regardless of gender, imbided a large amount of femininity from their mothers during nursing. Arthur F. Kinney describes the social attachment of breastfeeding thus: "[h]umoral medical theory supported breastfeeding by supporting circulation of fluids associating milk with blood and lactation with menstruation" (172).

Thus, breastfeeding was viewed as an extremely feminine act, just as giving birth was.

Shakespeare gave Lady Macbeth lines that call attention to her ability to breastfeed and therefore her femininity. Her speeches reveal instances where she challenges her gender's ideology and even suggests that gender is mutable. For instance, perhaps the most compelling maternal speech comes from Lady Macbeth when she is trying to convince Macbeth to murder Duncan. She declares:

> I have given suck, and know
> How tender 'tis to love the babe that milks me;
> I would, while it was smiling in my face,
> Have plucked my nipple from his boneless gums
> And dashed the brains out, had I sworn as you
> Have done to this. (I.7.54-59)

In this statement, Lady Macbeth builds up to what was considered the most unnatural and antimaternal action a mother could perform, infanticide, and she combines that image with an image of herself breastfeeding. On the surface, this appears as a heinous statement that no mother should utter as plainly as Lady Macbeth does. However, there are many more dimensions to this statement, one of which turns it into a tool that Lady Macbeth uses to guilt her husband into obeying her. Adelman states, "Lady Macbeth expresses here not only the hardness she imagines to be male, not only her willingness to unmake the most essential maternal relationship; she expresses. . . Macbeth's utter vulnerability to her" (138). This statement shows Lady Macbeth using shocking and horrifying things as a means to negotiate power. In this speech, she is comparing her husband's breaking of a promise to her to herself murdering an infant. By combining an image of the maternal power of breastfeeding and the gore of infanticide, Lady Macbeth asserts dominance over her husband.

Lady Macbeth's famous speech has inspired much debate among literary critics, who offer several conflicting opinions as to what Lady Macbeth actually means when she compares her husband to the life of an infant. Their arguments often hinge on whether or not she is making a feminine statement. On one hand, Adelman argues that Lady Macbeth uses imagery of infanticide to force her husband to succumb to "female forces" (134). On the other hand, Alfar claims that this speech is "not a lack of maternal feeling but of the monstrosity of her husband's forswearing his word" (126). Adelman goes on to maintain that Lady Macbeth is acting as a temptress, one who uses her feminine ways to control her husband (134). Her power, then, comes from the fact that she is female. Yet, Alfar argues that Macbeth's reply—"Bring forth men children only, / For thy undaunted mettle should compose / Nothing but males"—shows Macbeth's awareness of his wife's power (I.7.73-75). He "recognizes in his wife not only the fearlessness of a man, but the maker of men," (127). I agree with Alfar in the sense that Lady Macbeth's allusion to infanticide was an attempt to force her husband to realize how disgraceful it would be if he broke his oath to her. However, I believe Macbeth means more in this reply. Perhaps the reply contains praise; Macbeth is accusing her of being so full of masculine forces that she could not possibly create a female infant. In the masculine world of *Macbeth*, a woman who could produce only men would be ideal. Therefore, Lady Macbeth's power comes from her supposedly being full of masculinity despite her feminine gender.

Another aspect of Lady Macbeth's speech involves what it means to be a murderous mother. Mothers are typically depicted as nurturing, natural, tender beings who care for children, especially their own. A murderous mother violates not only nature but also the social construct of motherhood. Rose describes mothers as upholding and inhabiting a "private world" into which public affairs do not enter (301). Murder of any kind immediately becomes a public affair, something that the people outside of the home will notice and recognize. Keith M. Botelho also discusses the Renaissance assumption that wives and mothers should stay in the home; he relates it to the issue of infanticide, insisting that "a mother's capacity to produce and reproduce as well as to take away life, places her within a realm entirely different from that of a male murderer, a new sphere that could be inhabited only by a mother" (122). When a mother leaves the private realm of the home and begins to make her life outside of the home, it causes discomfort. Botelho's belief means that Lady Macbeth, labeling herself as a murderous mother, could have shocked Macbeth because of how far she stepped out of the private realm. She not only takes on the masculine act of murder, but the object of her murder is her child, from which she also withholds nourishment. Faced with this image, Macbeth has no choice but to listen to his wife.

The murder of an infant parallels the murder of gender roles. When Lady Macbeth gives up her duty as a mother, and therefore her primary duty as a Renaissance woman, she is yet again suggesting that her gender is mutable. Botelho suggests "[m]urder and the forgetting of maternal duty served as a way for any woman to resist or subvert subordination or confinement" (114). As previously mentioned, women were viewed as lesser partners in the marriage than their husbands and were therefore granted less power inside and outside of the home. Stephanie Chamberlain makes a similar statement to Botelho by indicating that Lady Macbeth's speech is a "profoundly defiant disclosure" and she is perhaps making a such a statement in order to break away from the "gendered constraints that bind her" (82). Botelho's and Chamberlain's beliefs go back to the main argument of this chapter: in order to create more conflict for the tragic hero, Shakespeare created his wife and mother characters to be outrageous in their allusions to their physicality. In an effort to mute her gender—in this case, the physical and social aspect of her femininity—Lady Macbeth makes a horrifying statement involving the murder of an infant. With this allusion, Lady Macbeth takes on a masculine trait of violence and casts aside the expectation of traditional mothers to care for their children above all else. However, the important thing to remember about this statement is the fantasy sense of it. Lady Macbeth, in a literal sense, is not stating that she has bashed a baby's head in; rather, she says she *would* bash a baby's head in, which suggests that she is making a hypothetical statement. But she could have also have constructed that response on purpose. In the masculine world in which she lives, Lady Macbeth must compete for attention in the only logical way, by crafting a hideous statement that catches her husband's attention.

Perhaps one of the most shocking elements of Lady Macbeth's infanticide allusion, at least for Macbeth, is that she suggests the destruction of an heir to the throne. *Macbeth* is very much a play emphasizing lineage or birth and the characters' dialogue conveys this by constantly mentioning blood. Blood, as previously discussed, was closely linked not only to birth, but to a woman's breastfeeding as well. In the opening scenes of the play, the witches give Macbeth and Banquo specific prophecies: Macbeth will receive the title of Thane of Crawdor and Banquo's children shall become kings. While Macbeth's prediction comes true, he fears later in the play that Banquo's may also, thus threatening his position on the throne. In a failed attempt to murder Banquo and his son, Macbeth feels "doubts and fears" (III.4.25). As previously discussed, Macbeth receives a prophecy from an image of a bloody child with the ironic message that no man born from a woman will harm him. The bloody child clearly embodies the image of a newborn baby, still covered with the blood of the mother. Perhaps this image of a freshly born infant both foreshadows Macduff's revelation about his birth and symbolizes the rebirth of both Macduff and Macbeth. Macduff is removed from his mother, presumably covered in blood; at that moment, seconds after his "birth," he experiences another birth which allows him to become a different person than he would have been if he had been naturally born. Macbeth also experiences a blood-covered moment. When he returns from slaying Duncan, Macbeth's hands are covered in Duncan's blood, signaling a rebirth. Macbeth was not born into a world in which he would be king; rather, he crafted his own world to be this way. At this point, he becomes a tyrant, a man who is not defined by what his wife tells him to do. From this point on, Macbeth no longer looks to Lady Macbeth for guidance because he has already followed her instructions.

Lady Macbeth also appears to go through a rebirth; however, her rebirth is much different from the men's. After the murder of Duncan, Lady Macbeth assists in the murder by removing the blood-covered knives from Macbeth's hands and, in the process, soiling her own hands. She then begins her descent into madness. Lady Macbeth exits the murder scene and states that she could have killed Duncan herself "Had he not resembled / My father as he slept" (II.2.12-13). Critics of Lady Macbeth's character seem to agree that this statement signifies that no matter how violent and masculine she acts, she cannot commit the ultimate masculine act of murdering a fellow man. It is important to note, though, that she goes through a rebirth in this scene, stripping her of her masculine toughness and changing the murderous mother character into a more feminine one. During Lady Macbeth's sleepwalking scene, she becomes more feminine. She states "Yet who would have thought the old man to have so much blood in him?" (V.1.38-40). As she continuously scrubs her hands, it appears that she has been shaken by the murder. She also refers to her physical gender in a slightly different way than earlier; she refers to her own hand as "this little hand" (V.1.51). Women are usually known to be daintier than men, especially in appendages such as the hands. Lady Macbeth's rebirth occurs prior to this scene, when her own hands are covered in blood, but the effects of that rebirth are present in this scene. She now refers to her gender, not muting it but embracing it. Perhaps this comes from a feeling of overstepping her own mental capacity. Strangely, after the ties that Lady Macbeth makes between blood and breast milk, she seems to have a sensitivity to blood after all.

Milk plays just as large a role as blood in the events of the play. While Lady Macbeth alludes to the act of breastfeeding to discuss femininity, she also makes remarks about milk's role in her life. In an attempt to suggest that her gender acts as a barrier, Lady Macbeth calls upon spirits that could possibly remove the femininity from her. She states "Come, you Spirits / That tend on mortal thoughts, unsex me here. . . Come to woman's breasts, / And take my milk for gall" (I.5.39-47). When read literally, Lady Macbeth calls the spirits to take a piece of her that makes her womanly, her milk. Breastfeeding generated the idea that a mother's milk contained not only nourishment but feminine qualities. By removing milk from herself, Lady Macbeth believes that she will become more masculine, and therefore stronger. Evidence in the play suggests that

Lady Macbeth views milk as something highly feminine. She states that Macbeth's nature is "too full o' th' milk of human kindness / To catch the nearest way" (I.5.16-7). From this statement one can infer that Macbeth is kind, and that kindness comes, metaphorically, from milk. He is so kind, so full of milk, that he, according to his wife, could not possibly take the quickest route to the throne, which would be to murder Duncan. Yet, Lady Macbeth comes up with this idea, even though as a woman she is full of milk. Perhaps this instance echoes the superstitions of Shakespeare's time. A man, becomes kind when receiving milk, but a woman does not necessarily become kind even though milk is inside her already.

As indicated earlier, a main message delivered by Shakespeare's tragedies illustrates the ways that love can kill. In order to create conflict with the tragic hero, Lady Macbeth not only uses her own physicality, but also her relationship with her husband. Lady Macbeth and Macbeth's relationship slowly deteriorates over the stress of hiding Duncan's murder. Perhaps, in this instance, the overindulgence of love takes a new form. Rose argues that, in addition to a possibility of an overindulgence of love, mothers can be tempted to coddle or even spoil their children (301). In their marriage, Lady Macbeth and Macbeth demonstrate that a mother-and-child relationship may exist alongside their husband-and-wife relationship and may interfere with it. Although they begin the play as partners, at various times one or the other takes control of the situation. Lady Macbeth convinces her husband to murder Duncan with her infanticide speech, to which Macbeth asks "If we should fail" and Lady Macbeth answers "We fail? / But screw your courage to the sticking-place / And we'll not fail" (I.7.60-62). This is an instance in which the partnership is still displayed; Lady Macbeth reassures her husband in a moment of insecurity and reminds him to be courageous when he must. Later, she takes on an almost motherly role over him in the sense that she takes over and enables him at the time of the murder. When Macbeth returns from Duncan's chambers, carrying the bloody dagger, Lady Macbeth tells him to take it to the room and "smear / The sleepy grooms with blood" (II.2.52-3). Macbeth cannot return to the scene to frame the guards, so Lady Macbeth takes the dagger, covering her own hands with blood and assuming authority over him. By helping him with the murder and covering for him for the rest of the play, Lady Macbeth proves her love to her husband while appearing to take authority over him in a nurturing, enabling way.

Macbeth creates women as a dangerous force to men. Alfar argues that the play "comprises a radical staging of female gender, contextualizing women's desire in hostile patrilineal structures and pointing to a cultural manufacturing of femininity as passive, tender, and merciful" (113). Indeed, I agree that *Macbeth* seems to push Lady Macbeth more toward a radical woman and less toward the passive woman seen in the character of Lady Macduff. Her own words illustrate her perception of herself; she incorporates masculine images into her own physical gender. Rather than talking about breastfeeding in a natural or beautiful sense, she adds the allusion to murder and gore. Her reasoning in making these speeches usually involves her need to be recognized as a powerful force. *Macbeth* involves war and war-related relationships. War is violent, masculine, and typically something that women support through their male relatives rather than actually taking part in any activities. Violence would usually drive women to stay in the background of wartime. Yet, Lady Macbeth involves herself in politics and war and establishes herself in the masculinity surrounding her. Alfar furthers her argument, stating that "Shakespeare uncovers the gender trouble behind the prescriptions that constitute femininity as compliance, masculinity as violence, and violence as power" (112). Perhaps the reason that Shakespeare's mother characters are so odd and yet maniacal is that he understood the hierarchy presented by Alfar combined with the ideas of a patriarchy: the only way to be powerful and successful is to be violent and masculine.

Shakespeare's take on motherhood and mother figures can signal a variety of things about the characters and his understanding of mothers in the first place. By having his mother figure characters act masculine and headstrong rather than feminine and tender, he creates tensions between the characters. Lady Macbeth creates this kind of tension because she exists in the domestic, private setting. The allusions to her physical, feminine attributes work as tools that Shakespeare uses to highlight the possibility that gender is mutable. In her speeches, Lady Macbeth challenges not only her husband but her gender by warping feminine images with violent and masculine undertones. The strongest evidence of this warping comes from her breastfeeding speech. When she compares the breaking of a promise to infanticide, she gains power over her husband and, thus, over others. By crafting his mother characters to have violent thoughts, Shakespeare gave Lady Macbeth power in the masculine world of *Macbeth*, in which the only way to gain power is through violence.

Works Cited

Adelman, Janet. *Suffocating Mothers: Fantasies of Maternal Origin in Shakespeare's Plays,* Hamlet *to* The Tempest. Routledge, 1992.

Alfar, Cristina León. *Fantasies of Female Evil: The Dynamics of Gender and Power in Shakespearean Tragedy*. U of Delaware P, 2003.

Botelho, Keith M. "Maternal Memory and Murder in Early-Seventeenth-Century England." *Studies in English Literature, 1500-1900*, vol. 48, no. 1, 2008, pp. 111-30. www.jstor.org/stable/40071324. Accessed Sept. 20, 2015.

Chamberlain, Stephanie. "Fantasizing Infanticide: Lady Macbeth and the Murdering Mother in Early Modern England." *College Literature*, vol. 32, no. 3, 2005, pp. 72-91. http://www.jstor.org/stable/25115288. Accessed Oct. 15, 2015.

Goldberg, Jonathan. *Shakespeare's Hand*. U of Minnesota P, 2003.

King, Margaret L. *Women of the Renaissance*. U of Chicago P, 1991.

Kinney, Arthur F. *Lies Like Truth: Shakespeare, Macbeth, and the Cultural Moment*. Wayne State UP, 2001.

Rose, Mary Beth. "Where are the mothers in Shakespeare? Options for gender representation in the English Renaissance." *Shakespeare Quarterly*, vol. 42, no. 3, 1991, pp. 291-314. www.jstor.org/stable/2870845. Accessed Sept. 13, 2015.

Shakespeare, William. *Macbeth*. Edited by Stephen Orgel. Penguin, 2016.

Sprengnether, Madelon. "Annihilating Intimacy in *Coriolanus*." *Women in the Middle Ages and the Renaissance*. Edited by Mary Beth Rose. Syracuse UP, 1986, pp. 89-112.

Dying Like a Man: Masculinity and Violence in *Macbeth*_____

Jim Casey

The queer and gender theorist Judith Butler has famously suggested that biological sex is not a "bodily given on which the construct of gender is artificially imposed," but rather a "cultural norm which governs the materialization of bodies" (*Bodies* 2-3). In the end, she claims, "There is no gender identity behind the expressions of gender; identity is performatively constituted by the very 'expressions' that are said to be its results" (*Gender* 33). This means that while the physical, biological sex of an individual's body may prescribe and proscribe specific gender expectations, gender itself must be continually "performed" through a set of socioculturally determined actions or "expressions" of maleness/femaleness. In the case of Shakespeare and Middleton's *Macbeth*, this theoretical frame has most often been used by critics to discuss the character of Lady Macbeth, but the idea of gender performance may also be applied to the men in the play.

Of all of Shakespeare's plays, *Macbeth* examines the theme of manhood most expansively and most explicitly. As D. W. Harding notes, "The nature of manliness is a question running all through the play, manliness as lived by the man and manliness seen in the distorting fantasy of the woman" (245). Repeated questions of sex and sexual performance—from the beards of the witches to the dirty jokes of the Porter—emphasize the point that manhood has to be repeatedly defined. For the most part, this definition of manhood seems to revolve around the performance of and participation in violent acts, as Robert Kimbrough suggests: "In *Macbeth*, [. . .] to be 'manly' is to be aggressive, daring, bold, resolute, and strong, especially in the face of death, whether giving or receiving" (177). Audience members first hear of Macbeth when the Captain gives his report of the battle to Duncan and describes how the traitorous Macdonwald was slain. The battle stood doubtful, he says,

> But all's too weak,
> For brave Macbeth—well he deserves that name—
> Disdaining Fortune, with his brandished steel,
> Which smoked with bloody execution,
> Like valour's minion carved out his passage
> Till he faced the slave;
> Which ne'er shook hands nor bade farewell to him,
> Till he unseamed him from the nave to th' chops,
> And fixed his head upon our battlements. (I.2.15-23)

Hearing this account, Duncan praises Macbeth, saying, "O valiant cousin, worthy gentleman!" (I.2.24). The words are not ironic—except perhaps to the audience—despite the gruesome actions described, yet the behavior seems particularly ungentlemanly, with the extreme violence suggested by "unseamed him from the nave to th' chops" only highlighting the barbarity of the moment. Therefore, it seems unlikely that what the king lauds in this passage is Macbeth's gentility.

Instead, what Duncan celebrates is Macbeth's martial prowess and deadly effectiveness. Macbeth gains worth here through military performance and declares his manhood through a willingness to risk his body, and indeed his life, for the good of the kingdom. Duncan and his kinsmen admire Macbeth not only for the wounds he inflicts, but also for those he receives. The Captain describes how, when the tide of the battle seemed to turn against them, Banquo and Macbeth carved yet another passage through the enemy as if "they meant to bathe in reeking wounds, / Or memorize another Golgotha" (I.2.39-40). Willing to sacrifice themselves for the good of the crown and oblivious to the threat to their own lives, Banquo and Macbeth become Scotland's saviors, with the allusions to Golgotha (where Jesus was crucified) and "reeking wounds" depicting the warriors as almost Christlike defenders of the realm. In their excessive bloodshed, Banquo and Macbeth themselves mirror the image of Jesus as *Christus miles* (Christ the soldier), recalling the messianic figures of both Isaiah 63:1-7 and William Herebert's "What is he, this lordling that cometh from the fight?" (both of whose garments are splattered with blood). In this way, Banquo and Macbeth are associated with the sacrifice of a martial Christ, who is both bleeding for the world and at the same time stomping sinners like grapes in a winepress. Duncan reiterates this assertion that a man's merit depends on both valor and physical sacrifice when he tells the Captain, who himself is injured, "So well thy words become thee as thy wounds, / They smack of honour both" (I.2.43-4). This theme of positive bodily destruction runs throughout the play, such as when Malcolm and Macduff first meet in England and Malcolm laments the state of their homeland. He suggests that they "seek out some desolate shade, and there / Weep our sad bosoms empty" (IV.3.1-2), but Macduff rejects this idea, offering a more warlike resolution: "Let us rather / Hold fast the mortal sword and, like good men, / Bestride our downfall birthdom" (IV.3.2-4). In this passage, Scotland is portrayed as a fallen comrade. According to Macduff, a "good" man would not weep over the fate of the country, but rather stand over the wounded homeland like a warrior over his fellow soldier, even if such an action might lead to his own death. To do less would be unmanly.

In fact, one of the defining characteristics of manhood in the play is the acceptance of one's own death and the willingness to meet it without fear. Thus, the only way the "unrough youths" of the rebel army can "Protest their first of manhood" (V.2.10-11) is with sword and shield. Until the young warriors prove their masculinity in battle, their manhood cannot be guaranteed, suggesting that undisputed recognition as a "man" requires violent performative action. When Macbeth enlists the aid of the two murderers to kill Banquo and his son, for instance, he asks them if they can forgive Banquo's supposed wrongs against them, and they simply reply, "We are men, my liege" (III.1.91). Because he wants to manipulate them into murdering his perceived rival, Macbeth retorts, "Ay, in the catalogue ye go for men, / As hounds and greyhounds, mongrels, spaniels, curs, / Shoughs, water-rugs, and demiwolves are clept / All by the name of dogs" (III.1.93-96). In this passage, Macbeth indicates that while biological maleness may make a person eligible for inclusion in the category of "man," there are gradations of manhood. Thus, although individual men in the play may each possess the physical and biological attributes that define him "in the catalogue" as a man, there is a hierarchy of manhood that may initially be based on physical attributes (male genitalia, deep voice, Adam's apple, beard) or class distinctions (king, aristocrat, commoner, slave) but ultimately comes down to how a man acts in the face of violence and death. Later in the play, when Old Siward learns that his son has been killed by a wound "on the front" (V.8.47), he does not lament the death of his son, as Macduff does with the news of his children's murder, but rather expresses his pleasure that his son died, as Ross says, "like a man" (V.8.43). Here, and elsewhere in the works of Shakespeare, there is a clear connection between an individual's manhood and his voluntary entrance into the realm of masculine violence. When challenged, a character can only "prove" his manhood by entering into the arena of masculine violence and submitting his body to possible destruction.

Shakespeare and Middleton emphasize this expectation by placing Young Siward's death at the end of the play, after a number of comparable events. Juxtaposed to the glory of this death, for example, is the murder of Macduff's son. R. S. White argues that

> The scene of the boy's killing is designed to stir feelings not of pathos, but of horror and anger. [. . .] Without the scene, the check upon our imaginative endorsement of Macbeth's compulsive ambition would be diminished, we should see the man more as victim than as murderer, and the play would be open to charges of uncritical sadism. However horrifying is the murder of the boy, its function is to bring us back to our moral senses. (51)

Yet while the scene does perform this necessary dramatic function, it also reemphasizes the difference between the prepubescent young Macduff and the armored Young Siward. As Stephen Greenblatt notes, young boys were characterized as still "effeminate" (78), and this makes the murder of Macduff's son reprehensible, because, like his mother (or any woman), he is not *supposed* to die. The characters who attack Fleance and Macduff's family are simply named "Murderers"; unlike the myriad bloody soldiers in the play, they lose honor and masculine fame because they prey on the helpless. Pieter Spierenburg observes that in almost all societies, "male honor is considered to be quite different from female honor. Men may take pride in attacking fellow men, whether they use this force to protect women or for other reasons. Passivity, in violent and peaceful situations, is a cardinal feminine virtue" (2). This gendered difference is articulated when Lady Macduff's plea to the murderers for pity is portrayed as a "womanly defense" (IV.2.78). Such passivity is set against the manly reaction to act, to fight against murderers and the injustices of the world. Moreover, this scene demonstrates that immature male bodies and all female bodies are inappropriate sites for masculine violence. Culturally, historically, these bodies are not *made* to die. In contrast, Young Siward—who kills and is killed by other men—gains honor because he engages in violence as a warrior. His death is acceptable because that is what the role of "man" expects of him. Even the treacherous Thane of Cawdor gains Malcolm's respect by the fortitude with which he faces death. Describing the traitor's execution, Malcolm notes admiringly that "Nothing in his life / Became him like the leaving it" (I.4.7-8). Despite his rebellious actions in life, the Thane demonstrates through his death that he is nevertheless a man. But note that what Malcolm praises here is not Cawdor's gentility, not his dignity, not his earlier admission of culpability, but rather how the man faced his execution "As one that had been studied in his death, / To throw away the dearest thing he owed, / As 'twere a careless trifle" (I.4.9-11).

Fear must be overcome in the man's world of *Macbeth*. When Macbeth recoils from the actual act of killing Duncan, his wife accuses him of cowardice. She asks him, "Art thou afeard / To be the same in thine own act and valor / As thou art in desire?" (I.7.39-41). He desires the crown, she says, but lacks the courage to take it. As a result, he must "live a coward," knowing that, despite his countless military accomplishments, he can no more perform the actions of a real man than a cat who fears getting his paws wet can catch fish (I.7.43-45). In his own defense, Macbeth responds, "Prithee peace. / I dare do all that may become a man; / Who dares do more is none" (I.7.45-7). This argues that there are limits to masculine violence, but Lady Macbeth will not acknowledge his protestations. To her, Macbeth only proves his manhood through his present actions. Until the performative act, she tells him, he is not really a man: "When you durst do it, then you were a man" (I.7.49). Despite her husband's previous acts of valor and deeds of bravery, he is no man until he performs the bloody action she demands of him. She has little patience for Macbeth's kindness and nothing but scorn for his fear. By the end of the play, Macbeth will have learned to master this fear. He will admit that learning about Macduff being not "of woman born" has "cowed [his] better part of man" (V.8.18,31), but when called a "coward" by Macduff (V.8.23), he proves that he has not been effeminized by fear and faces his opponent, and his death, like a man. This act is not framed as heroic, but rather simply as an expectation of manhood. Women may run from their fears, but men must stand and fight, as is evident throughout all of Shakespeare's plays. Retreating Roman soldiers in *Coriolanus*, for example, are described as having the "souls of geese" (I.5.5), and Fastolfe, who "like a trusty squire did run away" from battle (IV.1.23) in *Henry VI, Part 1*, is shamed and banished. In contrast, women such as Helena in *A Midsummer Night's Dream* may flee from conflict and confess to being a "right maid for [her] cowardice" (III.2.303) without any potential shame or banishment because female bodies are not compelled to run toward physical danger.

This gendering of fear and violent confrontation propels the action of the play. Macbeth tries to reassert his masculinity after seeing Banquo's ghost and hearing his wife's "Are you a man?" by claiming, "Ay, and a bold one, that dare look on that / which might appall the devil" (III.4.59-61). But she responds by stating that he sees only apparitions, like the floating dagger he imagined before, and that his fear would be more appropriate in a "woman's story at a winter fire, / Authorized by her grandam" (III.4.66-7). She frames this critique within the discourse of gender identity, ridiculing him for his womanish lack of courage and asserting that he has been "quite unmanned in folly" (III.4.74). Macbeth tries to object, declaring,

What man dare, I dare.
Approach thou like the rugged Russian bear,
The armed rhinoceros, or th' Hyrcan tiger;
Take any shape but that, and my firm nerves
Shall never tremble. Or be alive again
And dare me to the desert with thy sword.
If trembling I inhabit then, protest me
The baby of a girl. (III.4.100-07)

Like any great warrior, he says, he is willing to face any physical danger, despite the threat to his body. Banquo's ghost, however, threatens more than just his body. As a supernatural being it cannot be battled against with sword or shield and represents a danger not addressed in Macbeth's warrior's code. In fact, the apparition offers Macbeth no means by which to perform his manhood. Only when the ghost disappears can he say, "I am a man again" (III.4.109). After the encounter, however, Macbeth determines to defeat his emasculating fear, telling his wife, "Strange things I have in head, that will to hand, / Which must be acted, ere they may be scann'd" (III.4.140-1). At this point in the play, he succumbs entirely to his wife's notion of masculinity as action. Rather than pause and consider his conduct, Macbeth has decided to embrace Lady Macbeth's ideal of violent action over careful contemplation.

Earlier, Macbeth agonized over the death of Duncan and the uncertainty of the continuance of his own royal line. Now he merely acts, cruelly and without remorse. Viewed alongside Lady Macbeth's earlier soliloquy, this type of behavior is entirely consistent with what she imagines the attributes of a man (or at least *not* of a woman) to be. When she asks the spirits to "unsex" her, she urges them to fill her "from the crown to the toe topfull / Of direst cruelty" and to "Stop up th' access and passage to remorse" (I.5.41-43). Joan Larsen Klein contends that "as long as she lives, Lady Macbeth is never unsexed in the only way she wanted to be unsexed—able to act with the cruelty she ignorantly and perversely identified with male strength" (250). But this is male strength without any governing ordinances that limit masculine violence. As James J. Greene notes, "These lines leave no doubt that, for Lady Macbeth, masculinity is equated with cruelty, violence and murder, and femininity with their opposites" (158). Irene G. Dash makes a similar observation, arguing that "Lady Macbeth [. . .] misunderstands the meaning of manliness, interpreting it as ruthlessness" (166). Thus, Lady Macbeth's vision of masculinity is a horribly distorted one. The great tragedy of the play is that her husband accepts her definition as his own.

In opposition to this reading of Macbeth as culpable for his own decisions, E. A. J. Honigmann suggests that Macbeth is merely a victim of Lady Macbeth and the Weird Sisters: "Lady Macbeth appears to be somehow in league with evil and Macbeth its victim, a fly in the spider's web who struggles mightily but cannot escape" (139). But although the witches tell him that he will be king, he himself decides to murder Duncan. Similarly, although his wife goads and encourages him in the act, he is still the one who performs it. For many critics, Lady Macbeth and the witches are neither the victims nor the perpetrators of the crimes in *Macbeth*; they are merely the witnesses, the Others who cannot understand or fully participate in the experience of the masculine. In fact, some see the violence in the play as a reaction against the feminine. Jonathan Goldberg, for instance, argues that "The hypermasculine world of *Macbeth* is haunted [. . .] by the power represented in the witches; masculinity in the play is directed as an assaultive attempt to secure power, to maintain success and succession, at the expense of women" (259). Yet it must be remembered that in every case, any "assaultive attempt to secure power, to maintain success and succession" actually occurs at the physical expense of the male bodies, as masculinity demands.

So there are at least two competing views of masculine power in *Macbeth*. The first relies on what Alan Sinfield refers to as the "legitimate violence" that is licensed by the state (95), and the second depends on the boundless acquisitive violence that is advocated by Lady Macbeth. This second version violates all the early modern society's rules of manhood: it is for personal gain, it is enacted on inappropriate bodies, it endangers the security of the state. In addition, it forces a man to eschew womanly fear, compassion, sentiment, and remorse. He must sacrifice not only his own body but his emotions as well. Otherwise, he may become effeminized.

Women are leaky vessels (they lack retention), while men are taught to be retentive vessels (they take it like a man). When Macduff first learns that Macbeth has murdered his family, Malcolm urges him to "Give sorrow words" (IV.3.209), but he does not encourage some womanly reaction. Rather, he suggests that revenge will comfort Macduff's grief and provide a manly course of action against the murderer. At first, however, the great warrior is too overcome with sorrow to act, so that Malcolm, disturbed by the thane's emotional reaction, admonishes him to "Dispute it like a man" (IV.3.220). "I shall do so," Macduff replies, "But I must also feel it as a man" (4.3.220-1). Although he initially bids Macduff to express his sorrow, Malcolm becomes nervous when that expression involves performative acts that are normally associated with women. As Lady Macbeth does with her husband, Malcolm censures such an outpouring and tries to suppress Macduff's emotional reaction. He does not wish to stifle all feelings, however, just those unbecoming to a man. As Macduff himself expressed earlier in the scene, good men do not indulge in such effeminate luxuries as weeping and melancholy. The only emotions appropriate to a man are those that may be expressed on the battlefield, such as the "valiant fury" (V.2.14) attributed to Macbeth at the end of the play.

Accordingly, Malcolm redirects Macduff's grief toward an appropriately masculine action. He tells him, "Be this the whetstone of your sword. Let grief / Convert to anger; blunt not the heart, enrage it" (IV.3.228-29). Here is the expression of grief that Malcolm has been looking for, asking Macduff not to weep for his lost family, but instead to rage for them and to vow revenge. When Macduff recovers, he says, "O, I could play the woman with mine eyes / And braggart with my tongue" (IV.3.230-31); but he wants no intervening time between the present moment and the day when he faces Macbeth. Right now, he wants only revenge, with inappropriate personal feeling converted into authorized state service. Seeing that Macduff's manhood has been restored—that the warrior is willing to kill or be killed by his enemy—Malcolm states, "This tune goes manly" (IV.3.235).

Stephen Booth argues that the "generally debilitating scene is contrived in such a way as to emphasize Macduff's passivity and impotence" (106), but it may be that the critic here submits to the same distorted paradigm that Malcolm adheres to, equating emotion to weakness. Rather than viewing Macduff in this scene as passive and impotent, it might be more useful to read Macduff as asserting his own definition of masculinity, in which a man may possess powerful emotions yet not be mastered by them. Of course, this definition is not the prevalent one in the play. Instead, Malcolm's version of masculinity-as-suppression predominates.

Throughout the play, the audience is reminded that a real man does not bemoan his fate or attempt to reason with fortune. He takes arms against his sea of troubles and, by opposing, either ends them or dies in the attempt. Bold, resolute action defines manhood, always with the possibility of death as a result. When Ross tells Old Siward of his son's death, he stresses the fact that Young Siward died like a man. Ross says,

> Your son, my lord, has paid a soldier's debt.
> He only lived but till he was a man,
> The which no sooner had his prowess confirmed
> In the unshrinking station where he fought
> But like a man he died. (V.8.39-43)

Young Siward only becomes a man when he can die in battle, "unshrinking" from both the possibility of harm and the station of manhood. Old Siward receives the news of his son's death stoically. Unlike Macduff, whose son was still a boy, Old Siward apprehends his child's death as an acceptable outcome of war. He knows that young men die in battle; that is the expectation. As Duncan did earlier with the Captain, Old Siward equates his son's wounds with honor. When he learns that the Young Siward was wounded "on the front" (V.18.47), he says, "Why then, God's soldier be he. / Had I as many sons as I have hairs, / I would not wish them to a fairer death" (V.8.47-9). "This is chilling," Linda Bamber says of this passage. "Although Macduff's alliance is a benign version of the masculine-historical ideal, the ideal nevertheless demands the sacrifice of full emotional responsiveness" (107) Yet even more than the sacrifice of emotion, which is certainly a theme in the play, the passage implies that death may be the highest honor attainable for a man, consequently leading to the sacrifice of more male bodies.

In fact, many critics seem to admire Macbeth for his own courage, fortitude, and willingness to lay down his own body. Rather than "play the Roman fool" (V.8.1)—that is, commit suicide—for instance, Macbeth faces death like a man. J. M. R. Margeson suggests that the emphasis in tragedy on the "greatness of the tragic hero strongly suggests an anthropological background of the leader sacrificed or cast out of society for his defiance of the gods, which is secretly to be admired for its courage, but feared and publicly condemned for its blasphemy" (ix-x). More than merely admiring Macbeth, however, many critics assert that readers and viewers also associate with him. For example, Robert Bechtold Heilman suggests that "we have to consent to participation in a planned murder, or at least tacitly accept our capability of committing it. [. . .] We accept ourselves as murderers" (14), and Harold Bloom argues that

> The universal reaction to Macbeth is that we identify with him, or at least his imagination. [. . .] Shakespeare rather dreadfully sees to it that *we* are Macbeth; our identity with him is involuntary but inescapable. [. . .] Macbeth terrifies us partly because that aspect of our imagination is so frightening: it seems to make us murderers, thieves, usurpers, and rapists. (517)

Yet while this may be true of some who encounter *Macbeth*, the play itself acknowledges the savagery of the murders and challenges the simple definition of masculinity as action without question. When Lady Macbeth urges her husband to act and assert his manhood by murdering Duncan and he replies that he does "all that may become a man; / Who dares do more is none" (I.7.46-7), he recognizes that by moving beyond the bounds of acceptable violence, he actually mitigates his manhood. Ultimately, however, Macbeth does move outside the borders of appropriate masculinity. But the act of murder does not emasculate or effeminize him. Instead, as he oversteps the bounds of what is natural, he becomes more than a man. He becomes a monster.

Like the murderers (and his wife), Macbeth misunderstands the limits of masculine power and becomes a murderer himself. Elizabeth A. Foyster points out that during the period, "The two key 'male' characteristics were reason and strength" (29). When Macbeth's actions extend beyond the realm of reason, his power becomes perverted. That is not to say that the play advocates a complete abandonment of power. On the contrary, the value of masculine power is implicit throughout, especially in the depiction of King Duncan. In Shakespeare and Middleton's main source for the play, Holinshed's *Chronicles*, Duncan is depicted as a weak, old, ineffectual king. The rebel Macdonwald calls Duncan a "faint-hearted milkesop, more meet to gouerne a sort of idle moonks in some cloister, than to haue the rule of such valiant and hardie men of warre as the Scots were" (Boswell-Stone 19-20). *Macbeth* immediately establishes this soft, unmanly character of the king when Duncan does not participate in the battle against the rebels himself—and thus assert his own manhood on the battlefield—but rather relies on the military might of his generals, Macbeth and Banquo. In fact, in Holinshed's original, the people actually prefer Macbeth's rule over that of the impotent Duncan:

> Mackbeth, after the departure thus of Duncanes sonnes, vsed great liberalitie towards the nobles of the realme, thereby to win their fauour, and when he saw that no man went about to trouble him, he set his whole intention to mainteine iustice, and to punish all enormities and abuses, which had chanced through the feeble and slouthfull administration of Duncane . . . . Mackbeth shewing himselfe thus a most diligent punisher of all iniuries and wrongs attempted by anie disordered persons within his realme, was accounted the sure defense and buckler of innocent people; and hereto he also applied his whole indeuor, to cause yoong men to exercise themselues in vertuous maners, and men of the church to attend their diuine seruice according to their vocations. (Boswell-Stone 32)

In many ways, Duncan's lack of strength is as odious as Macbeth's abuse of it. To emphasize this point, Shakespeare and Middleton retain Holinshed's portrait of the weak king without maintaining the particulars. In the play, he depends on the strength and goodwill of his subjects, becoming, as Janet Adelman suggests, like the defenseless babe that Lady Macbeth famously imagines having "dashed the brains out" (I.7.58): "The satiated and sleeping Duncan takes on the vulnerability that Lady Macbeth has just invoked in the image of the feeding, trusting infant" (139). The goal for masculinity then is balance. Macbeth is reviled because he adopts his wife's view of masculinity as cruelty and violence, but Duncan is usurped because he fails to demonstrate adequate masculine power. As B. Riebling observes,

> Political tragedy studies the consequences of misrule, and *Macbeth* is no exception, censuring two extremes in civil malpractice. Although the majority of the play is taken up with Macbeth's criminal reign—a regime at odds with both Machiavellian and Christian precepts— Macbeth begins its exploration of tragic politics in Duncan's chaotic realm, presenting a brief but succinct portrait of the consequences of political innocence. (274)

Ideal masculinity in *Macbeth* exists somewhere between the caring nature of Duncan and the physical strength of Macbeth. Perhaps Macduff then becomes the play's ideal man: he has nurtured his children and feels tremendous pain when he learns of their murder, but he also has the power to act against tyrants such as Macbeth. More importantly, he does so not motivated by personal gain, but for the good of Scotland. The problem is that even with men of virtue, the damaging circularity of masculine death will continue because war and killing provide one of the few ways for men to unambiguously declare their manhood. R. A. Foakes remarks that *Macbeth* renews the cycle of violence in such a way that

> we are again asked at the end of the play to applaud in war that which fills us with revulsion in peace, as the head of Macbeth is brought onstage, replacing the head of Macdonwald, chopped off, as we

are told in the opening scene, by Macbeth. [. . .] Macbeth takes us beyond ordinary moral boundaries and judgments, for in the end, the play is less concerned with a murderer who deserves our moral condemnation, than it is with a great warrior who breaks through a fear-barrier in doing what he is good at, killing, only to find on the other side not the achievement and success he looks for, but rather a need to go on repeating himself in a desert of spiritual desolation. (154)

In a way, this returns us to Heilman's and Bloom's claims regarding the audience's own guilt and complicity, especially when we remember that *Macbeth* is a play that is meant to be staged. Not only do we not stop the violence onstage, but as audience members we actually help to perpetuate it. Yes, Macbeth continually repeats his actions in Foakes's "desert of spiritual isolation," but he also repeats these actions again and again throughout the play's performance run. We empower Macbeth by attending the play night after night, where night after night he kills and kills and society approves. In this way, we legitimize the violence that is authorized by the performance that is sanctioned by the society that approves of the violence onstage. Like Macbeth then, we have our own cycles of violence. And we too associate manhood with that violence.

Works Cited

Adelman, Janet. *Suffocating Mothers: Fantasies of Maternal Origin in Shakespeare's Plays*, Hamlet *to* The Tempest. Routledge, 1992.

Bamber, Linda. *Comic Women, Tragic Men: A Study of Gender and Genre in Shakespeare*. Stanford UP, 1982.

Bloom, Harold. *Shakespeare: The Invention of the Human*. Riverhead, 1998.

Booth, Stephen. King Lear, Macbeth, *Indefinition, and Tragedy*. Yale UP, 1983.

Boswell-Stone, W. G. *Shakespeare's Holinshed: The Chronicle Plays and the Historical Plays Compared*. Lawrence, 1896.

Butler, Judith. *Bodies That Matter: On the Discursive Limits of "Sex."* Routledge, 1993.

_____. *Gender Trouble: Feminism and the Subversion of Identity*. Routledge, 1990.

Dash, Irene G. *Wooing, Wedding, and Power: Women in Shakespeare's Plays*. Columbia UP, 1981.

Foakes, R. A. *Shakespeare and Violence*. Cambridge UP, 2003.

Foyster, Elizabeth A. *Manhood in Early Modern England: Honour, Sex and Marriage*. Women and Men in History Series. Longman, 1999.

Goldberg, Jonathan. "Speculations: *Macbeth* and Source." *Shakespeare Reproduced: The Text in History and Ideology*. Edited by Jean E. Howard and Marion F. O'Connor. Methuen, 1987, pp. 242-64.

Greene, James J. "*Macbeth*: Masculinity as Murder." *American Imago*, vol. 41, no. 2, 1984, pp. 155-80.

Greenblatt, Stephen. *Shakespearean Negotiations: The Circulation of Social Energy in Renaissance England*. U of California P, 1988.

Harding, D. W. "Women's Fantasy of Manhood: A Shakespearean Theme." *Shakespeare Quarterly*, vol. 20, no. 3, 1969, pp. 245-53.

Heilman, Robert Bechtold. "The Criminal as Tragic Hero: Dramatic Methods." *Shakespeare Survey*, vol. 19, 1966, pp. 12-24.

Honigmann, E. A. J. "*Macbeth*: The Murderer as Victim." *Shakespeare: The Tragedies*. Edited by Robert B. Heilman. Prentice-Hall, 1984, pp. 135-49.

Kimbrough, Robert. "Macbeth: The Prisoner of Gender." *Shakespeare Studies*, vol. 16, 1983, pp. 175-90.

Klein, Joan Larsen. "Lady Macbeth: 'Infirm of Purpose.'" *The Woman's Part: Feminist Criticism of Shakespeare*. Edited by Carolyn Ruth Swift Lenz, et al. U of Illinois P, 1980, pp. 240-55.

Margeson, J. M. R. *The Origins of English Tragedy*. Clarendon, 1967.

Riebling, B. "Virtue's Sacrifice: A Machiavellian Reading of *Macbeth*." *Studies in English Literature*, vol. 31, no. 2, 1991, pp. 273-87.

Shakespeare, William. *Coriolanus*. Edited by Johnathan Crewe. Penguin, 1999.

_____. *Henry VI, Part 1*. Edited by Norman Sanders. Penguin, 1995.

_____. *Macbeth*. Edited by Stephen Orgel. Penguin, 2016.

_____. *A Midsummer Night's Dream*. Edited by Stanley Wells. Penguin, 2005.

Sinfield, Alan. *Faultlines: Cultural Materialism and the Politics of Dissident Reading*. Clarendon, 1992.

Spierenburg, Pieter. "Masculinity, Violence, and Honor: An Introduction." *Men and Violence: Gender, Honor, and Rituals in Modern Europe and America*. Edited by Pieter Spierenburg. Ohio State UP, 1998, pp. 1-29.

White, R. S. *Innocent Victims: Poetic Injustice in Shakespearean Tragedy*. 1982. Athlone, 1986.

"Strange Images of Death": *Macbeth* and the *Vanitas* Still Life_____

Sophia Richardson

In the aftermath of a bloody battle against Norway, Ross rides onto the scene to inform Macbeth that he has been elevated to Thane of Cawdor to recognize his unflinching valor:

> The king hath happily received, Macbeth,
> The news of thy success; and when he reads
> Thy personal venture in the rebels' fight,
> His wonders and his praises do contend
> Which should be thine or his. Silenced with that,
> In viewing o'er the rest o' th' selfsame day,
> He finds thee in the stout Norwegian ranks,
> Nothing afeard of what thyself didst make,
> Strange images of death. (*Macbeth* I.3.93-101)

Although this report begins "happily" enough with "wonders" and "praises," it soon equates "success," ominously, with making "strange images of death." When Ross's speech foregrounds the "images" of death embedded within the linguistic play-text, he renders a visual medium within the verbal register. He "make[s] / [s]trange images" by delivering death unto others, and later he will "make" the image as he himself succumbs to death, beheaded and displayed to the army laying waste to his reign (V.8.23-7, 54-5). Repeatedly, the play connects death and images: before he murders the king, Macbeth imagines death's "horrid image" (I.3.135); Macduff, upon discovering Duncan's corpse, calls his sleeping compatriots (Banquo, Donalbain, Malcolm) to witness "[t]he great doom's image" (II.3.77); Lady Macbeth insists that "[t]he sleeping and the dead are but as pictures" as she chides her husband that "'tis the eye of childhood that fears a painted devil" (II.2.56-8), and terms Macbeth's encounter with death in the form of Banquo's ghost as "the very painting of your fear" (III.4.62). These figures notably call attention to the represented quality of the dead in this play. Related descriptions highlight not only representation, but also an aestheticization that seems specifically painterly, such as Macbeth's musing on Duncan's "silver skin laced with his golden blood" spilled from his stab wounds (II.3.110). Macduff's description of the scene as a "most bloody piece of work" whereby "[c]onfusion now hath made his masterpiece" underscores the king's death as a kind of artistic rendering (II.3.126, II.3.65).

The Rise of the *Vanitas* Still Life

The play's insistent emphasis on death's representations and representability engages the energies of a contemporary, newly popularized rendering of death: the *vanitas* still-life painting. *Macbeth*'s fixation on death aligns the tragedy with this emergent genre when it ponders mortality through metatheatrical turns and its pervasive visual vocabulary. Shakespeare's tragedy particularly draws on the ephemeral symbolic register of the *vanitas* tradition, which developed out of visual emblems of *memento mori* (reminders of death's approach) and still-life paintings. The *vanitas* gained unprecedented popularity around the turn of the sixteenth century as a favorite trope in the emergent Dutch still-life genre, and it migrated to England and through the Continent as painters, patrons, and paintings traveled abroad (Kelly 3-4). Alluding to the biblical reminder that "all is vanity" (*vanitas vanitatum,* Ecclesiastes I), the *vanitas* painting showcases the most ephemeral of objects to remind the viewer that life is fleeting and its pleasures are all ultimately merely empty "vanities" (De Pascale 99-101). Bubbles shortly to pop, candles burning out, and timepieces counting minutes, alongside worldly pleasures with a short shelf life (flowers beginning to wilt, fruit vulnerable to rot, wineglasses drunk dry), ornaments of material ambition (crowns, jewels) and evanescent entertainments (musical instruments, books, the cards and dice from games of chance) all serve as standard set pieces in the painted assemblages of the *vanitas* still life. In case the viewer might be distracted by all these shiny objects and forget their status as ostensibly worthless trifles, these paintings often borrow from the closely related *memento mori* genre

---

by incorporating a skull or bones into the image, often piling the objects around a skull to drive home the message that the painting (and life) centers around impending death.[1] Sometimes these images will even include written phrases to this effect, which *Macbeth* seems to pick up on in its fusion of the verbal and visual registers (see Figure 1).

Figure 1. *Vanitas Still Life.*

Andriessen, Hendrick. *Vanitas Still Life*. Flanders, ca. 1650.
In the collection of the Mount Holyoke College Art Museum
https://artmuseum.mtholyoke.edu/object/vanitas-still-life

The still-life paintings of which *vanitas* are a subset rendered household items and luxury goods in extreme detail. The rise of international trade and increased prosperity generated a class of newly wealthy merchants in nations like the Netherlands with both luxury possessions and the impetus to display them in paintings on the walls of their richly appointed houses (Liedtke). Among still lifes, *vanitas* paintings particularly exploited contradictions in this emergent social context: economic security and spiritual trepidation, artistic mastery and the debts of patronage. The striking visual qualities of *vanitas* favorites like bubbles, glasses, jewels, and complex blossoms offered the artist a chance to show off skills at painting reflections, transparent media, and ornate details. Simultaneously, the patron was afforded the chance to display copies of particularly costly possessions (crowns, jewelry, books, fine instruments) in a notably expensive medium (the commissioned oil painting).

Even more interesting, the way *vanitas* objects encode ephemerality and impending death jars against complacent luxuriating in material riches and conspicuous consumption that the still-life painting promotes. Thematically focused on death, the *vanitas* painting renders contemporary cultural crises of mortality as Reformist culture struggled with the new understandings of the afterlife following upon doctrinal abolition of purgatory, which had made death more definitive; among the cultural consequences of reimagining the afterlife were changes in mourning and memorial practices, including modes of painting. In the era of *Macbeth*'s first performances, moreover, questions about death could be even more radical than confessional variation: Robert Watson detects nagging skepticism about any afterlife at all: "Despite its ferocious displays of Christian conviction, Jacobean culture struggled with the suspicion that death was a complete and permanent annihilation of the self, not merely some latency of the body awaiting Last Judgment" (3). The particularly brutal plague epidemic of 1603 rendered the inevitability of death and the complete erasure of individuality it threatened particularly visible to Londoners as they witnessed the bodies piling up in the streets and piles of corpses thrown into mass graves (Neill 13-22). Indeed, the mass casualties of the London plague would presumably have been particularly resonant to audiences of *Macbeth*—probably first performed in London in 1606—who would have been unlikely to have forgotten that spectacle. The publication of plague pamphlets and literary accounts like Thomas Dekker's 1604 *News from Gravesend* suggest that the plague was indeed still at the forefront of the public imagination in the following years. In the early modern world, Watson argues, "[t]he prospect of personal annihilation was always asserting itself—staring up from plaguy corpses, rising in the inscrutable remains of classical antiquity, threatening to become legible even in the Bible itself. Jacobean culture was obliged to find ways to unthink that thought, to talk itself out of fear, to quarantine a potentially catastrophic cultural epidemic" (29).

In this context, the luxury economy and artistic *sprezzatura* of *vanitas* paintings—the nonchalance with which skilled painters rendered the most difficult subjects as they portrayed expensive goods like furs and satins and flower petals—appear a compensation for a real cultural anxiety about a death that lurks everywhere, strikes everyone, and offers no salvation. The *vanitas* trope both makes visible the ever-present lurking fear of death's inevitable and total annihilation of self and offers a way to materially counter this evisceration, providing a mode of artistic memorializing that might preserve oneself and one's possessions at least on earth.

The conventional subjects of *vanitas* paintings that pointedly engage these questions of persistence and ephemerality, autonomous agency and dissolution into dead matter, also suffuse rhetoric of the era, surfacing widely in sermons and in commonplace books. Archbishop of Canterbury George Abbot, for instance, preached in a sermon that "[w]e who know that flesh is grasse, and the grace of it but a flowre, that our breath is but a vapour, and our life but as a bubble, who speake much of mortality." *Macbeth* deploys this theatrically, borrowing key symbols of *vanitas* from visual art. Animating bubbles and candles on the stage alongside "vain" material gains (crowns and titles) and leisure activities (banqueting, riding), the play composes dramatic juxtapositions that reflect on cultural concerns with *vanitas*: that is, with ambitious self-fashioning (e.g.: Macbeth's "vaulting ambition" [I.7.27]), with the ephemerality of wordly gains, with the meaning of death.

"Whither are they vanished?": Bubbles and Ephemerality

Bubbles, a frequent element of the *vanitas* painting, might epitomize vanity. They are blown by fools and children for entertainment, offering purely aesthetic pleasure devoid of practical value. For the painter and patron, too, bubbles epitomize the artistic vanity of *sprezzatura*: because they reflect and distort light without being fully visible, bubbles challenge the painter despite their seeming simplicity. Painted bubbles augment the visual pleasure of real bubbles, as well as their inutility (see Figure 2). The *homo bulla* (man as bubble) moralizes *vanitas*, suggesting the emptiness and ephemerality of the human viewer. Bubbles encapsulate life's accoutrements as insubstantial, inconsequential vanities.

Macbeth presents the witches as bubbles. Confronted with the bizarre insubstantiality of the vanishing Weird Sisters, Banquo muses: "[t]he earth hath bubbles as the water has, / And these are of them" (I.3.79-80). The witches seem to suddenly appear and then vanish into thin air, just as bubbles swell and pop: "[w]hither are they vanished?" Banquo asks, and Macbeth responds "[i]nto the air, and that which seemed corporeal melted / As breath into the wind" (I.3.80, 81-2). Macbeth's letter to his wife describes the witches similarly: they "made themselves air, into which they vanished" (I.5.4-5). Not only the witches' appearance as related by others invoke bubbles; their own diction does as well. They "[h]over through the fog and filthy air" (I.1.13); Hecate announces "I am for th'air" (III.5.20); the witches instruct their cauldron to "bubble" and "boil." In their spell-work, the witches repeat "fire burn and cauldron bubble" three times; they require that the "fillet of a fenny snake / In the cauldron boil and bake" and that the whole concoction "like a hell-broth boil and bubble" (IV.1.11, 21, 36, 12-13, 19). Macbeth also accuses them

Figure 2. *Homo Bulla.*

From: Boissard, Jean Jacques. *Emblemes Latins [...] avec l'interpretation Françoise.* Metz : Jean Aubry and Abraham Faber, 1588. *Emblematica Online.* by permission of University of Glasgow Library, Special Collections." University of Glasgow. Web. 16 May 2017. http://www.emblems.arts.gla.ac.uk/french/dual.php?id1=FB Oa007&type1=1&id2=sm415-c4r&type2=2

This image is accompanied by facing-page text titled "l'estat de l'homme est moin qu'autre durable" ("the state of man is less than durable") and a poem that begins by describing a child playing with soap bubbles ("d'un savon limoneus c'est enfant qui se joue / enfle à discretion maints globes empoulés"), only to reflect on how quickly the bubble—like all human lives—will succumb to time. Below the image is a Latin text: "FLuxa quidem, & vana in nostrâ sunt omnia vitâ: / E Lachesis pendent omnia nostra colu. / Quàm citò bullatae pluvius tumor interit undae, / Tam citò certa obitus cuilibet hora venit." ("Transient and vain is everything in our life: everything hangs from the thread of Lachesis. As quickly as the wet swelling of the bubbled water perishes, so the certain hour of death comes to anyone." Latin translation provided by University of Glasgow website).

of sending the winds to create "yeasty" (frothy, bubbling) waves to "[c]onfound and swallow navigation up" (IV.1.75-6).

Embodying bubbles as they float through the air, liable to vanish at any moment, and also generating endless streams of further bubbles (in their cauldron, in the waves), the witches imitate not only the physical properties of bubbles, but also their *vanitas* connotations. The witches evoke the vain pleasures of worldly entertainment—specifically, the theatrical spectacle of *Macbeth* itself—as well as of the emptiness and intangibility of these pleasures. As in the painterly *vanitas* tradition, the witches are associated with set pieces that display finely wrought representational skills. It is the witch scenes in *Macbeth* that provide the occasion for music, dance, dumb show, and a masquelike procession of apparitions and kings, a profusion of staged media that illustrates all the vanities of the theater (III.5, IV.1). (Indeed, in William Davenant's 1687 *Macbeth* adaptation, the witches are even provided with flying machines and additional purpose-written music by John Eccles and Richard Leveridge to further intensify the experience of heightened mediation.) Like *vanitas* paintings that warn against worldly pleasures while luxuriating in the painter's virtuosity, the witches onstage recall the emptiness of theatrical illusion while at the same time embracing all the sensory pleasures of the entertainment. Both witches and bubbles reveal the perils and promises of spectacular "show." Banquo asks "[a]re you fantastical, or that indeed / which outwardly you show?" (I.3.53-4) and later determines "to you [Macbeth] they have showed some truth" (II.1.22). This language links the witches with the vain theatrical "show" that we enjoy but which is ultimately substanceless, a world that will be burst like a bubble by the audience's final applause. Visually, bubbles delimit negative space, temporarily marking an entity (a pleasure, an ambition) that is ultimately hollow, absent, empty—a substance hovering at the limit of insubstantiality, that will become entirely effaced and traceless after the bubble bursts. Accordingly, the witches arise bubblelike from the moors to provide prophecies that will fuel Macbeth's vain ambition to become king, then vanish, traceless, into the air. So too will Macbeth's pride inflate to the point of self-annihilation as the bubble of his vanity pops, leaving him with nothing. The rewards of his military campaign and political scheming are alluring but not enduring; his "fruitless crown" and "barren scepter" will be stripped away, leaving him with no titles, no holdings, no heirs (III.1.61, 62).

"Out, out, brief candle!": Self-Consuming Lives

If bubbles demarcate negative space, candles measure negative time. A candle shows how much time has passed by how much of the candle is no longer there. Unlike an hourglass, which conserves its total volume of sand even as it runs out on one side, a burning candle vaporizes wax or tallow into air and smoke—and vanishes forever. As bubbles expand to self-annihilation spatially, candles do much the same temporally. As the illustration *Quod nutrit me consummat* ("what feeds me consumes me") depicts, the candle extinguishes itself over its brief enflamed life (see Figure 3). As Ross articulates when he thinks Duncan's sons have ordered the murder of their own father in their quest for worldly success: "[t]hriftless ambition […] will ravin up / Thine own life's means!" (II.4.28-9). The candle, like life, is slowly converted to nothing, its alluring flame merely vanity.

Macbeth connects burning candles, evanescent time, and vanishing life force as he responds to his wife's death:

> She should have died hereafter:
> There would have been a time for such a word.
> Tomorrow, and tomorrow, and tomorrow
> Creeps in this petty pace from day to day
> To the last syllable of recorded time,
> And all our yesterdays have lighted fools
> The way to dusty death. Out, out, brief candle,
> Life's but a walking shadow, a poor player
> That struts and frets his hour upon the stage
> And then is heard no more. It is a tale
> Told by an idiot, full of sound and fury,
> Signifying nothing (V.5.17-28).

QVOD NVTRIT ME, CONSVMMAT.

Ce qui estoit pour nourriture tue,
Comme voyez ceste belle chandele.
Ainsi en prend à cestuy-la qui mue
La verité de Dieu, par sa cautele,
Bonne de soy : mais est par l'infidele
Souuent tournee à sa damnation :
Et au croyant donne vie eternele,
Lequel la tient au cœur sans fiction.
                          Voicy

Figure 3. *Quod nutrit me consummate.*

From: De Montenay, Georgette. *Emblemes ou deuises chrestiennes.* Lyon : Jean Marcorelle, 1571, pp. 54. Held at the Beinecke Rare Book and Manuscript Library, Yale University. Photograph by the author.

The poem below the illustration calls attention to the candle on the table in the image, explaining, "Ce qui estoit pour nourriture tue, / Comme voyer ceste belle chandele" ("That which serves as food kills / As you see in this lovely candle"; my translation).

Here, past time—"our yesterdays"—serves as the candles that "have lighted fools" on their journey toward "dusty death." Time is the beacon illuminating the path of life, but just as the candle burns and turns to air, so too do our bodies return to dust. The flame that lights our lives, then, is also the slow, eviscerating burn of death. When the "brief candle" is finally "out," we discover that it, like the witches, vanishes "[i]nto the air, and what seemed corporal melted" (I.3.81).

Like a melting candle, life as rendered in Macbeth's speech transmutes itself into empty air. Time itself is converted into language and performance: Macbeth laments that "there would have been a time for such a word," that the future, indicated by the repeated word "tomorrow," creeps until "the last syllable of recorded time," that a "poor player" in a meager "hour upon the stage" "struts and frets" away his time on the stage until all his lines have been delivered (V.5.21, 24-5). Like a real candle melting into air as time passes, the image of the candle-timepiece invoked by this speech is converted through time ("time," "tomorrow," "hour") into language ("syllable[s]" of time), which—like the vapors of a candle—is empty air, just breath shaped into a tale "signifying nothing." This evacuates the deictics ("hereafter," "tomorrow," "yesterdays") that offer illusory presence, but are ultimately vacant, an afternoon's theatrical entertainment that vanishes into nothing.

Negotiating "Nothing": Uncertain Ontology

Like the *vanitas*, the play presents life as "nothing": it is but a "shadow," only darkness. However, this evaporation of substance into language is also countered by the turn to the "poor player" onstage. While the image of life as "walking shadow" implies insubstantiality, as discussed above, the subsequent conflation of the "shadow" with a theatrical "player" also challenges this through the bodily presence of the actor delivering these lines. If the "poor player" standing before us on the stage is indeed "but a walking shadow," he is a thoroughly incarnated shadow. This challenges any conceptual dichotomy of substance and absence by positing the "shadow" as both the absence of a thing—*not* an object, but the immaterial outline of one, generated by a *lack* of light—and as the presence of the thing itself (the shadow is life, is a flesh-and-blood actor).The light of the candle thus, in one sense, serves as the energy that makes life visible. But it also eats away at life: the driving force toward death. Darkness is equally double: on the one hand, the "shadow" cast by the candle is proof of life (life is defined here as "a walking shadow"); on the other hand, death is figured as the total darkness when the candle goes out. Light and life, darkness at death are all at play here, but they are deeply and doubly entwined, refusing clean substitution of one term for another. This confusion aligns with the similarly uncertain figurations of absence and presence in the *vanitas* painting as the ostensible ephemerality of the items depicted is countered by the artistic immortalization of these very items as they are preserved on the canvas.

The candle as uncertain figure for both life and death resurfaces in plot-points and diction surrounding deaths throughout the play. The night that Macbeth murders Duncan, between when he has made up his mind to do the deed and when he actually has completed the crime, there is a brief interlude in which Banquo and Fleance discuss the time of night:

> BANQUO How goes the night, boy?
> FLEANCE The moon is down; I have not heard the clock.
> BANQUO And she goes down at twelve.
> FLEANCE I take't, 'tis later, sir.
> BANQUO Hold, take my sword. There's husbandry in heaven;
> Their candles are all out (II.1.1-7).

Whereas Macbeth's "Out, out, brief candle!" speech either dispassionately describes or passionately implores death, Banquo here illustrates how extinguishing a candle can preserve life. Banquo imagines that, by putting out the stars, heaven frugally husbands its resources. At the same time, however, these extinguished star-candles also seem to figure Duncan's death, only a few lines later in the scene. (Banquo's astute observation that the "candles are all out" may also foreshadow his own death a few scenes later in the play.)

When this second assassination scene arrives, extinguished lights—this time torches rather than candles—again figure death.

Banquo specifically requests a light ("Give us a light there, ho!" [III.3.9]) and by spying this light, the murderers locate and identify Banquo ("A light, a light! / 'Tis he" [III.3.17-18]). As Banquo dies, the light goes out, linking Banquo's light and his life: when he is alive he holds the torch; as he is killed, the flame goes out. However, the extinguished flame allows Fleance to escape with his life: the murderers' confusion suggests that it is because it is now too dark to see that they have lost Fleance in the night.

> THIRD MURDERER Who did strike out the light?
> FIRST MURDERER   Was't not the way?
> THIRD MURDERER There's but one down. The son is fled.
> SECOND MURDERER We have lost best half of our affair. (III.3.23-25)

Just as Duncan's destructive murder was matched with the conserving "husbandry" of candle-preservation, so too is Banquo's murder paired with Fleance's preservation by the extinguished torch. Similar rhetoric "enkindle[s] [Macbeth] to the crown" (I.3.121) while Lady Macbeth imagines the murder of the grooms who will be accused of killing Duncan as though she is turning them to plumes of smoke:

> […] his two chamberlains
> Will I with wine and wassail so convince
> That memory, the warder of the brain,
> Shall be a fume, and the receipt of reason
> A limbeck only (I.7.63-67).

While Macbeth flares up to receive "the ornament of life" (I.7.42) (the crown), the murderers' memory and reason evaporate, as in a distilling "limbeck" or alchemist's vessel. One flares into (short-lived) life while the others die, turned to smoke and "fume" before they are permanently snuffed out. Lady Macbeth's candles are multivalent in going out; after drugging the guards, she exclaims, "what hath quenched them has given me fire," correlating the extinguishing of their lives with the rekindling of her own (II.2.2). Just as Fleance is spared by the extinction of Banquo's torch, Lady Macbeth is enflamed by the impending death of Duncan's party. Eschewing a simple one-to-one correspondence between life and light, *Macbeth* situates candles (and their companions, torches and tapers) at the crossroads of life and death, allowing them to simultaneously figure multiple, seemingly oppositional concepts. Returning to the visual, we once again find a visual analog in the painted tradition of anamorphosis, a figure that appears as different images depending on the perspective of the viewer. Like the anamorphic skull hidden in Holbein's famous *vanitas* portrait of wealthy ambassadors, a single frame—or flame—figures both the "ornament[s] of life" (as Macbeth refers to the crown) and the lurking face of death (see Figure 4).

Signifying Nothing?

Deploying darkness and light, these passages foreground in visual terms a deep uncertainty about the ontology of absence and presence that haunts *Macbeth*, a problem it stages through both candlelight and bubbles. Both candles and bubbles offer a kind of fleeting visibility (of the candlelight, of the bubble's contour). Bubbles play with presence and visibility by presenting a form that melts into untraceable air as soon as the containing sphere dissipates. Candles' illuminated visibility, similarly, registers uncertainty about whether vision indexes ontological presence. Is darkness a presence or an absence? Is illumination presence or illusion? Ross articulates this conundrum as he wonders why it is so dark in the middle of the day: "[i]s't night's predominance, or the day's shame, / That darkness does the face of earth entomb / When living light should kiss it? (II.4.8-10). He attempts to determine here whether darkness is presence ("night's predominance") or absence (day that has fled in "shame"). Bubbles, too, play with the uncertainty of what counts as substance. They are effectively containers for nothing. And yet, this "nothing" exerts the pressure from within that causes the bubble to form and swell in the first place. This is the visual version of Macbeth's "tale full of sound and fury / signifying nothing." Just as with the darkness above, pockets of air (bubbles, tales of "sound and fury") simultaneously position themselves as sites of evacuated meaning (they do not signify) and as carriers of meaning (they signify nothingness). Or, as Macbeth puts

Figure 4. *The Ambassadors.*

Hans Holbein the Younger. *Jean de Dinteville and Georges de Selve ('The Ambassadors').* 1533. Image from *The National Gallery.* Accessed 16 May 2017. https://www.nationalgallery.org. uk/paintings/hans-holbein-the-younger-the-ambassadors

This portrait of two ambassadors is replete with the material vanities (instruments, books) possibly picked up from travels around the world (indicated by the mathematical or navigational instruments and the globes). What is remarkable about this painting is not only the rich color and detail of the ambassadors and their accoutrements, but also the skull painted diagonally in the bottom quarter of the painting. If one looks at this painting straight-on, the skull may disguise itself as a part of the floor's design, but if one looks at the image as though standing very close to the painting and looking up from the bottom left corner, the strange blob appears as a skull at an odd cross-angled perspective with the surrounding scene.

it, "nothing is / but what is not," positing "nothing" as both negation ("what is not") and positive presence (it "is" a particular state of being "what is not") (I.3.141-42).

These questions seem associated with spectacle, and indeed the play's metatheatrical lexicon (the "bloody stage," the "poor player," [II.4.6, V.5.24]) evokes the *theatrum mundi*, the Renaissance commonplace that all the world is a stage, and that the stage is a little world. These figures also, however, present the ontological uncertainty surrounding death throughout the play in ways that are specifically visual, and in terms that are painterly as well as theatrical. *Macbeth* is filled with ghosts, apparitions, hallucinations, and dreams—material 'nothings' that nonetheless exert tremendous pressure (see Macbeth's floating dagger [II.1.34-42], the "spot" on Lady Macbeth's hand [V.1.31], the appearance of Banquo's ghost at the banquet [III.4.42]). The play insists that we read "images of death" as figures of emptiness, of vanity. Just as Cawdor learned in his study of death "To throw away the dearest thing he owed / As 'twere a careless trifle" Macbeth insists that life is a vain game: "there's nothing serious in mortality; all is but toys" (I.4.10-11; II.3.91-2). At the same time, the play seems to take seriously the idea that "nothing" can be substantive, that "signifying nothing" can convey meaning rather than signal its evacuation.

The impetus to recast *vanitas* emptiness into a meaningful "nothing" is, I suspect, a way to work through the cultural anxieties about the ontology of death that were particularly pressing around the time *Macbeth* was written: the memories of plague victims piled up and stripped of their identities (Neill), a changing vision of the afterlife brought about by Protestant theology (particularly the abolition of purgatory), and an uncomfortable suspicion that death was not a vehicle into the afterlife but rather the annihilation of identity: completely evacuated, meaningless, nothingness (Watson). *Macbeth* does not deny death's emptiness, and its reliance on *vanitas* symbols (bubbles, candles, fruitless crowns) and tropes (life as "trifle," mortality as "toy") reinforces this. But apparently empty deaths come back to haunt the world of the play in a way that belies their total evisceration, deploying the artful outer surface of *vanitas* objects even as their hollowness is acknowledged. In the strange resonances and residues that that the "images of death" leave behind—as ghosts that "rise again," as "thoughts which should indeed have died / with them they think on" but do not (III.4.81; 3.2.11-12)—the play uses different media (the image and the theatrical performance) to stage competing yet coexisting understandings of death, as both eternal image and temporally unspooling dramatic performance, as both absence and lingering presence. If life is vanity and death is nothingness, the play seems to hope that perhaps these are at least "signifying" kinds of emptiness and "nothing."

Note

1. *Memento mori,* "remember death," was spoken into the ears of triumphant Romans by their slaves to encourage them not to become overly prideful (De Pascale 86). This message is often translated into visual media through skulls, bones, or other metonymies of mortality. Death has a rich visual tradition of representation, including the *memento mori,* but also encompassing scenes of contemplation of death (often featuring Mary Magdalene and Saint Jerome) and many tropes of personified death (the "black lady" of the plague, the leader of the "dance of death," the grisly lover of the deceased virgin). For a succinct illustrated overview of all the many visual conventions by which death has historically been represented in Western art, see De Pascale. For descriptions and examples specifically of *vanitas* paintings, see De Pascale pp. 99-101. For a brief history of *vanitas,* the cultural and economic factors occasioning its rise, and its distinction from other similar genres, see also Raymond J. Kelly.

Works Cited

Abbot, George. *An exposition upon the prophet Jonah Contained in certaine sermons, preached in S. Maries church in Oxford. By George Abbot professor of divinitie, and maister of Uniuersitie Colledge.* Imprinted by Richard Field, 1600. *Early English Books Online.* http://gateway. proquest.com/openurl?ctx_ver=Z39.88-2003&res_id=xri:eebo&rft_ id=xri:eebo:citation:99836358. Accessed May 16, 2016.

Andriessen, Hendrick. *Vanitas Still Life.* Flanders, ca. 1650. Mount Holyoke College Art Museum. https://artmuseum.mtholyoke.edu/ object/vanitas-still-life. Accessed 16 May, 2017.

Boissard, Jean Jacques. *Emblemes Latins [...] avec l'interpretation Françoise.* Jean Aubry and Abraham Faber, 1588. *Emblematica Online.* By permission. U of Glasgow Library, Special Collections. www.emblems.arts.gla.ac.uk/french/dual.php?id1=FBOa007&type1=1&id2=sm415-c4r&type2=2. Accessed May 16, 2017.

https://commons.wikimedia.org/wiki/File:Hans_Holbein_the_Younger_-_The_Ambassadors_-_Google_Art_Project.jpg.

https://commons.wikimedia.org/wiki/File:Hendrick_Andriezsoon_002.jpg.

Davenant, William. *Macbeth : a tragedy : with all the alterations, amendments, additions, and new songs as it is now acted at the Theatre Royal.* Printed for Hen. Herringman, and are to be sold by Jos. Knight and Fra. Saunders at the Blue Anchor in the lower walk of the New-Exchange, 1687.

Dekker, Thomas. *News from Gravesend: Sent to Nobody.* Printed by T[homas] C[reede] for Thomas Archer, 1604. Reprinted by Chadwyck-Healey, 2000.

De Montenay, Georgette. *Emblemes ou deuises chrestiennes.* Jean Marcorelle, 1571, p. 54. Held at the Beinecke Rare Book and Manuscript Library. Yale U. Photograph by the author.

De Pascale, Enrico. *Death and Resurrection in Art.* Getty Publications, 2009.

Holbein, Hans, the Younger. *Jean de Dinteville and Georges de Selve (The Ambassadors).* 1533. *The National Gallery.* www.nationalgallery.org.uk/paintings/hans-holbein-the-younger-the-ambassadors. Accessed May 16, 2017.

Kelly, Raymond J. *To Be, Or Not To Be: Four Hundred Years of Vanitas Painting.* Flint Institute of Arts, 2006.

Liedtke, Walter. "Still-Life Painting in Northern Europe, 1600-1800. *Heilbrunn Timeline of Art History.* Metropolitan Museum of Art, 2003. www.metmuseum.org/toah/hd/nstl/hd_nstl.htm. Accessed 16 May, 2017.

Neill, Michael. *Issues of Death.* Clarendon and Oxford UP, 1997.

Shakespeare, William. *Macbeth.* Edited by Stephen Orgel. Penguin, 2016.

Watson, Robert. *The Rest is Silence: Death as Annihilation in the English Renaissance.* U of California P, 1994.

Shakespeare in an Indian Classroom: Reflections on Guilt-Consciousness, *Rasa*, and Witchcraft in *Macbeth* _____

Rahul Chaturvedi

The usual Indian classroom is little interested in the historical Macbeth, who ruled over Scotland between 1040 AD and 1057 AD after killing his predecessor Duncan I. The Indian classroom mostly does not judge Macbeth's crime in relation to the common laws of Scotland of that time, where the crown used to be passed on to a brother or a cousin, not to the direct descendent of the king after his death. The question whether Duncan wronged Macbeth by introducing the practice of primogeniture and robbing him of what was his rightful claim is therefore also of marginal significance. The assumption that Macbeth is a play about Scotland dealing with the crisis of succession is of secondary importance to both students and teachers. So, what is an Indian classroom interested in? It is mostly concerned with the moral dilemmas and universal appeal of Macbeth. It is interested in a Macbeth who is at once innocent and despicable, who is caught in the apocalyptic conflict between good and evil suggesting the moral self-reflexivity of the human race.

Human, All Too Human

The orthodox reading of *Macbeth* is usually a moral reading wherein Macbeth suffers for the crime of murder. The traditional response to Macbeth's downfall provides a horrifying moral lesson that speaks of the consequences of overstepping the limits of human ambition. To uphold the ethical and moral order, Macbeth is bound to be sacrificed as he has violated the law under the spell of the inhuman ferocity of his ambition.

But is Shakespeare a moralist? Perhaps not. In *Macbeth*, Shakespeare is staging a fierce conflict between a very powerful human drive (ambition) and an equally strong social law (austerity) wherein the protagonist finally violates the codes of ethics and ceases to follow the laws necessary to be considered a moral individual. By defying the moral laws that prohibit Macbeth from murdering Duncan and others, *Macbeth* discloses a fictional vision of inhumanity in man, which mostly lies dormant but might come out if provoked when conditions are opportune.

Despite the fact that Macbeth has murdered his king, hired hitmen to get his friend, and a woman and a child murdered, Macbeth elicits the reader's sympathy. How? Perhaps in two ways that are common to every human being: by transferring of guilt onto some other subject and by simulating the feelings of guilt. In the play, Macbeth emerges as a somewhat moral being by staging the doubt in the minds of the audience that the three Weird Sisters and his wife were responsible for his tragic downfall. Most readers consider that, but for the suggestion of the witches, his ambition would have died within. But for the resolved reinforcement of Lady Macbeth, Macbeth, the noble warrior, would never have dared to murder Duncan.

Just before his assassination by Macduff, Macbeth—on coming to know that Macduff was untimely ripped from his mother's womb—accuses the witches of betrayal, a crime that he himself has performed:

> And be these juggling friends no more believed,
> That palter with us in a double sense,
> That keep the word of promise to our ear
> And break it to our hope. (V.8.19-22)

Here Macbeth is instilling a suspicion in the reader's mind that he is being ruined because of the three Weird Sisters, who are powerful demonic forces that have absolute control over his deeds and destiny. Here the audience is being duped into the belief that the naïve, credulous, innocent Macbeth would never ever have done these terrible deeds but for the provocation of the three witches.

Macbeth also draws out the audience's sympathy by simulating conscience before the murder and remorse thereafter. For instance, soon after the three Weird Sisters vanish after making the prophecy, Macbeth speaks in an aside:

My thought, whose murder yet is but fantastical,
Shakes so my single state of man that function
Is smothered in surmise and nothing is
But what is not. (I.3.139-42)

Under closer scrutiny, the words at this point seem to carry a double sense. Is Macbeth referring to the murder of his dormant ambition or to the murder of Duncan? It is not fairly evident. Macbeth has still not met with his wife, and he is thinking of murder (perhaps Duncan's murder). In the lines that follow, he says, "If chance will have me king, why, chance may crown me / Without my stir" (I.3.143-4). Do not these lines suggest that Macbeth has already disposed himself to the deed that he would refuse to name till he has actually performed it? Soon after Duncan's proclamation that Malcolm would be the Prince of Cumberland, Macbeth speaks in another aside:

Stars, hide your fires;
Let not light see my black and deep desires.
The eye wink at the hand; yet let that be,
Which the eye fears, when it is done, to see. (I.4.50-53)

Are not these lines a confession of Macbeth's black and deep desires, his ambition to possess the crown of Scotland? If this be so, what the three witches spoke is nothing but the articulation of his own inner desires. Therefore the censure that Macbeth successfully transfers onto them is nothing but duplicity of his will. Further, does the expression "which the eye fears, when it is done, to see" allude to the unnameable deed of murdering Duncan? Remember, Macbeth has not met with Lady Macbeth so far. Therefore the assumption that "Macbeth would never have done this" but for the motivation and insinuation that he received from Lady Macbeth, seems to be going awry.

If this be so, what is Macbeth implying when he tells Lady Macbeth that "[w]e will proceed no further in this business" (I.7.31)? What should one infer from the wavering of his mind? Is Macbeth sincerely feeling pity at the prospect of murdering virtuous Duncan or is it a mere pretence of pity that Macbeth is showing to beguile his viewers? How shall we interpret the words that Macbeth utters after he has murdered Duncan?

> Methought I heard a voice cry "Sleep no more!
> Macbeth does murder sleep"—the innocent sleep,
> . . . . Macbeth shall sleep no more. (II.2.38-39, 46)

We could argue that these lines express Macbeth's guilty conscience. Writing about the psychology of conscience in his *Genealogy of Morals*, Nietzsche says that conscience is not "the voice of God in man" and "it is the instinct of cruelty that turns back after it can no longer discharge itself externally" (qtd. in Leiter and Sinhababu 138-39). Therefore, it may also be argued that the shilly-shallying Macbeth shows might be possibly an effect of what Nietzsche would call *bad conscience*.

Nietzsche has argued that "What man wants, what every smallest part of a living organism wants, is an increase of power. Pleasure or displeasure follow from the striving after that" (qtd. in Leiter and Sinhababu 141). Following this, it may be deduced that Macbeth's desire to become King of Scotland is a natural human instinct that drives him to murder. In this case, the bad conscience, which may also be called pangs of conscience or guilt-consciousness, is an outcome of his moralization. In fact, his attempts to moralize the murder by means of invoking his pricking conscience before the murder and his verbal expressions of remorse after the murder are spurious masks of morality that he (ab)uses to simulate the image of a moral being. It may also be argued that Macbeth always has a screen between his authentic/natural self and his audience: "False face must hide what the false heart doth know" (II.7.82).

Is the "bad conscience" or the "consciousness of guilt" a process of self-destructive internalization of authentic guilt? Are the feelings of guilt that Macbeth shows on his wrongdoing genuine? Feeling authentic guilt involves an inner suffering that one undergoes for an act that one believes one ought not to have done, an act ethically and morally reprehensible. It requires experiencing a mental pain. Further, it leads to the projection of the self as an ideal victim. Thus a guilty conscience emerges both as the perpetrator and the victim of cruelty that the subject has performed. In the play, Macbeth's orchestrating narrative of "feeling guilty" and "having a bad conscience" may perhaps be considered a part of his self-justificatory story wherein the morally good person is what he thinks himself to be, not what he in fact does. Macbeth's moralization of the murder by using "pangs of conscience" is the elevation of feeling guilty into a virtue, which makes the audience pardon him for the monstrous acts of cruelty. By simulating conscience, Macbeth is able to persuade his audience that he is meting out to himself "self-punishment of feeling guilty" which is enough to allow him to be considered a morally good individual, the kind of a person almost everyone else is.

The Nine *Rasas*

Over the past few years, while teaching *Macbeth* to undergraduates, I have often conducted an informal experiment. Before I start discussing my own and other available theoretical and philosophical points of view about the text, I ask students to write down adjectives that describe their feelings about Macbeth. There is almost always a consensus that Macbeth evokes admiration for his heroism, disgust for his crimes, and pity for being an innocent loser.

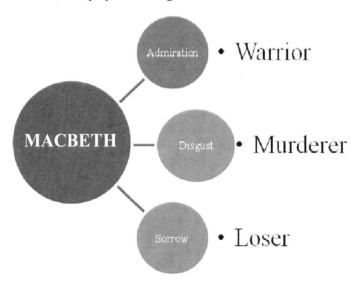

Figure 1. *Feelings Evoked by Macbeth's Disparate Actions.*

From this, I draw some general conclusions. First of all, in his final estimate, man—in this case Macbeth—is judged more by what he says than by what he does. Second, Macbeth evokes several conflicting *bhāva*s (emotions or states of mind) in the mind of the viewers. In view of the same, the question of dramatic effect of Macbeth upon the mind of the audience remains central in my classroom, which I mostly discuss with the help of *rasa* theory.

There is no exact equivalent for the Sanskrit word *rasa* in English. Etymologically, *rasa* refers to juice, or tasty liquid. In ancient Indian literature, it is referred to, variously, as the juice of a substance; in *Āyurveda*, as a chemical essence; in literature, as an experience of aesthetic enjoyment; in religion and spirituality, as transcendental bliss. Our concern here is limited to the meaning and usage of *rasa* in aesthetics, especially dramaturgy, where it has commonly been used to indicate the experience of delight born out of exposure to art (*kāvya*).

Bharata Muni's *Nāṭyaśāstra* is the most ancient treatise on *rasa* theory. Although the word *rasa* was in use before its exposition in *Nāṭyaśāstra*, Bharata Muni happens to be the first scholar who offered a comprehensive, elaborate and systematic account of *rasa* in *Nāṭyaśāstra*, which is an account of dramaturgy and its aesthetics. In this book, he has clearly written about the definition, nature, and constituents of *rasa*, their numbers, the processes/stages of the *rasa* experience. Therefore, *Nāṭyaśāstra* can be considered as a systematic and scientific enquiry into the nature of artistic experience from the points of view of the writer, the actor, and the audience. Defining *rasa*, Bharata Muni contends that *Vibhāvānubh āvvyabhicārisaṁyogāt rasaniṣpattiḥ*. Paraphrasing the verse, it can be argued *rasa* is produced/enacted/experienced when determinants (*vibhāva*), consequents (*anubhāva*), and transitory mental states (*vyabhīcāri bhāva*) combine to generate a more permanent mental state (*sthāyi bhāva*). In view of the same, it can be argued that *rasa* is the effect of synthesizing the amalgamation of various *bhāva*s. *Vibhāva*s (the determinants) are the root cause of *rasa* experience. They imply external stimuli that help emotional response to sprout within the subject. *Vibhāva*s are further divided into two kinds:

ālamban, the source stimuli, the first cause and prime mover of an emotional experience, and *uddīpana*, the excitant or aggravator stimuli. *Anubhāva*s (the consequents) are the externalized physical responses that follow *bhāva*s. In fact, the consequents manifest hidden and abstract emotions and reveal themselves through verbal and physical enactment of emotions. The consequents are theatrical elements and indicate performative, both oral and gestural, aspects of emotions. *Vyabhīcāri bhāva*s (the transitory mental states), thirty-three in number, are latent feelings that are fleeting in nature and get aroused in response to a stimulus. They designate conflicting impulses, psychological and physiological states of a human being. Although there is no mention of the word *sthāyi bhāva* (permanent mental state) in the verse, it is the final ingredient of the *rasa* experience. It is so called because it always remains latent within the experiencing subject (therefore permanent) and also coordinates conflicting psychological impulses and emotions to establish and maintain a state of equilibrium. In other words, *sthāyī bhāva*s are the realization and maturation of latent emotional states brought on by exposure to arts and literature and culminate in *rasa* experience—the pleasure of viewing art. These are nine in numbers: *rati* (love), *hāsa* (humour), *śoka* (sadness), *krodha* (anger), *bhaya* (fear), *utsāha* (courage), *jugupsa* (disgust), *vismaya* (wonder), *nirveda* (calmness). Consequently, the *sthāyi bhāva*s at the propitious moment are respectively realised into *nava-rasa*s (nine *rasa*s) namely, *Śṛiṁgāra* (the erotic), *Hāsya* (the humorous), *Karuṇa* (the tragic), *Raudra* (the furious), *Bhayānaka* (the fearful), *Vīra* (the heroic), *Bībhatsa* (the odious), *Adbhuta* (the wondrous), and *Śānta* (the peaceful) sentiments.

Another equally important consideration, is expressed through the word *niṣpattiḥ* in the foregoing verse, is the question of where the *rasa* that is being experienced lies. Bhaṭṭ Lollaṭṭa, a renowned commentator of *Nāṭyaśāstra*, argues that *rasa* is produced during the identification of the actor with the character on the stage. Thus he seems to be arguing that *rasa* lies in the character and actor both. Challenging Bhaṭṭ Lollaṭṭa's opinion, Śrī Śaṁkuka contends that *rasa* is not produced, but rather inferred. In his opinion, the audience identifies actors with real characters and infers pleasure in this identification. Thus *rasa* lies in the character being emulated, but realization of *rasa* is not possible without the use of inference on the part of the audience. Bhattnayak, refuting the arguments of both Bhaṭṭ Lollaṭṭa and Śaṁkuka, argues that *rasa* is neither produced nor inferred. Rather, it is experienced by the person reading or seeing a work of art. This experience of *rasa*, in his opinion, becomes possible through the process of *sādhārīkaraṇa*, the empathetic identification of the audience with the performer and the performance.

Figure 2. *Nava Rasa.*

From this perspective of *rasa* theory, *Macbeth* displays the presence of four very powerful *bhāva*s, courage, horror, disgust, and pity, corresponding to four *rasa*s: the heroic, the fearsome, the odious, and the tragic. The heroic sentiment, or *Vīra rasa*, is the *rasa* of fearlessness, heroism, valor, and sacrifice. When the play opens, Macbeth is reported to be displaying all of these heroic qualities. There is a rebellion, and Duncan is on the verge of defeat. However, Macbeth's bravery brings glory to his king and the country:

> For brave Macbeth—well he deserves that name—
> Disdaining Fortune, with his brandished steel,
> Which smoked with bloody execution,
> Like valor's minion carved out his passage
> Till he faced the slave;
> Which ne'er shook hands, nor bade farewell to him
> Till he unseamed him from the nave to th' chaps
> And fixed his head upon our battlements. (I.2.16-23)

The first impressions of Macbeth as a heroic figure are entrenched so deeply in the minds of the audience that they are unable to forget the valor that Macbeth exhibited in the war, and the loyalty to his king and his fatherland that he has shown by his readiness to sacrifice his life in the war. In this reported description of the war by a wounded captain, the determinant stimulus of heroic emotion is Macbeth himself. Rebel Macdonwald's treachery further stimulates this emotion. Duncan's spontaneous praise of Macbeth is the consequent. Feelings of enthusiasm, aggression, bravery, and pride are transitory mental states. The account of Macbeth's bravery is such that Duncan is spontaneously aroused to experience admiration for Macbeth's unrivaled gallantry, and the audience seems to share the same. Macbeth here incites the *Vīra rasa* in the reader/audience, exemplifying the life of honor, trust, faithfulness, and patriotism, and generating admiration and awe in the audience for his bravery, prowess, and perseverance.

It is also pertinent to outline here that *Indra*, the lord of Heaven, is considered to be the deity of the *Vīra rasa*. Interestingly, *Indra* is also the god of rain, thunder, and lightning, and this certainly reminds us of the opening lines of the play: "When shall we three meet again?/ In thunder, lightning, or in rain?" (I.1.1-2). Further, *Indra* is claimed to have killed a demon named *Vṛtra*, whose name alludes to the *vṛttis*, the fundamental psychological states of the human mind. True heroism is not only about the victory of self over the other by the power of the body, it also involves compassion to the other and self-control over the mind. And here Macbeth falters, falling into the trap of the evil witches' malicious designs. Macbeth is *Yuddh Vīra* (the hero of the war) but fails to become *Dharma Vīra* (the righteous hero)—it is relevant to mention here that Indian thought tradition speaks of four varieties of heroes, namely *Yuddha Vīra* (the hero of the war), *Dharma Vīra* (the righteous hero), *Dān Vīra* (the hero as the great benefactor), and *Dayā Vīra* (the compassionate hero). Thus Macbeth's heroism seems to be lacking in ethical righteousness and compassion. He may have overpowered his external opponents, but he has failed in disciplining his own inner adversaries, his *vṛttis*.

Secondly, Macbeth's nameless deeds are extremely terrifying and produce both horror and disgust in the audience. The first murder, of Duncan by Macbeth, generates *bhaya* (fear) from Macbeth and mercy for old Duncan:

> [T]his Duncan
> Hath borne his faculties so meek, hath been
> So clear in his great office, that his virtues
> Will plead like angels, trumpet-tongued against
> The deep damnation of his taking-off;
> And pity, like a naked newborn babe
> Striding the blast, or heaven's cherubin horsed
> Upon the sightless couriers of the air,
> Shall blow the horrid deed in every eye,
> That tears shall drown the wind. (I.7.16-25)

Macbeth himself claims to be moved by pity as he contemplates this murder he is about to do, which he calls the horrid deed in every eye. His forthcoming cruelty fills the audience's heart with fear. His next conspiracy and command to end life of Banquo and his son heighten our revulsion for Macbeth, whose wish to secure the crown is forcing him to grow ever more beastly. As his desire to become King of Scotland is fulfilled, so many other fears arise, especially the fear of losing the crown. The more powerful Macbeth becomes, the more fearful he grows, and with that the audience's illusory fears grow as well.

Soon the fearfulness in the audience is accompanied by the feelings of disgust for Macbeth. After coming to know that he must beware Macduff, Macbeth resolves

> From this moment,
> The very firstlings of my heart shall be
> The firstlings of my hand. And even now,
> To crown my thoughts with acts, be it thought and done.
> The castle of Macduff I will surprise,
> Seize upon Fife, give to th' edge o' th' sword
> His wife, his babes, and all unfortunate souls
> That trace him in his line. No boasting like a fool;
> This deed I'll do before this purpose cool.
> But no more sights. (IV.1.168-77)

Macbeth's fears now, triggered by the warning of the witches, force him to act instantly. His resolution to destroy not only Macduff but also his wife and children infuses terror tinged with disgust in the hearts of readers and audiences. In the scene that follows, in which Macduff's innocent son is having a childish conversation with his mother, we are appalled by the foreknowledge of the pitiless and brutal murder of that innocent child, who is unaware of Macbeth's savage design. On realizing how monstrous and beastly Macbeth is, we start feeling disgust at Macbeth who, blinded by his ambition, has dispensed with human morality. Thus, *jugupsa* also finds space because of the senseless, irrational murder of an innocent child, which produces the most undesirable and demonic *rasa* of *Bībhatsa*.

Despite the loss of Macbeth's primal innocence, obscuring his noble heroism, at the end of the play the audience experiences *śoka* (sadness and compassion) on the death of pitiless Macbeth. The soliloquy that he speaks on coming to know about the death of his wife makes us forget the horrors of his crime:

Tomorrow, and tomorrow, and tomorrow
Creeps in this petty pace from day to day
To the last syllable of recorded time,
And all our yesterdays have lighted fools
The way to dusty death. Out, out, brief candle,
Life's but a walking shadow, a poor player
That struts and frets his hour upon the stage
And then is heard no more. It is a tale
Told by an idiot, full of sound and fury,
Signifying nothing. (V.5.19-28)

How philosophical these words are that come out of a murderer's mouth (but that is forgotten by now). Poetry here overpowers reality. Rhetoric forces us to forget about justice. His sad declaration that everything is meaningless, nothing lasts, and the life that we live is nothing but *māyā* (illusion) shifts the audience's sympathies for Macbeth, and they begin searching for justifications to defend his crimes. Here, Macbeth becomes the determinant of sadness. The death of his wife and the impending in which he is about to lose his life turn excitant or aggravators. Macbeth's deep breaths, his sad existential pronouncement are consequents that manifest his inner sorrow. And the audience starts feeling attachment, even pain and so on, for Macbeth. This paves the way for the realization of *karuna rasa* (pity accompanied by compassion).

Thus we can contend that Macbeth marks the presence of four *rasas*, namely the *vīram*, *bhayanakam*, *bibhatsam* and *karunam*. However, the dominant *rasa* of the play is *vīram*, the heroic sentiment. Macbeth is shown as a warrior when the play starts and is shown dying as a warrior at the end. He refuses to run away or commit suicide. He prefers death by fighting like a noble warrior:

I will not yield,
To kiss the ground before young Malcolm's feet
And to be baited with the rabble's curse.
Though Birnam Wood be come to Dunsinane
And thou opposed, being of no woman born,
Yet I will try the last. Before my body
I throw my warlike shield. Lay on, Macduff[.] (5.8. 27-33)

Thus we see that Macbeth's story moves in the mind of the audience like the journey of person who evokes awe for his heroism but not without disgust, even terror, but tinged with pity.

Figure 3. Macbeth's *Rasa* Comes Full Circle.

Experiencing Witchcraft

For many young readers of *Macbeth* in an Indian classroom, the idea of witchcraft is perplexing, although not inconceivable. The question that lies before them is how to take the idea of witchcraft seriously even though they believe it to be untrue, superstitious, and unscientific. The two kinds of responses that one usually gets from the students can be categorized as either an *emic* (emerging from within the social group) or an *etic* (originating outside the group). The *emic* response in this case would be that the witches embody supernatural power, the agents of nemesis, which tempt Macbeth to his ruin. From this point of view, *Macbeth* seems to them a moral fable, a theological allegory, wherein the innocent Macbeth is duped by the wicked Weird Sisters who wield sinister satanic force toward his own tragic catastrophe. The *etic* response—wherein witchcraft is seen from the modern scientific perspective— is that that the three witches are external manifestation of Macbeth's inner, latent desire, giving expression to what Macbeth has always already wanted: the crown of Scotland .Thus, from the *emic* point of view, the three witches are real but supernatural; they exist, but ethereally. Their existence is objectively verifiable. From the *etic* point of view, they are (un)real, subjective hallucinations of Macbeth, airy externalizations of schizophrenic Macbeth's evil intent.

What these two perspectives lack is the New Historicist approach. In the debate whether the three witches in the play are real or not, the two approaches conceal the historical existence of women (occasionally men as well) branded as witches. The fiction of Shakespeare contains this veiled fact that there were witches and

Toad, that under cold stone
Days and nights has thirty-one
Sweltered venom sleeping got,
Boil thou first i' th' charmèd pot.
ALL: Double, double toil and trouble;
Fire burn and cauldron bubble.

SECOND WITCH: Fillet of a fenny snake,
In the cauldron boil and bake;
Eye of newt, and toe of frog,
Wool of bat, and tongue of dog,
Adder's fork, and blindworm's sting,
Lizard's leg, and owlet's wing—
For a charm of powerful trouble
Like a hellbroth boil and bubble.
ALL: Double, double toil and trouble,
Fire burn and cauldron bubble. (IV.1.4-21)

The song of the witches here noticeably reveals the secret information about the vessel, the ingredients, and the rituals performed during the witchcraft. Rituals are not only crucial here, but also properly formalized and systematic to elicit the profits of witchcraft. It is noticeable that the ingredients of the witchcraft are mostly body parts of animals—toad, snake, newt, bat, dog, lizard, owl, dragon, wolf, shark, goat, tiger, etc. —except the "liver of blaspheming Jew / ….Nose of Turk, and Tartar's lips" (IV.1.26,29).

Another interesting issue in the play is the witches' confession regarding the powers of witchcraft. Should this confession be considered as evidence that they were practicing real demonology? This question is key because the confession is made here without inquisition, without interrogation and torture. Through their confession, the Weird Sisters suggest that witchcraft is occult power.

The second part of Gaskill's definition of the witches is also very crucial to understanding the bewilderment of Banquo and Macbeth with regard to the witches. Gaskill writes that the witches are human, that they belong to society but are also unlike us. They represent the "other," embodying an alien culture of superstition, evil, and malevolence. In *Macbeth*, both Banquo and Macbeth are they were persecuted, and there were laws (Witchcraft 1563, 1604, 1735) that dealt with persons who claimed t power to call up spirits or foretell the future or who were harming other persons with the help of supernatural pow regard, Malcolm Gaskill writes:

> Between the 1480s and 1520s, Europeans were afflicted t crises which combined with fears about diabolic heresy an Apocalypse in deadly synergy. In these decades, witches in France, Italy, Spain, Germany, Switzerland, and the N A witch-hunt in the diocese of Como was particularly Dominican friar recorded that the Inquisition arrested 1,0 a year, executing one in ten. Early in the 16th century, a claimed to have acquired his powers in a land of fairies a triggered an investigation by the bishop of Trent, with t that he, like twenty other suspects, was burned at the stak

Thus the witches do not remain in a purely supernatura but rather also surface as a human phenomenon. So the qu arises is: What is witchcraft? Defining the practice of Malcolm Gaskill writes that it refers to "the practices or witches, especially the use of magic or sorcery; the supernatural power supposed to be possessed by a persor with the devil or evil spirits" (1). Writing about the w further states, "unlike monsters, they belong to society—a enemy within. They are 'other,' and yet they are also 'us are living projections of feelings that defy easy rationa reconciliation: amity and enmity, compassion and cru confidence and fear" (2).

This definition is crucial to understanding of the witches ir Because witchcraft is a practice, it must have had pra a specific methodology and laws of usage. In the play, witches are shown practicing sorcery. Here is a detailed d of their methodology:

> FIRST WITCH: Round about the cauldron go;
> In the poisoned entrails throw.

perturbed by the weird look of the witches. They try to discover whether the witches are "corporeal" or "ethereal" in nature. Banquo's anxiety is twofold. First, he is uncertain whether these creatures are real, because in his first impression he does not find them to be "th' inhabitants o' th' earth." Second, once he is partially convinced of their corporeality, he tries to position them in the category of gender. Should he call these creatures women because they look like women, or address them as men because they have beards:

> What are these,
> So withered and so wild in their attire
> That look not like th' inhabitants o' th' earth,
> And yet are on't? Live you, or are you aught
> That man may question? You seem to understand me,
> By each at once her choppy finger laying
> Upon her skinny lips. You should be women,
> And yet your beards forbid me to interpret
> That you are so. (I.3.39-47)

Banquo's description of the witches corresponds to popular stereotype of the witches in public imagination. The Elizabethan skeptic Reginald Scot has stated that "most people's idea of a witch was a woman who was 'old, lame, blear-eyed, pale, foul, and full of wrinkles,' usually a widow dependent on charity who 'waxeth odious and tedious to her neighbours'" (qtd. in Gaskill 33).

In *Macbeth,* this popular stereotype of the female witch, more specifically the malicious, spiteful, nasty crone, was thus powerfully reinforced by Shakespeare. Perhaps he was trying to engage with the complexities of witchcraft, which was usually attributed to women because they were identified as the "weaker vessel." Perhaps to challenge this popular stereotype, Akira Kurosawa in *Throne of Blood* and Vishal Bhardwaj in *Maqbool*—which are cinematic adaptations of Shakespeare's play in Japanese and Hindi respectively—perform a kind of gender-corrective surgery by assigning the witches' roles to males. Writing about the public perception of the witches and their supernatural powers, A. R. Braunmuller writes in his Introduction to the Cambridge UP edition of *Macbeth*:

English "witches" were typically old women without familial or communal support; their supposed "crimes" were practical and often economically destructive—causing a cow to stop giving milk or some other domestic beast to die, causing butter not to churn properly, crops to fail—or highly personal—causing a family member to die inexplicably, or a man to become sexually incapable, or a woman to be infertile. According to both popular belief and legal claims, accused witches contracted their souls to the devil in return for a familiar," usually a common animal such as a toad, cat, fly, or dog, which assisted her (only rarely "his") demonic designs. (30)

Corresponding to this popular belief, the three witches in the play are more than once addressed as old hags. Further, they themselves are shown confessing their occult powers. The conversation among then in which they discuss the plan of taking away a sailor's life can be cited as an evidence of confession:

> He shall live a man forbid.
> Weary sev' nights, nine times nine,
> Shall he dwindle, peak, and pine.
> Though his bark cannot be lost,
> Yet it shall be tempest-tossed. (I.3.21-25)

However, witchcraft is not merely a European historical problem of the medieval era. There have been instances of belief in witches in India as well, as witness the following instances of witch-hunting due to a death being attributed to witchcraft:

> Case I: On the night of August 7, 2016, and in the morning that followed, five women were tortured to death. Branded as witches, they were dragged out of their homes in the dead of the night, stripped and beaten, assembled before the tree and hacked with an axe which is used to chop wood.
> . . . .
> The death of a boy on August 2, he adds, had triggered murmurs in the village that it was the work of witches—something Karamdeo at that time had not paid much heed to. The 28-year-old farmer is still unable to understand the reason for the mindless violence against the

women. "We did not fight with anyone in the village. Why did they do this to us?" he says.

Case II: On December 9 [2016], a similar rerun took place more than 150 km away. An elderly woman, Susari Buru, was put on fire by her neighbour Anita Somasoe in Mander area of Khunti district. The accused believed that Susari indulged in witchcraft and blamed her for the death of her twin daughters. (Singh)

If this newspaper report is to be believed, "the Rajya Sabha was informed in June this year that 127 women branded as witches were killed in Jharkhand between 2012 and 2014. And as per police records, there have been 98 deaths and 1,857 incidents of witch-hunt from 2014 to June 2016 in the State" (Singh). It is pertinent to mention here that there is a law in place titled *Jharkhand's Witchcraft Prevention Act, 2001*, which has been very effective in curbing the menace of witch-hunting.

The purpose of using such recent instances of witch-belief in a classroom is to make the students aware that witchcraft is a social evil rooted in superstition. And Shakespeare's *Macbeth* facilitates such discussion by staging witchcraft as real and demonstrable, arousing incredulity and skepticism toward it, thereby questioning the popular Elizabethan belief.

What you have read in this chapter is a somewhat disjointed reflection on the complex response that the play evokes. However, the reader can imagine some kind of unity because these reflections are part of Macbeth's experience. Perhaps Shakespeare was not intending to create a hero when he wrote *Macbeth*. His tragedy was not meant to foster hero worship but sought to bring the virtues and the vices of a powerful man to the fore so that the audience could understand the human fact that the uncontrolled pursuit of power can convert an innocent man into an evil one. Perhaps through Macbeth he wanted to stage a reluctant villain whose will to self-destructive power, amidst awareness of the transience of human life, conflicts with the will to goodness. In *Macbeth*, Shakespeare is diving deep into the dark labyrinthine lanes of the human soul with a view to humanizing a frightening criminal. This is perhaps the reason that Shakespeare's hero, at times, seems to be a witch who speaks ambiguous philosophical rhetoric to justify his criminality. However, I don't have any final word on Macbeth. How you yourself experience (*rasa*) a witch, his wife, and the other three witches in the play, I leave to you and your readings.

Works Cited

Bharata Muni. *Nāṭyaśaṣtra of Bharat Muni*. Chaukhambha, 1978.

Braunmuller, A. R. "Introduction." *Macbeth* by William Shakespeare. Cambridge UP, 1997.

Gaskill, Malcolm. *Witchcraft: A Very Short Introduction*. Oxford UP, 2010.

Leiter, Brian, and Neil Sinhababu. *Nietzsche and Morality*. Oxford UP, 2007.

Singh, Shiv Sahay. "The 'Witches' of Jharkhand." *The Hindu*, Dec. 27, 2016, www.thehindu.com/news/national/The-%E2%80%98witches%E2%80%99-of-Jharkhand/article16933528. ece. Accessed June 26, 2017.

Shakespeare, William, *Macbeth*. Edited by Stephen Orgel. Penguin, 2016.

Living with Macbeth: Circles of Tragedy_____

Daniel Bender

Linear Time versus Circular Time

Is Macbeth a scarier play now than it was when first staged? Its theatrical action—staged in 1605—has not stayed put in a comfortably remote past. On the contrary, Macbeth's rapid sequence of political and interpersonal violence, one feeding the other, continues to play out in the modern world. Violence accelerates because its localized forms—street fight, political rivalry between two people—gains members from outside of locality, spreading violence from a locality to a national scale. In this process the initial triggering process is no longer contained in a past, separate from the present or future. As more members of antagonized groups join, the conflict spreads over time, so that yesterday's conflict is replaced by today's; the bitterness of that conflict fuels future conflict, creating a warped, unnatural, frozen chronology where tomorrows are repetitions of the present. In our late-modern epoch, with group membership able to take on global dimensions, the distant moors and castles of Scotland seem safely contained. So does the tragedy: Macbeth is a tragic figure from a Shakespearean play, and the drama of his violence is 400-plus years old, safely removed from our time and place. Or is it? If we take as premise that Macbeth stages exponential violence—the first act of violence leading to another, followed by another—we need to consider, as this chapter does, that the dramatic principle of the tragedy is transhistorical, that our own times can be subject to what I will call the Macbeth effect. Violence, reciprocated many times over, grows into catastrophe.

Macbeth has always made a claim to jump across time: tomorrow's unfolding was predicted in yesterday's prophecy, carried out the next night, and repeated into indefinite tomorrows. The idea that the past is a weary repetition of the present makes Macbeth famously joyless: "Tomorrow and tomorrow and tomorrow creeps in this petty pace from day to day" (V.5.19-20). *Macbeth* rejects calendar time, and gives instead something we sense uncomfortably at times in our own lives: the reappearance of the past in the present, as if the present had vanished, the past standing in as a witchy surrogate.

Macbeth establishes the circularity of time in its opening stage direction: "Thunder and lightning. Enter three Witches." We might think that Shakespeare's call for thunder and lightning is merely appropriate: a creepy atmosphere is right for the Three Sisters' stage entrance. But thunder and lightning is periodic, sure to happen again when heat, humidity, and ambient electricity converge. This circular sense of time applies with stunning effect in the catastrophic violence that is *Macbeth*. In Act I we learn that there was a civil war where men emerged from battle smoking in hot blood, but we soon discover that this past event is not past: violence with swords and daggers moves into the present, expanding in a widening circle across Scotland, replacing each present day with a page from the past.

This is not the whole basis of *Macbeth*'s tragic terror. The exponential, snowball effect of violence in *Macbeth* is eerily familiar. Although Scottish castles and sword-bearing warriors give the play an historically remote, even archaic feel, a new methodology in literary study known as presentism has urged readers to allow their personal beliefs and current preoccupations to enter into readings of a text. Presentism does not mean that the historical integrity of the work of art is something to disregard; rather, presentism urges us to treat the work of art as a delicate negotiation of the past and the present. The work of art carries deep historical significance for its original audience, but this does not mean that current study of a work of art can or should be understood as independent from our concerns, interests, and values in the present. As Hugh Grady and Terence Hawkes explain, students of literature quietly bring their own perspective to bear on a text produced in ages long gone:

> The truth is that none of us can step beyond time. The present can't be drained out of our experience. As a result, the critic's own "situatedness" does not—cannot—contaminate the past. In effect, it constitutes the only means by which it is possible to see and perhaps

comprehend it. And since we can only see the past through the eyes of the present, few serious historians would deny that the one has a major influence on their account of the other. Of course we should read Shakespeare historically. But given that what we term history develops out of a never-ending dialogue between past and present, how can we decide whose historical circumstances will have priority, Shakespeare's or our own? (Grady and Hawkes 3)

That we construct the past in light of present mentalities is one tenet of presentism. This chapter, however, draws on a presentist way of reading in response to the tragic dynamic specific to Macbeth. For the multiplying, radiating violence in Macbeth—from battlefield to moors to castle to homes across Scotland—offers us a way of understanding tragic experience in the recently expired twentieth-century America, where violence works by Macbeth principles of imitation and repetition. If we examine major domestic and international conflicts, we find that a first violent event—the initiating one—produces a surging set of violent acts, each imitating or at least echoing the violence of the initiating event. In the presentist reading I offer here, Macbeth is a diagnostic tool for understanding catastrophic violence not in medieval Scotland, but within civilian society of the United States and in the international conflicts that tore through the twentieth century.

As a first illustration that *Macbeth*'s law of exponential violence operates in the real world of international relations, I turn to United States history and two major wars overseas to suggest the extension of Shakespeare's play into modern cultural conditions. A reasonable person would assume that the military munitions expended in a world war would far exceed the munitions expended in a war contained to a small geopolitical zone; we would assume, in other words, that the United States military had dropped many more bombs in World War II, since the various theaters of war—Europe, the Pacific Islands, and Japan—represented a vast terrain of conflict. Yet study of bombing tonnage that juxtaposes World War II tonnage to tonnage dropped in Southeast Asia during the Vietnam War reveals our commonsense surmise to be incorrect:

By the time the United States ended its Southeast Asian bombing campaigns, the total tonnage of ordnance dropped approximately tripled the totals for World War II. The Indochinese bombings amounted to 7,662,000 tons of explosives, compared to 2,150,000 tons in World War II." (Clodfelter 225)

These unlikely-looking statistics become more plausible if we consider the multiplying effect of military violence set forth in Shakespeare's tragedy. Macbeth returns from the bloody field of civil war where he has defeated the traitorous leader of the rebel leader, Macdonwald, and displayed Macdonwald's severed head on a pike. The King of Scotland, grateful and relieved, promises that Macbeth will see his political career advance, that he will be rewarded for his services: "I have begun to plant thee/And will labor to make thee full of growing" (I.4.28-9). The king's commendation renders the battlefield violence not only acceptable but laudatory: if Macbeth repeats such violence he will again experience—though in a warped, no longer appropriate way—the feelings of personal triumph and valor that had gained him the warm praise of a king. By the same principle of positive violence, the victory of World War II—always associated with a moral victory over evil—becomes the initiating event, since military victory could be experienced again in a military campaign against the Viet Cong. That the bombings did not have the intended effect is not the immediately relevant point. The desire to repeat one's successes is a powerful but sometimes tragic motive, because the past performance, duplicated in the present, lacks the moral context in which victory can be called that.

My discussion of saturation bombing in Vietnam is meant to suggest that the theatrical violence staged in Macbeth carries a transhistorical, structural principal of conflict: military conflict in modern times works from an initial positive kind of violence to become more drastic, intensive, and thus tragic.

We can see Macbeth's rise from theatrical event to explanatory model of intensified violence in the twentieth century by examining sites of civilian violence during the Vietnam war. In various cities and university campuses across America, groups protested US military actions in Vietnam; In protesting, blocking the streets, closing stores, stopping the normal sequence of business as usual, the protestors formed into a kind of civilian militia, picking up the militancy first seen in military campaigns abroad. In some cases, frustrated by their government's refusal to leave the Southeast Asian country alone, protestors started fires, shattered windows, walked out of classes, boycotted companies that contributed to the war effort. The war, as they say, had come home.

How is that outcome a presentist epiphany of the *Macbeth* effect? Aristotle was the first to note that humans are "the most imitative creatures in the world" (*Poetics* Book 4). According to a latter-day version of Aristotle's theory of imitation known as *social learning*, individuals and groups are emboldened to act when they see others performing a roughly similar action and wish to bring this action into their repertoire of actions (Bandura 580; Whiten 2417-2428). They observe a model accomplishing something, recognize that the accomplishment can be reproduced in the present, and then devise their own method to attain the imitated goal (Bandura 580-582). The imitator learns how to tie a shoelace or how to distinguish a good candidate for office from a bad or—moving into the realm of tragedy—how to defeat an enemy.

Social learning helps to understand *Macbeth*'s reign of terror and the violent protests that turned Vietnam-era America into a war zone as events that share a common time scheme: the present. Both episodes of violence are initiated by legitimate, organized, openly avowed forms of violence. King Duncan declares that a Scottish thane, Macdonwald, is the enemy, though we never hear from Macdonwald or hear his reasons for starting a civil war. The United States declared the North Vietnamese desire to have political control of South Vietnam to be an act of aggression. Just as Macbeth begins a reign of violence after seeing socially accredited violence on the battlefield, so too bombing campaigns such as "Operation Rolling Thunder" (1965) triggered expanding circles of learned violence.

Waves of civilian unrest followed. Church bombings occurred in Birmingham, Alabama, racial riots roiling the land from Baltimore to Detroit to Los Angeles; young black men in Oakland, California, traded civilian clothes for the militant uniforms of the

Black Panthers For Self-Defense. Water cannons dispersed antiwar protesters in the streets of Washington DC and outside the 1968 Democratic National Convention in Chicago. Radiating circles of unrest widened. Women's rights marches were greeted with scorn and mockery. Martin Luther King, Jr., the outspoken advocate of peace and critic of the Vietnam war, was assassinated in April 1968—the year of the Tet Offensive against American military offensives. Presidential candidate Robert Kennedy was gunned down in a hotel kitchen in November 1968. The imitation-induced violence spelled out in Macbeth's duplication of battlefield violence in civilian life was replayed on the stage of American domestic life. The repetition of a chaos proposed here is already operating in the repetitions of natural turmoil that Shakespeare builds into his play. The opening stage direction of Act I, Scene 1—"thunder and lightning"—is heard again in Act IV, Scene 1: "Thunder. Enter the Three Witches." War in our own times or as depicted in Shakespearean tragedy has yet another feature, connecting the historically distant tragedy to tragic potentialities in our own time and place.

War: The Present as Past, the Past as Present

War produces a special kind of person, calling for our admiration and offering us comfort and reassurance: the war hero. A war hero is decorated, held up for the adulation and careful observation of the citizens of the warring country. We do not say, "That person killed." We say, "That person defended her or his country." This means that war takes part in the dynamics of social learning and its imitative sequence: one sees the soldier, the admiring looks and public praise, and imagines oneself assuming that role too. The learner understandably wants to duplicate the role of soldier that is so honored. Macbeth has returned from a civil war where his "brandished steel" has left many Scots bleeding and rebel leader Macdonwald sliced open "from the nave to th' chaps" (I.2.17, 22). Yet Macbeth's day of glory on the battlefield takes us from Shakespearean play to disturbing clinical diagnosis of battlefield trauma. The same sequence of valor and psychological distress after the event shows up in a psychiatric diagnosis of posttraumatic stress disorder (Jaech 292).

Although Shakespeare did not have the term for post-combat mental disturbance that we have, his tragic figure's symptoms closely resemble those identified by medical and psychiatric science. The Veterans Administration website on PTSD symptoms names major disturbances: a person returning from a war zone may have nightmares : "You may have a hard time sleeping" (US Department of Veterans Affairs). In an uncanny echo of Shakespearean military hero turned into a creature of disturbed psychological function, Macbeth confesses his own symptoms: "Methought I heard a voice cry, 'Sleep no more! / Macbeth does murder sleep'" (II.2.38-9). Macbeth also experiences the Veteran Administration symptom of a trigger: "Whence is that knocking? / How is't with me when every noise appalls me?" (II.2.60-1). The knocking at a medieval gate has the same present time effect as a truck engine: backfiring, the noise jolts a sleeping army veteran into agitated wakefulness. A further transhistorical parallel between and the current reality of PTSD forms an ironic comment, almost a choric refrain on Macbeth's descent into tragic emulation of his battlefield: "You may not have positive or loving feelings toward other people and may stay away from relationships" (US Department of Veterans Affairs). A final parallel between PTSD and Macbeth's deterioration will help us to recognize Macbeth's transhistorical emergence into the present. "You may think the world is completely dangerous, and no one can be trusted" (US Department of Veterans Affairs). Macbeth does more than think the world is dangerous; he hires spies in every noble household, perceiving compatriots to be enemies.

Double Trouble: War in the Streets

The catastrophic violence of Shakespeare's *Macbeth* can reach into the most ordinary of domestic spheres and into the twenty-first century. An initial tragic event on the streets of a quiet city reproduces a cascade of reciprocating violence. "[B]lood will have blood" (III.4.124)—Macbeth's calm description of how reprisal works—also describes recent turmoil in Ferguson, Missouri. After the controversial shooting death of Michael Brown in 2014, the local police department materialized in media coverage as a paramilitary organization. Heavy armored vehicles—vaguely familiar as war matériel seen in Iraq—were deployed on the streets of Ferguson. As in the terrible assassination of the king in Act I of *Macbeth*, where members of the nobility must take refuge from the unknown assassin in their midst, the citizens of St. Louis group together in a defensive formation, a reactive citizen army, alarmed by an event that seemed to threaten them as the next in line.

A similar infusion of war zone behavior into civilian codes of behavior is traceable in the tragic events of Orlando, Florida. A resident of Orlando, sympathetic to the cause of Muslims but also suffering disturbances of his own, opened fire in a nightclub and killed fifty people. While the motives of the gunman cannot be known with certainty, what is clear is that an anarchic desire to inflict pain indiscriminately and in large numbers moved the shooter on the night of the massacre (NY Times). In his cold indifference to the question of who should be treated as an enemy and who should be spared as an innocent, Omar Mateen reiterated the tragic lack of deliberation and sense of responsibility that Macbeth shows in his indiscriminate violence: "this my hand will rather / The multitudinous seas incarnadine, / Making the green one red" (II.2.64-6).

Women and Violence, Then and Now

Although the tragedy of *Macbeth* is focused on masculinist violence, cross-gender violence is woven into the play, so that Lady Macbeth, relegated to the role of lady of the castle and staid organizer of domestic matters, appears as an embittered woman, left at home. The segregation of women into domestic work is a long-running conflict—a cold war of the sexes—in our society. But this war of men against women has its own renaissance in Shakespeare-era advocates and theorists of chauvinism. As the cultural historian and feminist Hanna Fenichel Pitkin argues, a major political theorist during the Renaissance age, Niccolò Machiavelli, did not want male supremacy to be merely accepted or reaffirmed. He wanted to give male superiority a boost. For Machiavelli, the world of politics is for men whose virility (Latin *vir* refers to man*)* makes them the rightful participants in games of thrones. Women are linked to the Goddess Fortuna, and men were symbolized, in spiteful intent, as women: a man may be successful and hard-working, but Fortune will throw him down, for no apparent reason. Woman cannot take part in politics, according to Machiavelli. "Women are dumb, fearful, indecisive, and dependent," according to Pitkin's reading of Machiavelli. Pitkin finds hostility in Machiavelli's view of women to be a consistently held view: women are "childishly naïve" and "easily manipulated" (Pitkin 110).

What was life like for Lady Macbeth in her youth? Machiavelli gives us solid grounds for speculation. The experience of seeing men as doers and women as passive subjects has inflicted its own kind of posttraumatic stress disorder on Lady Macbeth, whose distrustful, embattled, hostile state of mind parallels that of her husband. While the shocking violence of war is the decisive experience of Macbeth, a parallel universe of shocking violence has engulfed Lady Macbeth. She has observed men training for greatness with axes, swords, spiked flails. She has witnessed the failure of negotiation, perhaps a pseudomasculinist refusal to even consider negotiation. She has seen Duncan arrive at her home, cheerful, able to detach from the extreme violence without the slightest self-scrutiny. As an elite member of the Scottish nobility, Lady Macbeth may have had social contact with treacherous Macdonwald, leader of the opposition. Might Macdonwald have had a legitimate grievance in young Lady Macbeth's eyes? She could not risk saying so.

Lady Macbeth is not a 1950s housewife of immaculate dress and perfect hairdo but she is expected to be an attentive hostess in her castle. "Your majesty loads our house. For those of old, / and the late dignities heap's up to them, / we rest your hermits" (I.6.19 21). She seems to chafe at her role. Hermits were assigned to accompany the king and his entourage and pray for their health—especially after periods of military violence and postwar executions. Assuming this humble role as a prayerful subordinate, she assures Duncan that she and her husband will "rest your hermits." But the extreme deference raises our doubts about women's role as providers of hospitality, removed from the political discourse that is reserved for elite Scottish males. As a recent analysis of hospitality in *Macbeth* has suggested, the act of providing home comforts to a man who has overseen large-scale battlefield violence and is now in need of dinner may be more than Lady Macbeth can stomach (Lupton 372-73).

The idea that women in *Macbeth*'s Scotland chafe beneath their social subordination and long for the autonomy accorded to men gains support in the famous soliloquy where Lady Macbeth renounces her gender:

> The raven himself is hoarse
> That croaks the fatal entrance of Duncan
> Under my battlements. Come, you spirits
> That tend on moral thoughts, unsex me here
> And fill me from the crown to the toe topfull
> Of direst cruelty. Make thick my blood;
> Stop up the th'access and passage to remorse,
> That no compunctious visiting of nature
> Shake my fell purpose nor keep peace between
> Th' effect and it. (I.5.37-46)

In a society that values military victory as the highest form of achievement, Lady Macbeth has clearly been left out. Her social subordination is a form of oppression.

Lady Macbeth's rejection of a submissive gender role reappears in twentieth-century America, though in a fortunately civil variation. In 1964, with war policies in Vietnam gaining strength and male generals holding the public stage as grand strategists, Bette Friedan wrote *The Feminine Mystique*, a text that rained thunder and lightning on male supremacy. Friedan proposes that women no longer be hermits or cheerleaders, praying or cheering for male well-being. She hoped to see women as participants in business and politics and decision-making—an arrangement that would open the gate of social importance and significance. Though Friedan would be resented for overturning conventional thinking, she points out the passivity and dependency that men have tried to identify as women's rightful role. "Anatomy is woman's destiny, say the theorists of femininity; the identity of woman is determined by her biology" (10). Friedan goes on to argue that the problem is women needing to mature and find their human identity. The following passage reveals a latter-day circle of gender violence emanating from Lady Macbeth's soliloquy:

> The problem that has no name –which is simply the fact that American women are kept from growing to their full human capacities—is taking a far greater toll on the physical and mental health of our country than any known disease. Consider the high incidence of emotional breakdown in the "role crises" of their twenties and thirties, the alcoholism and suicides in their forties and fifties; the housewives' monopolization of all doctors' time. Consider the prevalence of teenage marriages, the growing rate of illegitimate pregnancies and even more seriously, the pathology of mother-child symbiosis. Consider the alarming passivity of American teenagers. It will continue to produce millions of young mothers who stop their growth and education short of identity, without a strong core of human values to pass on to their children. We are committing, quite simply, genocide, starting with the mass burial of American women and ending with the progressive dehumanization of their sons and daughters." (495)

Friedan's pioneering work on new identities for women does not call for assassination, nor does she ask malign spirits to "unsex me here," but the violence of gendered domination would, starting in the 1960s, be the cause for widespread resistance, resentment, refusal to accept the standard of male privilege. The female character in *Macbeth* chooses violence to replace "the man"—the figure of male authority associated with brutal conflict followed by smiling sociability. The feminist movement is a continuation by nonviolent means of Lady Macbeth's gender-motivated resistance. Marches and rallies—necessary to move masculine society toward respect for gender equality—are the latter-day embodiments of Lady Macbeth's tragic style of resistance (Hampton 327-29).

The Weird Sisters: Double Talk and Psychological Operations

The exclusion of women from the consultations of men, and the consequent withdrawal from men is highlighted in the character of the weird sisters. Despite the fact that they hover in the marshy margins of the Scottish landscape, they are attuned to the inevitability of violence; they take pleasure in imagining its future manifestations and enticing Macbeth to choose violence over peace. The sisters of fate are not physically violent; they choose a method of enticement that leads men to make destructive choices. Macbeth does not have to be worried about being killed, since "no man of woman born" excluded women; outcasts, they exist as a sinister government of witches, able to bring down kings, set up new ones, and then see the cycle repeated when, in Act V, Malcolm, son of Duncan, is hailed as king with the newly decapitated body of Macbeth nearby. The witches use the sword of suggestion and seduction: "Macbeth shall never vanquished be until / Great Birnam Wood to high Dunsinane Hill / Shall come against him" (IV.1.114-16). Or he will never be killed by "man of woman born," though the Weird Sisters (derived from *wyrd,* archaic term for fate), aka the witches, withhold the crucial detail that Macduff, having been born by Cesarean birth, is technically not born in the natural way.

The verbal and psychological violence of the witches continues into our present: powerful modern governments have agents of psychological warfare. Like the sinister predictions of the witches, disinformation and false guidance is fostered by nations having a foreign intelligence arm. The conventional and long-standing name for this form of mind-gaming is PsyOps (Psychological Operations). PsyOps use "grey" and "black" information to cause the enemy to be paralyzed by fear, to feel guilty about personally held values and beliefs, or to lose confidence in the outcome of a conflict and give up. *Grey information* is misinformation that may or may not be from the enemy government (Melton 25-30). It is intended to create discontent with the existing government, especially governments that, in the eyes of the foreign intelligence service, bear an independent outlook or are friendly with rival nations. *Black misinformation* is deliberate deception that creates an image of credible reality, and allows a government to engage in extreme violence on the "strength" of their fabricated international incident. In studies of the notorious event that led to a declaration of war, scholars have found evidence that contradicts the official narrative that North Vietnamese boats fired on a US ship. A 1996 study reviewed radio transmissions on the night of the alleged incident and casts serious doubt that such an attack occurred. (Moise 145-6, 207)

Even the most neutral description of the world's secretive intelligence agencies brings up remembrances of the Weird Sisters' methods. Government agents seeking to destabilize another government can also disrupt, confuse, and delay the adversary's decision-making process, using such covert means as sunspots to disrupt radio transmissions and stories of antigovernment plots. The witches' friendly greeting "Banquo and Macbeth, all hail" (I.3.69) is the opening gambit in their psychological operations. By praising two war veterans as equal heroes and then predicting that one will outshine the other, they create the ground for Macbeth's vicious assassination plans. The witches are medieval epicenters of a misinformation campaign that will develop into the modern techniques of state-sponsored deception of violence. This political form of violence spreads across centuries; the techniques of espionage and dirty tricks change, the motives remain constant. Recall, for example, the widespread allegation of deceitfulness in the Bush administration's explanation for renewing the war in Iraq. Uranium could be used to create weapons of mass destruction, the public was warned; on March 19, 2003, President Bush explained to the American public that Iraq possessed such weapons. Despite feverish attempts to find WMD, none were ever found. (Stein and Dickinson)

Conclusion

This essay has identified tragic structures in twentieth-century and twenty-first-century societies that are traceable to the dynamics of tragic experience in *Macbeth*. The thesis does not produce a feeling of well-being and certainly entitles the reader to ask: If multiplying circles of tragedy are a continuous feature of human societies, what hope does an individual have to avoid being encircled by a post-modern state rife with violence? (Lowrance 825-7).

Literature is said to be a powerful source of learning; we see the compulsion of the tragic hero, Macbeth, and understand that he might have acted differently. The concept of involuntary action is the ethical principle underlying all tragic actions. Is there a way for individuals to avoid the circle of tragedy? One answer might be found when we turn to a very distant past, ancient Greece, and an ancient philosopher, Aristotle. In his *Nichomachean Ethics*, Aristotle meditated on the causes of poor choice: anger, appetite, ambition. These are instinctive drives that cause us to act suddenly, without deliberation. But the ability to deliberate on the means to achieve our goals, Aristotle tells us, is a saving power we hold within us. Macbeth could have found a constructive way to realize his desire to power; the king had promised to "plant" him and let him "grow." In deliberation, Aristotle tells us, we might foresee the consequences of bad choices and then deliberate about civil means to achieve our goals.

Works Cited or Consulted

'Always Agitated. Always Mad': Omar Mateen, According to Those Who Knew Him By Dan Barry, Serge F. Kovaleski, Alan Blinder and Musib Mashal, June 18, 2016. https://www.nytimes.com/2016/06/19/us/omar-mateen-gunman-orlando-shooting. Accessed October 18, 2017.

Aristotle. *Poetics.* http://classics.mit.edu/Aristotle/poetics.1.1.html. Accessed June 21, 2017.

_____. *Nichomachean Ethics.* http://classics.mit.edu/Aristotle/nicomachaen.html. Accessed June 21, 2017.

Bandura A, Ross D, Ross S. Transmission of aggression through imitation of aggressive models. The Journal Of Abnormal And Social Psychology [serial online]. November 1961;63(3): 575-582. Available from: PsycARTICLES, Ipswich, MA. Accessed October 19, 2017.

Clodfelter, Michael. *Vietnam in Military Statistics : A History of the Indochina Wars, 1772-1991.* McFarland, 1995.

Friedan, Betty. *The Feminine* Mystique. 1963. Norton, 2013.

Grady, Hugh, and Terence Hawkes. *Presentist Shakespeares*. Routledge, 2007.

Hampton, Bryan Adams. "Purgation, Exorcism, and the Civilizing Process in *Macbeth*." *SEL: Studies in English Literature 1500-1900*, vol. 51, no. 2, 2011, pp. 327-47.

Jaech, Sharon L. Jansen. "Political Prophecy and Macbeth's 'Sweet Bodements.'" *Shakespeare Quarterly*, vol. 34, no. 3, 1983, p. 290.

Lowrance, Bryan. "'Modern Ecstasy': *Macbeth* and the meaning of the political." *ELH*, vol. 79, no. 4, 2012, pp. 823-49.

Lupton, Julia Reinhard. "Macbeth's Martlets: Shakespearean Phenomenologies of Hospitality." *Criticism*, vol. 54, no. 3, 2012, pp. 365-76.

Melton, H. Keith and Robert Wallace. *The Official CIA Manual of Trickery and Deception*. Harper Paperback, 2010.

Moise, Edwin E. *Tonkin Gulf and the Escalation of the Vietnam War*. U of North Carolina P, 1996.

Pitkin, Hanna Fenichel. *Fortune Is a Woman: Gender and Politics in the Thought of Niccolò Machiavelli*. U of Chicago P, 1999.

"Psychological Operations." https://en.wikipedia.org/wiki/Psychological_ Operations_(United_States). Accessed June 21, 2017.

"Psychological warfare (United States)." *Wikipedia*. Apr. 13, 2017. https:// en.wikipedia.org/wiki/Psychological_warfare. Accessed June 21, 2017.

Shakespeare, William. *Macbeth*. Edited by Stephen Orgel, Penguin, 2016.

Stein, Jonathan, and Timothy Dickinson. "Lie by Lie: A Timeline of How We Got Into Iraq." *Mother Jones*, 2006. www.motherjones.com/ politics/2011/12/leadup-iraq-war-timeline. Accessed June 21, 2017.

U. S. Department of Veterans Affairs. www.ptsd.va.gov/public/family/ ptsd-and relationships.asp. Accessed June 21, 2017.

Whiten, A., et al. "Emulation, imitation, over-imitation and the scope of culture for child and chimpanzee." *Philosophical Transactions of the Royal Society B: Biological Sciences*, vol. 364, no. 1528, 2009, pp. 2417-28.

RESOURCES

1564	William Shakespeare born to John and Mary Arden Shakespeare in Stratford- upon-Avon. While no record exists to give the precise date, tradition celebrates his birthday on April 23, three days before his baptism at Holy Trinity Church. Shakespeare's fellow playwright Christopher Marlowe is also born this year, roughly two months earlier.
1566	James Stuart, later to be James I of England and James VI of Scotland, is born to Mary Stuart, known as Mary Queen of Scots.
c. 1569	Shakespeare almost certainly educated at the King's New School in Stratford, along with the other children of prominent local citizens such as his father.
1572	Poet John Donne and poet/playwright Ben Jonson born.
1577	Raphael Holinshed publishes his *Chronicles of England, Scotland, and Ireland.*
1580	Sir Francis Drake returns triumphantly from his circumnavigation of the globe.
1582	Wedding license issued on November 28 for the union of Shakespeare, age 18, and Anne Hathaway, age 26.
1583	On May 26, six months after their marriage, Anne and William christen their first child, Susanna.
1584	Sir Walter Raleigh establishes the colony of Roanoke in Virginia.

1585	On February 2, twins Judith and Hamnet are baptized.
1586	The Babington Plot, which attempted to install Mary Queen of Scots on the English throne in the place of Elizabeth I, is thwarted.
1587	Mary Queen of Scots executed on February 8.
1588	The Spanish Armada threatens to invade England, but is defeated on August 8.
1589-90	Estimated date of Shakespeare's arrival in London and commencement of work as an actor and playwright.
1592	Shakespeare attacked as an "upstart crow" by Robert Greene, who despised what he saw as the pretension of a young man with no university education attempting to write plays.
1593	London theaters closed in January on account of the bubonic plague. Shakespeare turns to poetry, dedicating his first published work, the mythological narrative poem *Venus and Adonis*, to his patron Henry Wriothesley, Earl of Southampton. Christopher Marlowe slain outside a tavern in Deptford.
1594	The theaters reopened following the cessation of the plague, and Shakespeare sees the publication of his second major poem, *The Rape of Lucrece*, and his first printed play, *Titus Andronicus*.
1595	Shakespeare becomes a sharer in the theater company known as the Lord Chamberlain's Men, for whom he acts and writes plays exclusively from this time on.

1596	Shakespeare's only son, Hamnet, dies. The cause is not known to history.
1597	Shakespeare uses the proceeds from his share in the Lord Chamberlain's Men to purchase New Home, the second-largest house in his birthplace of Stratford-upon-Avon.
1598	Francis Meres publishes *Palladis Tamia*, a volume of literary criticism in which he praises Shakespeare highly for his eloquence, love poetry, tragedies, and comedies, listing both of his major poems as well as his as-yet-unpublished sonnets and a dozen of his plays.
1599	The Lord Chamberlain's Men build the Globe Theatre.
1601	The Earl of Essex attempts a rebellion against the Queen, but fails and is beheaded. Shakespeare's father dies.
1603	Queen Elizabeth I dies, and James VI of Scotland ascends the throne as James I. James elevates Shakespeare's company to royal favor, and the Lord Chamblerlain's Men become the King's Men. The first edition of *Hamlet* is published.
1605	The Gunpowder Plot, an attempt by Guy Fawkes and other Catholics to assassinate the Protestant king, fails. Shakespeare alludes to this in *Macbeth*.
1606	*Macbeth* performed at court for King James.
1607	Jamestown, the first permanent English colony in America, established.

1608	The King's Men begin performing in the indoor Blackfriars Theater in addition to their outdoor venue of the Globe.
1609	Shakespeare's *Sonnets* published.
1611	The King James version of the Bible is published.
1613	The Globe Theatre burns to the ground during a performance of Shakespeare's *Henry VIII*. Around this time Shakespeare writes his final plays—several collaborations with John Fletcher, his successor as playwright for the King's Men—and retires to Stratford.
1616	Shakespeare finalizes his will in March, (in)famously leaving his wife the "second-best bed," and dies on April 23—his fifty-second birthday. Two days later he is buried in Holy Trinity Church, the same church where he was baptized as an infant.

Works by William Shakespeare

The following list of works is divided into four sections. The first two are based on genre, and include all the extant works that modern scholars attribute to Shakespeare as either sole author or primary author in a collaboration. The third section lists extant works in which Shakespeare is believed to have played some part as a collaborator, as well as works in which a Shakespearean attribution is actively disputed by modern scholarship. The final, brief section lists the two plays that were mentioned in Shakespeare's lifetime but that have not survived in any known manuscript or printed edition.

Plays

All's Well That Ends Well

Antony and Cleopatra

As You Like It

The Comedy of Errors

Coriolanus

Cymbeline

Hamlet

Henry IV, Part I

Henry IV, Part II

Henry V

Henry VI, Part 1

Henry VI, Part 2

Henry VI, Part 3

Henry VIII

Julius Caesar

King John

King Lear

Love's Labor's Lost

Macbeth

Measure for Measure

The Merchant of Venice
The Merry Wives of Windsor
A Midsummer Night's Dream
Much Ado About Nothing
Othello
Pericles
Richard II
Richard III
Romeo and Juliet
The Taming of the Shrew
Tempest
Timon of Athens
Titus Andronicus
Troilus and Cressida
Twelfth Night
The Two Gentlemen of Verona
The Winter's Tale

Poems

"A Lover's Complaint"
"The Phoenix and the Turtle"
The Rape of Lucrece
Sonnets
Venus and Adonis

Partial, Disputed, or Collaborative Works

Arden of Faversham
Double Falsehood
Edward III
"Funeral Elegy"
Sir Thomas More
Two Noble Kinsmen

Lost Works

Cardenio

Love's Labor's Won

Bibliography

Ackroyd, Peter. *Shakespeare: The Biography*. Anchor, 2006.

Adelman, Janet. *Suffocating Mothers: Fantasies of Maternal Origin in Shakespeare's Plays*. Routledge, 1992.

Alfar, Christina León. *Fantasies of Female Evil: The Dynamics of Gender and Power in Shakespearean Tragedy*. U of Delaware P, 2003.

Bamber, Linda. *Comic Women, Tragic Men: A Study of Gender and Genre in Shakespeare*. Stanford UP, 1982.

Bloch, Marc. *The Royal Touch: Sacred Monarchy and Scrofula in England and France*. Routledge, 1973.

Booth, Stephen. *King Lear, Macbeth, Indefinition and Tragedy*. Yale UP, 1983.

Brooks, Cleanth. "The Naked Babe and the Cloak of Manliness." *The Well Wrought Urn.* Harcourt, 1947. Reprinted in *Macbeth* by William Shakespeare, edited by Sylvan Barnet. New American Library, 1963, pp. 196-221.

Butler, Judith. *Bodies That Matter: On the Discursive Limits of "Sex."* Routledge, 1993.

_____. *Gender Trouble: Feminism and the Subversion of Identity*. Routledge, 1990.

Calogeras, R. C. "Sleepwalking and the Traumatic Experience." *International Journal of Psychoanalysis*, vol. 63, 1982, pp. 483-89.

Carroll, William C., editor. *Macbeth: Texts and Contexts*. Bedford/St. Martin's, 1999.

Chamberlain, Stephanie. "Fantasizing Infanticide: Lady Macbeth and the Murdering Mother in Early Modern England." *College Literature*, vol. 32, no. 3, 2005, pp. 72-91. http://0-search.ebscohost.com. carlson.utoledo.edu/login.aspx?direct=true&db=edsglr&AN=edsg cl.135022676&site=eds-live. Accessed Oct 15, 2015.

Cooper, Joel. *Cognitive Dissonance: 50 Years of a Classic Theory*. Sage, 2007.

Dash, Irene G. *Wooing, Wedding, and Power: Women in Shakespeare's Plays*. Columbia UP, 1981.

Davenant, William. *Macbeth : a tragedy : with all the alterations, amendments, additions, and new songs as it is now acted at the Theatre Royal*. Printed for Hen. Herringman, and are to be sold by Jos. Knight and Fra. Saunders at the Blue Anchor in the lower walk of the New-Exchange, 1687.

Empson, William. *Seven Types of Ambiguity*. 1930. Penguin, 1995.

Erne, Lukas. *Shakespeare as Literary Dramatist*. Cambridge UP, 2003.

Evans, Robert C. "Trauma in Shakespeare's *Macbeth*." *Critical Approaches to Literature: Psychological*. Edited by Robert C. Evans. Salem, 2017, pp. 101-18.

Foakes, R. A. *Shakespeare and Violence*. Cambridge UP, 2003.

Frye, Roland Mushat. "Launching the Tragedy of *Macbeth*: Temptation, Deliberation, and Consent in Act 1." *Huntington Library Quarterly*, vol. 50, 1987, pp. 249-61.

Gaskill, Malcolm. *Witchcraft: A Very Short Introduction*. Oxford UP, 2010.

Grady, Hugh, and Terence Hawkes. *Presentist Shakespeares*. Routledge, 2007.

Greenblatt, Stephen. *Shakespearean Negotiations: The Circulation of Social Energy in Renaissance England*. U of California P, 1988.

_____. "Shakespeare Bewitched." In *Shakespeare and Cultural Traditions*. Edited by Tetsuo Kishi, Roger Pringle, and Stanley Wells, U of Delaware P, 1994, pp. 17-42.

_____. *Will in the World: How Shakespeare Became Shakespeare*. Norton, 2005.

Greene, James J. "*Macbeth*: Masculinity as Murder." *American Imago*, vol. 41, no. 2, 1984, pp. 155-80.

Hampton, Bryan Adams. "Purgation, Exorcism, and the Civilizing Process in *Macbeth*." *SEL: Studies in English Literature 1500-1900*, vol. 51, no. 2, 2011, pp. 327-47.

Harris, Anthony. *Night's Black Agents: Witchcraft and Magic in Seventeenth-Century Drama*. Manchester UP, 1980.

Holinshed, Raphael. *The Chronicles of England, Scotland, and Ireland*. 1587. 6 volumes. J. Johnson, 1807-08.

Hope, Jonathan, and Michael Witmore. "The Language of *Macbeth*." *Macbeth: The State of Play*. Edited by Ann Thompson, Bloomsbury, 2014, pp.183-208.

Honigmann, E. A. J. "*Macbeth*: The Murderer as Victim." *Shakespeare: The Tragedies.* Edited by Robert B. Heilman, Prentice-Hall, 1984, pp. 135-49.

Howell, Maria L. *Manhood and Masculine Identity in William Shakespeare's* The Tragedy of Macbeth. UP of America, 2008.

Janoff-Bulman, Ronnie. *Shattered Assumptions: Toward a New Psychology of Trauma.* Free Press, 1992.

Kaaber, Lars. *Murdering Ministers: A Close Look at Shakespeare's Macbeth in Text, Context and Performance.* Cambridge Scholars, 2016.

Kelly, Raymond J. *To Be, Or Not To Be: Four Hundred Years of Vanitas Painting.* Flint Institute of Arts, 2006.

Kermode, Frank. *Shakespeare's Language.* Penguin, 2000.

Kimbrough, Robert. "Macbeth: The Prisoner of Gender." *Shakespeare Studies*, vol. 16, 1983, pp. 175-90.

Kinney, Arthur F. *Lies Like Truth: Shakespeare, Macbeth, and the Cultural Moment.* Wayne State UP, 2001.

Knights, L. C. "How Many Children Had Lady Macbeth? An Essay in the Theory and Practice of Shakespeare Criticism." In *Explorations.* New York UP, 1964, pp. 15-54.

Kranz, David L. "The Sounds of Supernatural Soliciting in *Macbeth*." *Studies in Philology*, vol. 100, 2003, pp. 346-83.

Levin, Joanna. "Lady Macbeth and the Daemonologie of Hysteria." *English Literary History*, vol. 69, 2002, pp. 21-55.

Mele, Alfred. *Self-Deception Unmasked.* Princeton UP, 2001.

Moschovakis, Nick. "Dualistic *Macbeth*? Problematic *Macbeth*?" *Macbeth: New Critical Essays.* Edited by Nick Moschovakis. Routledge, 2008, pp. 1-72.

Mullaney, Stephen. "Lying Like Truth: Riddle, Representation and Treason in Renaissance England," *ELH*, vol. 47, 1980, pp. 32-47.

Orgel, Stephen. *The Authentic Shakespeare: And Other Problems of the Early Modern Stage.* Routledge, 2002.

Palfrey, Simon, and Tiffany Stern. *Shakespeare in Parts.* Oxford UP, 2007.

Rose, Mary Beth. "Where are the Mothers in Shakespeare? Options for Gender Representation in the English Renaissance." *Shakespeare*

Quarterly, vol. 42, no. 3, 1991, pp. 291-314, www.jstor.org/stable/2870845. Accessed Sept. 13, 2015.

Roychoudhury, Suparna. "Melancholy, Ecstasy, Phantasma: The Pathologies of *Macbeth*." *Modern Philology*, vol. 111, 2013, pp. 205-30.

Scot, Reginald. *The Discoverie of Witchcraft.* 1584. Southern Illinois UP, 1964.

Shapiro, James. *The Year of Lear: Shakespeare in 1606.* Simon, 2015.

Shoenbaum, Samuel. *Shakespeare: A Documentary Life*. Oxford UP, 1975.

Venuti, Lawrence. "Adaptation, Translation, Critique." *Journal of Visual Culture*, vol. 6, no. 1, 2007, pp. 25-43.

Watson, Robert. *The Rest Is Silence: Death as Annihilation in the English Renaissance.* U of California P, 1994.

Welsh, James. "What Is a "Shakespeare Film," Anyway?" *The Literature/Film Reader: Issues of Adaptation*. Edited by James M. Welsh and Peter Lev. Scarecrow, 2007, pp. 105-14.

White, R. S. *Innocent Victims: Poetic Injustice in Shakespearean Tragedy.* 1982. Athlone, 1986.

Williams, Glenn. "A Very Brief Survey of the First Three Hundred Years of Commentary on Shakespeare's *Macbeth*." http://www2.cedarcrest.edu/academic/eng/lfletcher/macbeth/papers/gwilliams.htm. Accessed 30 July, 2017.

Willis, Deborah L. *Malevolent Nature: Witch-hunting and Maternal Power in Early Modern England.* Cornell UP, 1995.

William W. Weber became fascinated with Shakespeare at an early age, and developed this fascination into an abiding passion while studying literature as an undergraduate at the University of the South at Sewanee, Tennessee. After earning his BA with a major in English and a minor in Latin, he continued his studies at Yale University. There he began his teaching career and wrote a dissertation, "Shakespearean Metamorphoses," exploring the interpretive and instructive dynamics of Ovidian allusions in Shakespeare's poetry and drama. Excerpts of this dissertation have appeared in *Shakespeare Survey* and *Studies in Philology*, with the article from the former winning the 2014 Renaissance Society of America—Text Creation Partnership Article Prize for Digital Renaissance Research. He augmented his research and teaching at Yale with adjunct teaching jobs at the University of New Haven and Fairfield University, and in 2014 both received his PhD and accepted a job as visiting assistant professor of English at Centre College in Danville, Kentucky.

At Centre, William taught introductory courses in the interdisciplinary Humanities program as well as upper-level courses on Shakespeare, Revenge Drama, and the English sonnet. In addition to teaching, he founded, advised, and coached the Centre College Rugby Football Club, and won multiple institutional awards for service and scholarship.

Contributors_____

Daniel Bender teaches at Pace University (New York) and specializes in the literature of the English Renaissance. His research agenda centers on innovative methods for classroom study of this period's artistic products. His article on "Native Pastoral in the English Renaissance: Kett's Rebellion and the 1549 Petition,"(2015) argues for recognition of artistic qualities in writing by commoners who had urged what appear to be merely economic and political policy reforms in Tudor England His article "'...appertaining to thy youth': The End of the Academe in *Love's Labour's Lost* and A Curriculum for the Future" (2016) advocates the integration of practical life skills into classroom study of this comedy's depiction of a profoundly impractical curriculum. "Living with Macbeth: Circles of Tragedy" contributes to the critical studies movement known as presentism, whereby the work of art gains immediacy and relevance by being granted transhistorical reality in the here and now.

Jim Casey is an assistant professor at Arcadia University in Philadelphia. Although primarily a Shakespearean, he has published on such diverse topics as fantasy, monstrosity, early modern poetry, medieval poetry, textual theory, performance theory, postmodern theory, adaptation theory, old age, comics, masculinity, Shakespeare, Chaucer, and *Battlestar Galactica*.

Rahul Chaturvedi teaches literature at the Department of English, Banaras Hindu University, Varanasi, India. Prior to joining Banaras Hindu University, Varanasi , he also taught at the Centre for English Studies, Central University of Jharkhand, Ranchi, India. He obtained his PhD from Banaras Hindu University on the topic *Postmodernist Narratives: A Reading of Select India Fiction in English*. His current areas of interest include world literature, contemporary literary theory, political philosophy, and translation studies.

David Currell is assistant professor of English at the American University of Beirut, where he teaches early modern drama and poetry. He has published on Shakespeare in *Critical Survey* and *Shakespeare Survey*. He is coeditor of a special issue of *English Studies* devoted to the topic *Reading Milton through Islam*, and of the forthcoming book *Digital Milton*.

Mohammad Shaaban Ahmad Deyab is an associate professor of English literature in the English Department, Faculty of Arts, Minia University, Egypt. He received his PhD from Southern Illinois University at Carbondale. His writing has been published in both academic and professional journals, and he has presented papers at conferences from Cambridge, UK, to Virginia, USA. Currently, his research interests include ecocritical, feminist, postcolonial, and comparative studies.

Robert C. Evans is I. B. Young Professor of English at Auburn University at Montgomery. He earned his PhD from Princeton University in 1984. In 1982 he began teaching at AUM, where he has been named Distinguished Research Professor, Distinguished Teaching Professor, and University Alumni Professor. External awards include fellowships from the American Council of Learned Societies, the American Philosophical Society, the National Endowment for the Humanities, the UCLA Center for Medieval and Renaissance Studies, and the Folger, Huntington, and Newberry Libraries. He is the author or editor of more than thirty-five books and of more than four hundred essays, including recent work on various American writers.

Pamela Royston Macfie teaches Shakespeare, Dante, and early modern poetry at the University of the South in Sewanee, Tennessee, where she is the Samuel R. Williamson Distinguished University Professor. Her published work, which includes essays on Ovid's appropriation by Dante, Spenser, Shakespeare, Chapman, and Marlowe, concentrates on the poetry of allusion in early modernity. Her most recent publication, "The sonnets and narrative poems: Shakespeare, Ovid, reversal, and surprise," appears in *The Routledge Research Companion to Shakespeare and Classical Literature* (2017).

Fernando Gabriel Pagnoni Berns (PhD student) works at Universidad de Buenos Aires (UBA)—Facultad de Filosofía y Letras (Argentina)—as professor in Literatura de las Artes Combinadas II. He teaches seminars on international horror film. He is director of the research group on horror cinema "Grite" and has published articles on Argentinian and international cinema and drama in the following publications: *Imagofagia, Vita e Pensiero: Comunicazioni Sociali, Anagnórisis, Lindes,* and *UpStage Journal* among others. He has published chapters in the books *Horrors of War: The Undead on the Battlefield,* edited by Cynthia Miller; *To See the Saw Movies: Essays on Torture Porn and Post 9/11 Horror,* edited by John Wallis; *Critical Insights: Alfred Hitchcock,* edited by Douglas Cunningham; *Dreamscapes in Italian Cinema,* edited by Francesco Pascuzzi; *Reading Richard Matheson: A Critical Survey,* edited by Cheyenne Mathews; *Time-Travel Television,* edited by Sherry Ginn; *Critical Insights: Paranoia, Fear & Alienation,* edited by Kimberly S. Drake; and *Deconstructing Dads: Changing Images of Fathers in Popular Culture,* edited by Laura Tropp, among others. He is currently writing a book about the Spanish horror TV series *Historias para no Dormir.*

Sophia Richardson is a graduate student in the English department at Yale University working primarily on early modern drama and verse. She graduated from Oberlin College in 2015 with a BA in English, comparative literature, and German. She coauthored a review essay on *Sleep No More* in *Borrowers and Lenders* and is currently working on the connection between Margaret Cavendish's interest in the sartorial and her vitalist materialist natural philosophy.

Bryon Williams earned his PhD in English from Duquesne University and his MA from Stanford University. He has been teaching *Macbeth* and other Shakespeare works to university and high school students for more than twenty years. He has led multiple literary and historical tours of England, where students attend performances of the Royal Shakespeare Company and visit Stratford, the Globe Theatre, and other sites central to Shakespeare's cultural context. His scholarly interests include ecocriticism and the medical humanities. He has published scholarship on Homer, Percy Shelley, Henry David Thoreau, and Robinson Jeffers, and his recent work focuses on issues of race and gender in American nature writing. Bryon is Teacher of Integrated Humanities at The Academy at Penguin Hall in Wenham, Massachusetts.

Savannah Xaver is a first-year graduate student of English at the University of Toledo. A native of Toledo, Savannah graduated from the University of Toledo in 2016 with a degree in English and a focus on British Literature. Her current focus is on sixteenth- and seventeenth-century literature, specifically the works of Shakespeare and Donne; however, she also enjoys Victorian tragic novels. She hopes to continue her education and is currently applying to doctoral programs in Renaissance Literature. When she is not reading, Savannah hosts live trivia games and tutors in writing.

Horace 5
Howell, Maria L. 35
Hughes, Ken 71, 76, 79
hysteria 87, 101

iambic pentameter 58, 68
illusion 153, 159, 175
indeterminacy 85
infanticide 116, 121, 122, 124,
    126, 128
intention xxi, 141
internalization of authentic guilt
    167

James I of England xxx, 12, 22
James, Sid 77
James VI of Scotland xiv, xxx, 12,
    22
Janoff-Bulman, Ronnie 98
Joe Macbeth ix, 71, 76, 77, 78, 79,
    80, 81
Johnson, Samuel 5
Jorden, Edward 87
Joseph of Arimathea 17
jugupsa 170
justice xx, xxiii, 44, 175

Karuṇa 170
kāvya 169
Kelly, Raymond J. 162
Kennedy, Robert 188
keywords 56, 57, 60, 63, 69
Khan, Iqbal 88, 90
Kimbrough, Robert 130
King Duncan 32, 74, 141, 187
King Lear xxx, 4, 6, 70, 98, 113,
    143
King Lucius 17
King, Margaret L. 116, 128

King, Martin Luther, Jr. 188
King of Scotland 12, 39, 167, 174,
    186
King's Evil viii, 12, 14, 17, 22, 23,
    24, 26
Kinney, Arthur F. 120
Klein, Joan Larsen 136
Knight of the Burning Pestle, The
    xv
Knights, L. C. 7
Kranz, David 58
krodha 170
Kurosawa, Akira 179
Kurzel, Justin 74, 92

Lacan 8
Lady Macbeth x, xvi, xviii, xix,
    xxv, 7, 8, 11, 25, 27, 33, 34,
    35, 36, 48, 49, 51, 61, 62,
    65, 66, 79, 80, 81, 92, 93,
    96, 98, 99, 100, 101, 102,
    103, 104, 105, 106, 107,
    108, 109, 110, 111, 112, 113,
    115, 116, 117, 118, 119, 121,
    122, 123, 124, 125, 126,
    127, 128, 130, 135, 136,
    137, 138, 140, 142, 144,
    146, 158, 161, 165, 166,
    190, 191, 192, 193
Lady Macduff 90, 115, 118, 119,
    127, 134
Language 27, 41, 48, 70
Lapotaire, Jane 109
Laurie, Piper 108
Lennie 77
Leveridge, Richard 153
Lollatta, Bhaṭṭ 170, 171
Lord Chamberlain's Men xxix,
    xxx